Heavy Wings

Heavy Wings

Zhang Jie

Translated from the Chinese by

Howard Goldblatt

GROVE WEIDENFELD
New York

Copyright © 1981 by Zhang Jie
Translation copyright © 1989 by Howard Goldblatt

First published in China as *Chenzhong de chibang* in 1980
by the People's Literature Publishing House, Beijing

Published by Grove Weidenfeld
A Division of Wheatland Corporation
841 Broadway
New York, NY 10003

Library of Congress Cataloging-in-Publication Data

Chang, Chieh, 1937–
    Heavy wings.

    Translation of : Ch'en chung ti ch'ih pang.
    I. Title.
PL2837.C486C4813   895.1'35   88-27100
ISBN 0-8021-1039-8

Manufactured in the United States of America

This book is printed on acid-free paper

Designed by Sue Rose

First Edition 1989

1   3   5   7   9   10   8   6   4   2

Dedicated to all those who work for the future of China,
even at the expense of their own.

Translator's Preface

IN the early 1980s, the Chinese Writers Association honored Mao Dun, the recently deceased novelist and former minister of culture, by creating a national prize for fiction in his name. *Heavy Wings* was the second winner of that prize (1985). Originally published in 1981, Zhang Jie's novel was in the vanguard of the "reform literature" that dominated the early 1980s, a corpus of influential writing that took the "Four Modernizations" as its subject matter.

Although the book version of the novel was consulted for this translation, the primary text, in response to the author's wishes, was the serialized magazine version, which appeared in 1980 in the literary quarterly *Shiyue* ("October"). Some deletions have been made at the request or with the approval of the author. The pinyin system of romanization has been used throughout.

Terms of address in Chinese differ in many respects from those in the West. *Lao* (old) and *Xiao* (little), which are not to be interpreted as pejorative or condescending, are the most common terms of address among peers, relative age usually determining which is to be used.

Characters

Chen Yongming	Manager of Morning Light Auto Works; husband of Yu Liwen
Fang Wenxuan	Bureau director in Ministry of Heavy Industry
Feng Xiaoxian	Bureau director in Ministry of Heavy Industry; responsible for political and personnel affairs; former manager of Morning Light Auto Works
Ge Xinfa	Worker in Morning Light Auto Works
Guo Hongcai	Section chief in Ministry of Heavy Industry
He Jiabin	Cadre in Ministry of Heavy Industry
Ho Ting	Department head in Ministry of Heavy Industry; party branch secretary
Ji Hengquan	Secretary to Vice-Minister Zheng Ziyun
Kong Xiang	Vice-minister of Heavy Industry
Li Ruilin	Caretaker at Morning Light Auto Works; former party secretary
Lin Shaotong	Secretary to Minister Tian Shoucheng
Liu Yuying	Hair stylist; wife of Wu Guodong
Luo Haitao	Cadre in Ministry of Heavy Industry
Lü Tou	Caretaker at Morning Light Auto Works; father of Lü Zhimin
Lü Zhimin	Worker at Morning Light Auto Works
Mo Zheng	Adopted son of Ye Zhiqiu; son of persecuted intellectuals

Shi Quanqing	Cadre in Ministry of Heavy Industry
Song Ke	Bureau director in Ministry of Heavy Industry; former manager of Morning Light Auto Works
Tian Shoucheng	Minister of Heavy Industry
Wan Qun	Cadre in Ministry of Heavy Industry
Wang Fangliang	Vice-minister of Heavy Industry
Wu Bin	Worker at Morning Light Auto Works
Wu Guodong	Workshop foreman at Morning Light Auto Works; husband of Liu Yuying
Xia Zhuyun	Wife of Vice-Minister Zheng Ziyun
Xiao Yi	Secretary to Minister Tian Shoucheng
Yang Xiaodong	Workshop team leader in Morning Light Auto Works
Ye Zhiqiu	Journalist; adoptive mother of Mo Zheng
Yu Liwen	Doctor; wife of Chen Yongming
Zheng Yuanyuan	Photojournalist; daughter of Zheng Ziyun and Xia Zhuyun
Zheng Ziyun	Vice-minister of Heavy Industry; husband of Xia Zhuyun; father of Zheng Yuanyuan

Prologue

What is life?

A friend says, "Life is finding happiness in hardships."

"No!" I say. "Life is the eternal struggle of Man with his Fate."

Heavy Wings

One

*Let us find salvation in a simple statement
from an ordinary person: Practice is the
sole criterion of objective truth.*

F rom the kitchen come the tantalizing aroma of beetroot soup
and the spirited sounds of a cleaver on a chopping board.
One of those rare sunny winter days. Ye Zhiqiu, just over an
illness, is in a mood to match the weather, and surprised to find
she's regained the hearty appetite of her school days, when she
could finish off three bowls of rice at a sitting. Feelings like this,
buried in her past, have nearly disappeared from her life, and now
she feels like playing a schoolgirl prank.

But no, not a woman whose hair is already turning gray. She
can't even let go at home, for if it became a habit and followed her
to the office or out in public, that would *really* get people talking.
Though she always watches her step, some people still consider her
behavior preposterous. Even if she went out and performed ten
good deeds a day, no one would notice. They'd be too busy

recalling some careless little act and would resent her for being out of step with the times. Such a simple woman, actually, about as complicated as an amoeba. Forty years old and she still hasn't figured out what life is all about. When she has time to think, she becomes aware of her own defects, but as soon as she gets worked up over something, she's her old self again.

So she forces herself to suppress this happy urge, as any proper middle-aged Chinese woman would do. Apparently, however, she has less willpower than desire, for no sooner is the urge restrained than it resurfaces as a long-forgotten French phrase shouted into the kitchen: "Qu'est-ce qu'on va manger aujourd'hui pour le déjeuner?"

"De la soupe aux betteraves, et du saucisson avec du pain."

Good for Mo Zheng, he hasn't forgotten! Of course, that comes from growing up in a cultured family.

"Cultured family"? Maybe so, but now he has nothing. An orphan, just like her.

What does it mean to be "cultured" anyway? Back then it was just an intolerable extravagance, a catchword for "bourgeois."

Human beings were stupid to have created material culture! If they'd only stopped evolving at the time of the Creation and were still crawling around on all fours, how simple everything would be!

Mo Zheng's parents were professors of French at a major university back in the 1950s. Ye Zhiqiu was their student.

It's not just that Mo Zheng is a penniless orphan, but that life's hardships have robbed him of his birthright and forced upon him things he should have been spared. After the violent death of his parents during the Cultural Revolution, he roamed the streets, living on what he could steal, like a wild dog. The first time she brought him home from the precinct station, he repaid her kindness by biting her savagely. He nearly turned her place inside out. Maybe only a wild dog could know the pain he was feeling, having learned that an extended hand had but one intention—to beat him. How could he conceive of a hand offered in kindness?

But once again Ye Zhiqiu brought him home from the precinct station, without quite knowing why. Maybe because she, too, was

4

an orphan and knew the pain of being at the mercy of people's fickle attitudes. It was this pain that bonded them.

Maybe she knew that the prospect of maternal love was forever lost to her and, like women everywhere, desperately needed a release for her maternal instincts.

Nothing is harder for a woman to bear than the curse of ugliness.

Taken individually, there's nothing wrong with Ye Zhiqiu's features, but overall, there are surely few women as ugly as she. Her hair matches her character—coarse, shaggy and wiry, unstylish. Yet she refuses to let a hairdresser give it a more modern look or thin it a little. Short and bushy, it sticks out in all directions, like a soldier's helmet seen from afar.

She has no feminine curves, no glamour. Her square shoulders make her look like an aging tree stump hewn by a woodcutter—hewn not sawed.

No man in his right mind would marry a woman like that.

The hardest hearts may, after all, be the most fragile. For one that has grown callous and cold under the constant threat of being trampled underfoot, ravaged, destroyed, the greatest taming force in the world is tenderness. Its arrival is a godsend. From Ye Zhiqiu Mo Zheng received more than tenderness—she gave him true motherly love.

Here comes the food.

Mo Zheng carries in a bowl of steaming beetroot soup in one hand and two plates of sausage and bread in the other, like an experienced waiter. Balanced atop the plates is a small dish of jam. The thin slices of sausage are neatly fanned out around the edges of the plates: the bread has been cut into thick slices so uniform they might have been measured with a ruler.

The sight of Mo Zheng expertly busying himself in the kitchen with one of his meals, the inscrutable smile of a chef on his face as he playfully clanks his spatula against the wok, has always given her mixed feelings. She never knows whether to laugh or cry. He seems so much better equipped to survive than people of her generation. She still, for instance, doesn't know how to cook, and if it weren't for him, she'd be eating the insipid canteen food, which all tastes the same, whether it's braised pork or stewed chicken. She enjoys good food, but she's never been willing to spend the time to prepare it, and even if she were, it wouldn't make any difference. Her life is a mess. . . . No, it's all a matter of getting by.

She knows there must be better ways to describe their differences, so why has she settled on something as trivial as this? In the end, whatever he puts his hand to—cooking, playing the piano, studying French—he does it so much better. So why is he content to serve her like this? Not that there's anything wrong in serving her, that's not it; it's just . . . well, what exactly is it? Her thoughts begin to drift.

Mo Zheng blows on his fingers after setting the bowl of scalding soup down on the table.

Those hands ought to belong to an artist: long, powerful fingers; broad, thick palms; strong knuckles and wrists. She knows he studied piano as a child, when his legs were still too short to reach the pedals. Yet even at that tender age all thoughts of food and games were driven out as he banged away at the keys. And now, after all these years, whenever she sits down at the dust-covered piano to play a tune with fingers too stiff to do her bidding, he runs into his room as soon as he hears the music, as though the sound holds hidden dangers.

What does she mean, "ought to"? Mo Zheng isn't a little boy in light blue flannel anymore. He's a tall, strapping young man in a wrinkled green army-surplus jacket whose five original buttons have been replaced by a random assortment. His baggy denims look like half-filled sacks draped around his long, skinny legs; like every pair he owns, they have tattered cuffs, a result of snagging them as he works around trees—pruning, watering, spraying insecticide. . . . But that doesn't stop the girls from falling for him, so long as they're ignorant of his past. They love his square jaw; his full, even mouth; his soft black hair, parted in the middle and loosely combed back, as though professionally styled, and the neat, straight eyebrows that stop at his temples, except for one or two hairs that arch slightly upward and give him the appearance of being in motion even when he's still. Maybe because his dark eyes are slightly larger than most people's, his gaze seems more solemn, more deliberate, even somewhat aloof. More than anything else, it's this contrast between his eyes and his eyebrows that gives him such a striking appearance.

Mo Zheng slides a rickety stool out from under the table with his foot. It creaks as he sits down, as if unable to withstand the sudden weight bearing down painfully on it.

The sound frightens her. How many times has she told him to fix it or throw it away! Sooner or later it's going to give out and send someone sprawling. But Mo Zheng has never shared her anxiety. "Don't worry about it," he says casually. "As long as *you* don't sit on it, there's no problem." It's not laziness; he simply refuses to believe that the possibility of a little fall is worth getting all worked up over. Why worry about it! So what can she do, except look anxiously at the stool every time he sits down on it? This time he's seen through her attempt to mask her concern. She really ought to stop worrying so much.

"Well, how's it taste?"

She bends over and blows on the scalding soup before trying it. "Not bad." She smiles. "Perfect, in fact, just like your French."

His spoon freezes in midair. Why must she dredge up the past? That's the last thing he wants to think about, but somehow it keeps popping up, following him everywhere, wrapping itself around him and never letting go. Just one more thing to worry about, although worrying never seems to do any good. He gulps down some soup, angrily, as if trying to swallow his irritation along with it. The creases on his brow gradually smooth out as he tears off a piece of bread with his strong white teeth.

Crash! For a moment she thinks his stool has collapsed under him. But no, the sound came from overhead. They must have knocked over something up there. Then some howls from Xiao Zhuang, some loud shuffling, and the muffled sobs of Liu Yuying, his mother.

"Just like characters out of Gorky," he says with a sneer.

Ye Zhiqiu stops eating.

"What's wrong?" The sneer freezes on his face.

An embarrassed smile. She feels like a high-strung child whenever she's around him; he's so much more worldly than she, and less easily moved. "I don't know why, but I always lose my appetite when I hear someone cry."

"Spoken like a true Christian."

"Mo Zheng!" Angry, her feelings hurt, she stands up and tries to leave. Mo Zheng sticks out one of his long legs.

"Take it easy. There's nothing you can do. They'll be back at it in a couple of days anyway."

He's right, of course. The children upstairs cry all the time, their parents are always fighting. Not that the adults enjoy arguing or that the children are delinquents—why do they let life get them down like this?

"Sit down and eat," Mo Zheng urges sympathetically. "It's getting cold."

But she's lost her appetite, along with her high spirits. She shakes her head and walks silently over to the desk, where she sits down and leafs through the stack of newspapers that had lain unread during her illness. Out of habit she glances at the production figures from new factories and the reports of enterprises that have exceeded their annual production quotas. . . . She's reminded that the year is coming to an end. Another month or so and it will be 1980. Recalling an article she'd been rushing to finish before she fell sick, she searches for the draft.

That's strange! Where could it be? I'm sure I put it on top of the pad of writing paper, but it's not there. Maybe I stuck it in one of the drawers.

She opens them all, one after the other, each of them a jumble of diaries, old letters, stamps, envelopes and pocketbooks with money inside, ID cards, eyeglass cases (several of these), prescription bottles (some empty, others full); only someone with the patience of Job could stand to look for anything in this mess. Sadly, few people have less patience than Ye Zhiqiu; every time she searches frantically for something in these drawers, she vows to straighten them up someday and throw out all the useless junk, of which there's plenty: This bunch of old letters, and look, this prescription bottle is empty. *Clunk!* She tosses it into a corner of the room.

But as always, as soon as she's calmed down a bit, the vow is forgotten, and the accumulated junk stays right where it was—in one of her drawers. Besides, even though the letters aren't from close friends or relatives, she can't bear to throw them away. They are a record of her life and her spectacular failures.

She's always getting involved in things that don't concern her. Predictably, her involvement seldom makes any difference. Every time she returns from one of her frenzied "missions," beaten and exhausted like a fly that's futilely banged itself against a wall, she sits at her desk and leafs through these old letters, feeling guilty about deceiving such decent, sincere people. And yet no one has ever felt that she was untrustworthy. God, it's hard! Visitors suddenly turn up on her doorstep, rubbing their bony hands and smiling bashfully as their faces redden. Their grievances could fill an entire night. It's gotten so bad that Mo Zheng's room has been turned into a sort of way station.

Where in the world is that draft?

"Mo Zheng, have you seen that sheet of paper I left on the desk?" No need to mention that it's a draft, since it couldn't possibly make finding it any easier. He's never been interested in her work and doesn't even glance at anything she writes.

"What sheet of paper? I never took any paper off your desk!"

"A sheet of writing paper, with some writing on it!"

Suddenly it dawns on him. "Oh! A couple of days ago Xiao Zhuang was playing down here, and I gave him a piece of scrap paper from your desk to wrap up some candy."

That hurts. "Oh, no! That was the draft of an article I'm writing on year-end production figures. It wasn't scrap paper!"

"How was I supposed to know it was a draft?" Not a hint of concern or contrition.

"How many times have I told you not to touch any paper I've written on! I *meant* don't touch it! Everything I say to you goes in one ear and out the other!"

A look of remorse finally appears on Mo Zheng's face, not because the draft has been destroyed, but because he sees her anger and hears the despondent tone of her voice. "You know," he says repentantly, "you really ought to be resting. Why all the rush? Besides, those reports are a bunch of nonsense. Who reads them? Who *believes* them?"

"How can you say that? Where do you get such crazy ideas?" She bangs the desk.

He holds his tongue to keep from angering her even more. He lowers his head and concentrates on eating, trying to appear casual. The silence of the room is broken only by the sound of his spoon hitting the sides of the bowl and his chewing.

They argue frequently, and he generally gives in. He hates to make her angry, for she is an oasis in the desert of his heart. She's the only person on earth who loves him, gives him warmth, and never holds his past against him, even though he is one of those people who feels that his generation is superior to the one before.

Sometimes he finds it hard to believe that a mere twenty years separate them, given the enormous differences in their understanding of life's realities. It's incredible! Is everyone of her generation like this? Yes, probably so. They are so good, so trusting and innocent, yet they stubbornly cling to their outmoded ideas!

She usually feels maligned by these arguments, for she has never considered herself an empty-headed woman, and there's nothing outmoded about her, although his generation thinks so. As far as they're concerned, getting old means lagging behind the times.

She has been a reporter for more than twenty years, ever since graduating from college in 1956. Through her job she meets all sorts of people and has a better understanding of what's going on than most. She has developed her own views of certain incidents, and even though these incidents try her patience, she constantly reminds herself: Ye Zhiqiu, no matter what you write, don't let yourself become a hypocrite or take advantage of people.

During the Cultural Revolution, for instance, she found all sorts of excuses to stop writing altogether rather than join the chorus of two-faced theoreticians. She knows that this was prompted more by a fortuitous ignorance of theoretical issues than by courage. But then, she's always been a coward. And whose fault is that? She belongs to a generation of cowards.

Her job brings her into contact with lots of grass-roots comrades on the front lines of industry, honest people doing honest work. To her, these production figures, considered nothing but dry statistics by some, represent familiar faces, molten steel, revolving turbines, a vast network of electrical transmission lines . . . She takes comfort in knowing that this essential work is still being done. Her job, too, is essential, one worth doing, and doing well. So how can Mo Zheng talk about it like that? It's absurd!

Her jaw quivers with anger.

Realizing that things are getting out of hand, Mo Zheng stops eating. She's got it all wrong. He wipes the sneer off his face and grows deadly serious. "I'm not talking about your job. It's those interminable statistics. Lots of people think that those figures are sent up from below, one level at a time, but in fact they're worked out on an abacus just so they can coincide with the demands of some graph. As I see it, anything can be falsified, including Chairman Mao's 'Supreme Instructions.' The newspapers are always reporting that industrial production for the second half of the year has outstripped the first half by so many percent, and that this year's has outstripped last year's by so many percent. Nonsense! It doesn't mean a thing. I'm not saying that the figures lie, but that they don't mean anything. Take Lao Wu, the worker who lives upstairs. What kind of life does his family lead? That's what people ought to be writing about. We need more honest reporting about the lives of people who've spent years sweating away at jobs that create the nation's wealth and insure our future survival. That's the way to gauge whether or not our industrial production is developing, and how fast. If our living standards keep lagging behind capitalist societies, what does all our crowing about superiority accomplish? Does it win the hearts of our own people? What good are all those figures? Have you ever thought about that? They're nothing but phony, self-deceiving window dressing!" He is letting off steam for a change, talking faster and faster. He shoves his bowl away with such force that the soup spills and runs over the edge of the table onto his pants. Pulling out a wadded-up, grimy handkerchief, he wipes his pants, over and over, more as a release for his feelings than to clean his pant leg.

Mo Zheng's words have taken the edge off Ye Zhiqiu's pent-up resentment. He's making sense. Painfully, she thinks about all the mistakes made in economic policy since 1956, and all the failures. If it weren't for those interminable twists and turns, the people might be enjoying a better life now. Still, they're better off than before Liberation.

"At least the figures show that our economy keeps improving every year," she says feebly. "Compared to the years before Liberation . . ."

Mo Zheng stops rubbing his pant leg. "I knew you'd say that! You can't keep making that comparison forever. We're talking about two totally different ways of life! How can you compare our socialist society to the old society? If you're going to be content making simple comparisons like that, then maybe we should still be living like slaves. Don't forget the tremendous advantages they had over primitive man!" With a look that shows that the discussion is over, he flings his handkerchief into his soup, as though it were a dishrag, and gets to his feet, livid with anger. Scooping up the dishes, he heads toward the kitchen, but stops at the door and turns, the dark clouds on his face seemingly blown away by a gust of wind. "You really ought to give some thought to why Lao Wu's family is always fighting and arguing," he says with genuine concern.

She is moved by the force of his sincerity. Mo Zheng, who has always felt that tenderness is a sign of weakness in a man, seldom shows this side of his character. It's a luxury he can't afford, something only a fool who doesn't know his own limits would give in to. He knows he has to suppress any yearnings for tenderness if he's to avoid the pain that comes from giving in to its seductiveness.

Lao Wu and his family have been their neighbors for years. Ye Zhiqiu hasn't forgotten what a loving, considerate husband and handsome young man Wu Guodong was at first. Everyone in the building teased him for being so attentive to Liu Yuying during her first pregnancy. Auntie Wang, their neighbor on the second floor, said to him more than once, "Xiao Wu, don't make such a fuss! Having a baby is like laying an egg, so don't get all worked up. You'll scare the wits out of Xiao Liu!" But in spite of all their advice, Ye Zhiqiu knew that if he could get away with it, he'd carry Liu Yuying around all day long, as though she were a freshly laid egg rather than a laying hen. Xiao Liu had once been such a lovely young bride. Now, ten years later, where has it all gone? How could everything have changed so completely? How could Lao Wu have turned into such a coarse, prematurely balding man? And where did all the wrinkles on his wife's forehead come from?

Two

The perm has turned out nicely, just the way Xia Zhuyun likes it, softly waved and brushed elegantly over to the side. Now that she's getting on in years, she can't do her hair up in tight little curls like the young women. That vulgar style is fine for working girls who can only afford to perm their hair once a year and want those tight little swirls to stay as long as possible.

Using the mirrors in front and behind her, she surveys her hairdo from every angle, slowly, with a smile. She nods her approval to Liu Yuying, who stands behind holding the mirror for her.

This hairdresser knows her job. No wonder she comes so highly recommended. But why does she look so sad? Awfully despondent for such a young woman. Something is certainly preying on her mind.

Xia Zhuyun relaxes as she waits for the hairdresser to bring her handbag and coat.

The coat, a thick gray worsted made from the best wool, is light as a feather. Her unusual handbag isn't one of those common boxy things, but a wide, flat purse with an embossed pattern that her husband brought back from an official trip to England the year before.

It's become a sort of ritual: whenever the old fellow goes on one of his trips he brings something back for her. And each time he hands her a present, her face lights up like an empress receiving tribute. But she probably wouldn't be smiling if she knew how he always says condescendingly, "This is for the little woman," whenever he buys her something like a tin of Hangzhou's famous Dragon Well tea.

Liu Yuying watches Xia Zhuyun slowly put on her coat, then place her scarf over her head, taking care not to ruin her new hairdo, before opening her handbag. She's not making a show out of her slow, deliberate actions; this is just how wives of influential husbands do things, a way of life for the leisure class, people who are accustomed to being treated with deference. They know that others will wait patiently and respectfully on their every movement, whether they have something more important to do or not. It is a slowness reserved for women getting on in years.

Xia Zhuyun reaches into her handbag and takes out an expensive tan embossed leather wallet with two gold-colored snaps.

The wallet contains at least five or six ten-yuan bills, roughly a month's wages for Liu Yuying, maybe more. The only time she carries that much money is on payday. She seldom carries more than one yuan.

Xia Zhuyun removes one of the bills and rubs it hard between her fingers, as though trying to produce another one. Then she hands it to Liu Yuying.

Xiao Gu, the cashier, notices the exhaustion on Liu Yuying's face, put there by all her worries. She glances at the clock on the wall as she hands the customer her change. "It's already five-thirty, time for you to go home!"

Liu Yuying acknowledges Xiao Gu's concern with a smile. So

what if I do go home now? What do I have to look forward to there but more worries?

The money is filthy and all crumpled up, especially the ten-fen bills. Xia Zhuyun distastefully picks them up with the tips of her fingers, remembering to count them carefully before putting them into her wallet and snapping it shut. Then with a final glance into the mirror, she heads out of the beauty shop, hearing a soft "goodbye" from the hairdresser just as she reaches the door. She quickly turns back. "Goodbye!" she says with a pang of regret, not because she hadn't rewarded the hairdresser for her labors (she paid her, after all), but because she feels she's slighted her somehow. Why, she wonders unhappily, didn't she say goodbye first? It makes her appear unmannerly. Who'd have thought that a mere hairdresser would have better manners than she!

As she emerges from the beauty shop, Xia Zhuyun glances at her gold wristwatch. More than four hours just to have her hair permed! But her only real concern about time is how to find enough activities to fill it. The maid takes care of everything around the house, and her youngest daughter is already grown and out working. Since she has a good job as a photojournalist, all her mother has to worry about now is finding her a suitable husband.

Xia Zhuyun goes to work sometimes, when her health and mood permit. But her weak heart keeps her home most of the time. And yet she can't spend the rest of her life in bed! She tried her hand at knitting, but at the rate she works she'd be lucky to finish one garment every few years. Her husband once commented playfully, "By the time this sweater's finished, my beard will have turned from gray to green."

She wasn't sure if he was joking or complaining. But who cares, as long as it helps to pass the time.

Since she has plenty of time to read, she subscribes to several periodicals and newspapers; so many, in fact, that she spends most of her waking hours reading. There is a difference between her and the other wives of senior cadres—she's been to college. But the corrosive effects of affluence have begun to diminish her abilities to pursue, understand, even remember things related to cultural life. She can't retain anything she reads in all those books, magazines, and newspapers.

On nights when the old fellow is at a meeting at the Ministry and her daughter is out, she stays home alone and stares at the twenty-inch Japanese color TV from the living-room sofa. She usually dozes off as she sits there facing the screen, so when she goes to bed, she can't sleep and must find something to think about; insomnia doesn't worry her, since she can sleep as late as she wants the next morning. Most of the time she thinks about her daughter's marital prospects. Deputy Commander Wang's second son is still single, but he's such an indifferent boy and not particularly talented. Then there's Ambassador Yu's son, but his health is so fragile he might make her a young widow. Minister Wang's third son is a good-looking boy, and intelligent, a translator by trade, but he might already be spoken for . . . on and on she thinks, finally getting out of bed and going over to knock on the door of her husband's study. No answer. Has he fallen asleep or is he just ignoring her, knowing that it can't be important anyway? Whatever the reason, he doesn't come to the door.

Naturally, at her age she's not spending all that time on her appearance to make herself attractive to anyone in particular, but has simply fallen into a habit formed over many years of being fastidious; it's also a good way to show off her status. Her husband, who is always working, attending meetings, busying himself with the grass-roots-level units, or talking on the telephone, never notices how she dresses or does her hair. And all those phone calls! It's getting impossible for her to even leave the house, and that's led to plenty of grumbling: "All I ever do is answer your phone calls!" "No one's forcing you!" he says. But she's not about to let him stop her. Answering the phone is her job. How else is she supposed to exercise her authority as the lady of the house and show off her husband's importance?

Once, in 1956, she dragged him off to a ball at the Beijing Hotel. The next day she asked him, "How did you like the dress I wore last night?"

He thought long and hard. "Not bad. The yellow complemented your complexion."

His thoughtful, earnest response stunned her. Once the shock passed, she fired back angrily, "Have you become color-blind all of a sudden? I wore a purple taffeta cheongsam last night!"

He laughed. "Well then, I guess you'll have to go out and have a yellow one made!"

But by the time she got around to having the dress made, when she modeled it for him, he'd completely forgotten his comment about how the color complemented her complexion. "Why yellow? That's not a very flattering color on you!"

But that was about the only complaint she had with him. He'd been a handsome, distinguished man in his youth, and she'd been the envy of plenty of women. He was also a faithful husband, never taking an interest in other women. In fact, he treated her like an ornament that he could take or leave. They had been sleeping in separate rooms for years, and she wondered if he regretted getting married in the first place. Maybe he had mistaken youthful ardor for love when he decided to propose. Was it possible he'd never actually loved her and had put all his passion into his work? She complained to him sometimes: Work, always work, nothing but work, almost as though the family, daughters included, didn't belong to him. If she hadn't pulled the right strings, their daughter would never have landed a job as a photojournalist, a high-status, cushy occupation that brought her into contact with the upper crust and provided a ringside seat for national affairs.

Then, too, they'd needed suitable living accommodations once her husband got his job back, but Ministry quarters were hard to find back then—it always seemed strange to her that the Ministry put up so many buildings, yet somehow neglected to build any for senior cadres of ministerial rank—so they had to content themselves with staying where they were. What kind of home was this for a vice-minister, a measly five rooms on the fourth floor? What other vice-ministers had to live like this? Naturally, Xia Zhuyun wasn't advocating that the Ministry build them a special home, but at least they ought to be moved into more appropriate quarters. That seemed only fair. After all, she had a heart condition and her husband had asthma! But since he couldn't be counted on to do anything about it, it was all up to her.

* * *

Liu Yuying feels as though her customer has taken her last ounce of energy out the door with her. She's afraid she's coming completely unglued. She didn't sleep a wink last night and left for work without breakfast. Then at lunchtime she ate only a few bites. Anger has formed a lump in her throat that won't go away. No matter how depressed she is, she won't allow herself to sit down and rest; she needs a distraction, anything to keep her from crying, so she picks up a broom and begins sweeping the floor.

Never in all her years had she even been yelled at, not by her father, not by her mother, not by anyone. But yesterday she was slapped across the face, and by whom? By the husband for whom she would have willingly laid down her life. And why? Because Xiao Zhuang broke a thermos bottle. Wu Guodong slapped his son without so much as asking whether or not he'd been scalded. "It's only a thermos bottle," she said to him, "worth a yuan or so. So why'd you hit him?"

"To hear you talk," he argued, "you'd think you were married to a cabinet minister or something! Only a yuan or so! Just how many 'yuan or so's' do you have?"

She could manage a yuan or so at the time, but by month's end, scraping that much together would take all the budgeting wizardry she could manage. Only someone who's lived on the margin like this can truly understand what a yuan or so means in the life of a housewife. . . .

After Wu Guodong contracted hepatitis and had to take sick leave, he received sixty percent of his original salary, a total of forty-nine yuan a month. Her monthly salary, including allowances, was just over fifty. Out of that they had to feed a family of four and send fifteen yuan a month to Wu Guodong's parents. And now that Wu Guodong was sick, he needed more nutritious food than usual. But how could he eat it under the envious stares of his children? It stuck in his throat.

They got by somehow, and although the times were tough, they could have been worse. But even that was only possible through plenty of hard work by Liu Yuying.

In order to save a few fen, she never bought cut or even dried noodles, but made her own from scratch, even if she'd been on her feet all day long until her legs were puffy and her back bent from soreness.

She always passed up fresh seasonal vegetables, buying rejects for ten fen a bunch at sidewalk stalls. Her sister wrote her from Xinjiang to complain about the high cost of food there, and by comparison Beijing wasn't all that bad: at least there were plenty of substandard goods—vegetables, fish, fabric, shoes . . . and Liu Yuying knew which markets cheaply sold the things she needed.

To save on detergent, she made full use of her organizational skills: first she washed all the light-colored clothing, then the dark, then scrubbed the children's shoes, and finally used the no-longer soapy water to clean the mop.

She employed all of her feminine talents and knowledge in the service of getting through these troubling days. Before her marriage she'd never experienced times like these, never been put through so much. But things had been different then, and she thought back wistfully to the days before 1958, when life had been so much easier for everyone. Since 1965 everything had gone from bad to worse.

She didn't want her parents to know how hard it was, first, because they'd be worried about her, and second, because their life was no bed of roses either. Father had retired from the factory and her younger brother had brought a wife home, so what was to be gained by adding to their worries? Every time Liu Yuying took her husband and children to visit her family she made sure they looked as good as they could, and she always took along some snacks as a gift, even if it was only a box of little cakes that sold for seventy fen a catty or some fruit cakes that went for sixty fen. But nothing ever escaped the sharp eyes of her mother, who always managed to find a way to help out: on the children's birthdays or on New Year's, she gave her daughter what she could, always in such a way as to keep her son-in-law in the dark. The last thing in the world she wanted was to destroy his self-respect.

And there was more: Liu Yuying suppressed her feminine desire to be as attractive as possible. Several days before, she'd gone out to buy some material for a winter jacket, and her first choice had been a piece of beige Dacron fabric with green and blue flecks. But when she calculated that the jacket would cost her over ten yuan, she couldn't bring herself to buy it. She paced back and forth in front of the counter before finally settling on some cotton fabric instead. The money, she felt, was better spent on nutritious food for Wu Guodong. Besides, the children needed new felt shoes. . . .

But none of this ever earned her a word of thanks. It was as though it was expected of her. All that her efforts and sacrifices ever earned her was derision and taunts, but even that would have been bearable if he hadn't taken his anger out on the children. And not just once or twice, either! What are the children guilty of? If you didn't have what it takes to support a family, you shouldn't have gotten married in the first place! But now that you have a family, you have an obligation to do whatever it takes to support it, or else you'll never be able to call yourself a man! If you only know how to go around complaining, beating your children, and yelling at your wife, then you're not a man in my book! Growing angrier and more bitter, she replied caustically, "Maybe I *should* have married a cabinet minister!"

"Well, why didn't you?"

Filled with grievances and bitterness, and convinced of each other's heartlessness, neither was in a mood to make up. Back and forth it went, one hurtful comment after another, building in intensity, with Xiao Zhuang right in the middle. Then as Liu Yuying was trying to keep her husband from hitting Xiao Zhuang, he suddenly slapped her across the face. Even he was shocked by his own action. What the hell am I doing! he thought.

Liu Yuying stood there and glared dry-eyed at her husband, as though only now did she really know this man with whom she had lived for over ten years.

There had been plenty of arguments in recent years, but nothing like this had ever happened before. What had caused it? Who was to blame?

The slap seemed to bring Wu Guodong to his senses. He suddenly realized that Liu Yuying was the mainstay of the family. Without her it would fall apart. Had he ever asked her how she managed on their paltry income? Never. Had he ever given a single thought to any of her needs? Never. She, on the other hand, had willingly sacrificed everything. Steadfastly and without a word of complaint, she had taken all the burdens of the family onto her soft, weak shoulders.

Maybe women are actually stronger than men, more determined, and more capable of self-sacrifice!

And yet for some perverse reason, he couldn't bring himself to apologize. Maybe he sensed how inadequate it would be, maybe he underestimated the seriousness of what had just happened, or maybe he assumed that she could neither forgive him nor understand why he had done it, and that anything he did now would only infuriate her more.

Liu Yuying's mind is flooded with thoughts. Maybe I should die here and now, and let Wu Guodong spend the rest of his life filled with remorse. But then who'd take care of the children? Maybe they'd wind up with a mean stepmother! Tears come to her eyes as she recalls horror stories from her own childhood about cruel stepmothers. No, I mustn't die! How about a divorce? But what kind of a solution is that? Everyone would assume I'd done something disgraceful. Well, wouldn't they? Don't people treat divorced women with disdain and suspicion? No, she'd never allow herself to be talked about like that. She could pack up and move back to her parents' home, but that wouldn't work either since there's no room, and it would only add to her aging parents' problems. . . . All day long, ever since morning, she's been thinking, but still no idea of how to give Wu Guodong what he deserves.

God, why is my life so bitter! What a different life that last customer must have. She must be so happy, so content, married to a man who wouldn't even raise his voice at her, let alone hit her!

Her tears begin to flow again, but she quickly dries her eyes before anyone notices.

It begins to snow; tiny, fluffy, pure white snowflakes drift to the ground, dancing happily in the cold gusts of wind. The first snowfall of the year, it reminds her of her girlhood—so happy and carefree, such wonderful days!

A young couple walks in just then. The cold air has turned the girl's cheeks a deep red, accentuating her bright, lively eyes.

The boy is carrying two large shopping bags filled with packages from local department stores. Once inside, he just stands there with a silly grin on his face, not because anything is particularly funny, but because he is so happy he can't help himself.

Liu Yuying's experience tells her at a glance that the youngsters standing in front of her are about to get married.

"Comrade," the girl says to Liu Yuying, "I'm looking for a hairdresser named Liu . . ."

"What do you want her for?"

The boy clears his throat, probably to underscore the importance of what he has to say. "We want a perm, and we've heard she's the best in the business!"

"In this shop it doesn't matter who takes care of you," Xiao Gu cuts in, "since all the girls are good stylists!" She is concerned about how Liu Yuying looks. Is she sick? Then why not get some rest? She tries too hard, and her heart's too big for her own good. She doesn't know how to turn down a personal request for her services.

The boy is embarrassed. He's obviously never been in a situation like this before and doesn't know how to make them understand how important this request is to him and to his fiancée. "It's like this . . ." He doesn't know what to say.

But Liu Yuying knows only too well that at this moment his entire life revolves around his fiancée, and that even the most trivial matter takes on enormous proportions. She's exhausted, she's upset, and she has a bellyful of grievances, but she is moved by the young man's naive zeal. "I'm Liu," she says in spite of herself.

"Okay," Xiao Gu says, "I'll give you a ticket for her!" She turns to Liu Yuying and says reproachfully, "Your face is all puffy!"

"I want a cold perm," the girl says as she pays the cashier.

Xiao Gu abruptly pushes the money back as she looks up at the clock: "I'm afraid there won't be enough time for a cold perm."

The innocent young couple, nearly blinded by their happiness, are suddenly struck by the realization that the affairs of the world don't necessarily revolve around them. They stand there looking at each other, not knowing what to do.

"How am I supposed to find the time to come back tomorrow? There's no way I can make it . . ."

Liu Yuying signals Xiao Gu with her eyes. "All right," she says compassionately, "here's your ticket. But don't forget to show your appreciation to Stylist Liu when she's finished."

The girl stands in front of the glass surveying the different hairstyles, a bemused smile on her face. She turns to the young man. "Which style would look best?"

Wearing the same sort of smile on his face, he merely parrots her: "Which style would look best?" Then suddenly, struck by a husbandly inspiration, he says, "Stylist Liu, why don't you pick out the one that suits her best."

The girl echoes his sentiment: "Right, that's the idea!"

"All right," Liu Yuying says, "if that's what you want, just leave it to me." She lifts up the girl's braids, but just as she is about to cut them off, she looks over at the young man and notices the mixed emotions in his eyes.

What can be going through his mind? Maybe he's thinking: As soon as those braids are cut off, she'll be entering a new stage of life. Maybe I should be the one to lead her into that new life with my own hands.

Liu Yuying pauses, then says to him, "Why don't you do it?"

How in the world could this middle-aged woman with sad eyes and a puffy, wrinkled face, someone probably no wiser than they, so unerringly and immediately understand the sacred sense of responsibility and unadulterated trust they feel toward each other, particularly since they have only a vague understanding of it themselves? How does she do it?

The young man, scissors in hand, hesitates. Then, after snipping off her braids, he gazes at them for a long moment before gently putting them into a small plastic bag. The whole scene reminds Liu Yuying of a similar incident nearly twenty years earlier between herself and Wu Guodong. What's with me today? Why does everything remind me of Wu Guodong and me?

Liu Yuying is putting the finishing touches on the girl's perm with the hair dryer.

The two faces in the mirror represent two worlds. Next to the

rosy-cheeked, bright-eyed face of the girl, Liu looks even more
pale and drawn than usual. Wasn't she once rosy cheeked and
bright eyed, too? As she looks at the girl's reflection she is moved
to wish, "Oh, my dear, I hope you stay this beautiful, this fresh
looking forever!"

As the hair dryer hums softly, Liu Yuying twists the hair behind
the girl's ears into curls that fall onto her cheeks, highlighting her
youthful charm. The girl looks bashfully at her reflection in the
mirror, barely able to recognize herself. It will take some time for
her to get used to her new appearance.

Somehow the two youngsters are aware that the unspectacular
event unfolding in this beauty shop on the night before their
wedding and the unspectacular hairdresser they have encountered
will have a lasting impact on their life together.

The young man, excited and flustered, reaches into one of the
shopping bags, takes out a wrapped package, and hands it to Liu
Yuying. "Stylist Liu, this is for you, it's . . . it's our wedding
candy!"

"I can't take that, but thank you for the thought."

But after having had it thrust upon her several times, she knows
it would be ungracious not to accept the gift, so she opens the
package, takes out two candies wrapped in thin red paper with the
"double happiness" sign stamped on them, and puts the box back
into the shopping bag. Then she escorts them out of the beauty
shop.

At this hour there aren't many people on the street, which is
covered by a thin layer of snow. Liu Yuying remains standing on
the sidewalk watching the happy couple walk off. Once again she
makes a silent wish: "I hope you stay this beautiful forever!"

She waits until they walk into the night and are out of sight
before turning to go back inside. Suddenly she spots Wu Guodong
leaning against a tree next to the door of the shop. He must have
been standing there a long time, since his tattered cap, his shoulders, and his scarf are covered with snow. Liu grips the two pieces
of candy tightly in her hand as she watches him walk slowly toward her.

Three

He Jiabin is looking sternly, even somewhat gloatingly, into the man's fat, greasy face. It's huge, so much larger than an ordinary face. He can barely keep himself from shouting in the affected manner of a Beijing Opera aficionado: "What a face, oh, what a huge face!" Or even more cuttingly: "Now there's a face that'll give you plenty of face!"

His greasy-faced host is still quite young, but a lifetime of rich food and drink has given him sagging jowls, a double chin, and a drooping belly.

"Worried, are you?" He Jiabin is thinking. "Well, you've got every right to be. Maybe if I get you good and worried you'll lose some of that fat!"

But the man isn't as worried as He Jiabin thinks. It's all an act. His experience as a purchasing agent has taught him how to deal with all sorts of people. His facial expressions serve the same function as the made-up faces of Beijing Opera actors; he tailors his role to the audience and makes up his face accordingly. Someone like He Jiabin is putty in his hands. Although he is only an intermediary, it is still a good idea to win him over; this is what's called "the toast." If that fails, he can always bypass him and go straight to Director Feng, an old comrade-in-arms of the local Party secretary. Director Feng was the one who had let him in the "back door" to supply the equipment for the power plant, and by comparison, what he's trying to arrange this time is chicken feed. Naturally, he can't go running to Director Feng for every little thing that crops up. Knowing how to use connections takes brains; you have to be alert to spot the right opportunity at the critical moment. It's like a savings account—you maintain a healthy balance only by limiting your withdrawals and making deposits whenever possible.

The man smiles ingratiatingly. "Would you mind checking with the factory one more time to see if they could adjust the voltage level? We were so rushed when we signed the purchase order we didn't have time to recheck the figures."

"Nonsense! How could the people who signed the order not know that a piece of equipment with these specifications requires a generator motor that supplies six thousand volts, not three hundred eighty? Were they drunk? This is supposed to be the work of professionals, not someone from off the street looking for a handout!" He bangs the table on which the crumpled purchase order is lying. "Besides, there's nothing I can do about it anyway. That power plant of yours isn't in this year's state plan, so you're not supposed to be ordering equipment from us anyway. We're only supposed to supply capital construction that falls within the state plan. What puzzles me is how you managed to get the basic equipment in the first place."

He Jiabin is venting his anger on this man. He often laments how hard it is to do his job. Maybe he'd be better off just letting things slide because all he's ever gotten from his work is a bellyful of anger.

He knows that the man in front of him, for example, was once a store clerk, and if he'd been content to work hard, who knows, he might have turned out all right. But he chose the path of corruption, for which he seems perfectly suited, and now here he is, a purchasing agent, which some people assume is little more than a traveling salesman who deals in needles and thread, cabbages, and the like. How did he get the job? His brother-in-law ran the power plant, and that connection set him up over all the loyal, hard-working employees and led to this ridiculous state of affairs. What difference does it make to him that all of this costs the state a fistful of money, since none of it comes out of his pocket?

None of this comes as a surprise to He Jiabin, who has seen shady dealings and nepotism like this many times before. And not just in small power plants, but in big operations too. Back in 1975 a high-ranking official permitted the installation of a set of 125,000-kilowatt generators without obtaining official permission, since the on-site director of construction had been his wartime bodyguard, which gave him all the clout he needed. He Jiabin has worked at the Ministry of Heavy Industry for years, and during the Cultural Revolution, he saw one high-ranking official after another personally approve all sorts of construction, year in and year out. What did it matter if they weren't in the state plan? Who took the state plan seriously anyway? Every year there were complaints of overextended construction, but what did they expect? Even with all their carefully formulated plans (just how scientific those plans were is something better left unexplored), anyone who pleased could add an item. So a meal for five was laid out for ten people, and no one ever had enough. It was always the lame argument, "There's food on the table, so everyone eats."

Keep cutting back! Tighten your belts! But where could you do the cutting, since everyone had their powerful backers? By taking what was available, construction progressed at a snail's pace, and it was common for projects to be drawn out for eight or even ten years. No one seemed concerned since none of it came out of their hides.

This man, the brother-in-law of a highly placed official, is a perfect example, for although he's never been anyone's bodyguard, he has plenty of well-placed connections. He recently delivered a large quantity of walnuts, dates, eggs, and the eagerly sought bamboo-leaf liqueur, which he made available to everyone. It was all paid for, so who could refuse, particularly since it was so hard to get the stuff locally and it was dirt cheap? Even He Jiabin bought ten catties of eggs, since, as a bachelor, he doesn't have the luxury of a family ration book, which would give him an allowance of two catties every month.

They want for nothing here—chrysanthemums, edible fungus, peanuts, ginseng. Every province in the country needs power plants, and every one of them produces local products for export. The supplier of electricity can demand anything he wants. His wishes are their command, and for anyone who can't deliver, he can always lower the voltage or turn off the power. No unit can function without electricity, including the suppliers of local products. Units wanting to build power plants and get them up quickly have to compete not only for capital and the basic construction materials—lumber, steel, concrete—but for the timely arrival of the appropriate type and quantity of machinery as well, which is just as critical; for this you have to rely on contacts among the distributors. It's a snap when you deal with friends who can tip the balance in your favor where supply is concerned, and easily speed up delivery.

That's how things are done.

Reportedly, this small provincial power plant had even sent five or six people to Beijing for additional funding (since county funds alone were insufficient, they had to make up the deficit through state support), materials, and equipment. They stayed in a guest house for several months, and took taxis everywhere they went, to the tune of more than six hundred yuan, paid for by the blood and sweat of the peasants back home.

What's going on here? He Jiabin wonders with a sneer.

Of course, he knows that losing his temper or making sarcastic remarks would be as useless as throwing a childish tantrum. He is approaching the age of fifty, has worked for over twenty years, and is still a stickler for procedures. But his hands are tied in matters like this, and, besides, with this fellow he is up against a master. If

He Jiabin refuses to go along with him, the man can run to Director Feng, who will hand the matter over to Department Head Ho, who will in turn get some clever comrade to take He's place. There is, after all, no one assigned to the case, since it falls outside the state plan. Department Head Ho could, for example, hand it to Lao Shi, who has been looking for a chance to settle scores with He Jiabin. He'd be only too happy to wax eloquent on the importance of supporting agricultural construction, and how this power plant is a significant step in that direction and, therefore, an integral part of agricultural modernization. When Lao Shi isn't playing fast and loose with the truth, he's running over to report to Department Head Ho and Director Feng. He has his heart set on joining the Party.

Shi Quanqing always keeps close tabs on He Jiabin without letting on what he's doing. As far as he's concerned, He Jiabin is juvenile to the point of absurdity. In all the years they have worked together, he has watched He Jiabin stumble or be rebuffed time and again. He has spotted every obstacle that has confronted He Jiabin waiting to send him sprawling, but he has never once alerted him to the danger; he couldn't wait to see him fall flat on his face.

The world is guided by a remarkable law of symbiosis: some organisms exist by attaching themselves to others, like mosses and creepers that attach themselves to old trees; but unlike the organisms that grow on dead tree trunks, some parasites pillage living trees and suck the life out of them.

Although Shi Quanqing can't take immediate advantage of what He Jiabin has been saying and doing in this particular matter, it could certainly be stored away for the future.

The door slides open just a crack before being noisily flung open as Department Head Ho Ting enters the room. She is upset—her step and pained look make that clear—and Shi Quanqing knows at once that she's come looking for He Jiabin.

Ho Ting reads Shi Quanqing's expression and guesses correctly that He Jiabin is chewing out a "comrade from a grass-roots unit."

Shi's face has traces of anger, sympathy, censure . . . the look of a fair-minded man who doesn't like what he's seeing.

Ho Ting pulls a long face and knits her short eyebrows. The way her face changes every time she sees He Jiabin is a familiar sight to Shi Quanqing.

Wearing the dignity of her position, she walks up to He Jiabin's desk, but just as she is about to say something to him, the telephone rings.

A long-distance call, for sure, given the frequency and persistence of the rings.

He Jiabin picks up the telephone. "Hello, who's this?"

"Long-distance operator. There's a call for He Jiabin."

"That's me, go ahead."

"Hello, hello, is this Lao He? It's me, Lao Cai from the Taojiang hydroelectric plant!"

"What's up?"

"Hello, hello, I say hello——"

"Stop with all the hellos. What's on your mind? What's the problem? You've already used up a minute of this call with your infernal hellos. This is costing money!"

"It's like this. We ordered a hydraulic turbine from Austria . . ."

"I'm aware of that."

"Well, we just received the main engine specs, and a lot of the equipment we ordered from you last time doesn't meet those specs. So we want to cancel that part of the order!"

The nerve of that guy! Not a trace of embarrassment or discomfort in his voice. He Jiabin bellows into the phone, "I told you to your face to be patient and wait for the specs before ordering the equipment, but you wouldn't listen! Now you come to me, after the factory has already started production. If you cancel the order, where'll that put us?"

"Why blame us? We were authorized by our superiors to order the equipment. If we hadn't ordered it at the time, we'd have been accused of delaying the production schedule, and you know what that would have meant for us. Besides, we're operating within the state plan, so everything's aboveboard!"

He's right, how could they be blamed? Those in charge had

prescribed that every capital construction project move forward in accordance with strict procedures if it was to be included in the state plan: design permits, responsibility charts, design approval documents, all the materials, blueprints, the specifications for major and secondary equipment . . . all were required before any orders could be placed. But at this summer's meeting, representatives from three unauthorized power plants in provinces within He Jiabin's territory were there to place orders. One of them hadn't decided yet whether to import the main turbine or purchase one that was locally made; another hadn't even selected a building site, nor did he know if they'd be using oil or coal for fuel, which meant that they hadn't even begun to think about a turbine. Then there was the hydroelectric plant represented by Lao Cai, which had only signed a letter of intent with an Austrian company, not an actual contract. Before the main engine specs were in hand, Cai's superiors insisted on purchasing the supporting equipment. So what good were all those strict capital construction procedures in the first place?

"Who's going to take responsibility for the losses?" He Jiabin asks in exasperation. What a stupid thing to say! Who would take the responsibility? No one, that's who. Better to put it in meaningful terms. "Will you compensate the factory for its losses?"

"Sure!" Lao Cai says without hesitation. A wily old bird.

"Here's what we'll do," He Jiabin says with a slight change of heart. "Since we can't just cancel the order and forget about it, why don't you write up a report to explain what happened, and we'll pass it on to the factory."

"Fine, that's what we'll do."

"Okay, let's do it that way."

He Jiabin hangs up the phone, making a mental note to write a citizen's letter to the State Council about the chaotic situation regarding state plans and capital construction. Problems that had cropped up before the fall of the Gang of Four could in retrospect be blamed on them. But now, the situation in economic development has become so chaotic that it's going to be impossible to utilize the limited available resources—manpower, material, and capital—to the best advantage while minimizing waste. And if they can't manage this, what's the use in talking about speeding up the Four Modernizations?

While He Jiabin is still mopping his sweaty brow, after all that shouting into the telephone, and still thinking about plans and capital construction procedures, Ho Ting impatiently taps his desk top with her finger. He has been blissfully unaware that she wants to talk to him. But he's not about to ask what she wants, since he's never been able to please her, and he knows that if he opens his mouth, she'll probably read him the riot act, as usual. Over the past few years, lots of people have forgotten that respect for others is a reflection of one's own ethical level.

"Your section chief tells me you haven't turned in your summary on what you learned from Daqing, is that right?"

"I told him I have no intention of writing one!"

Looking like a judge about to pronounce sentence, she says, "All right then, Director Feng wants to see you."

The greasy-faced man grins spitefully.

Shi Quanqing quickly lowers his eyes so as not to reveal the happiness that fills them. Shi Quanqing's attitude toward He Jiabin is particularly baffling since He has never done anything to hurt or offend him. Why does he hate him so? Actually, it wouldn't make any difference if He had done anything to him, or offended him, since their incompatible personalities make them natural enemies.

As for Ho Ting, she and He Jiabin had once gotten along well enough, but ever since the Party branch elections of the year before, relations between them have soured. If it had really been a matter of having Lao Luo replace Guo Hongcai because the latter wasn't up to the propaganda duties assigned him, things might have worked out all right. But this was actually nothing but window dressing, and it soon became clear that the real reason Guo was replaced was that he always took contrary positions at the Party branch meetings. For instance, Ho Ting and Luo Haitao were promoting Shi Quanqing's application for Party membership, but the majority of the members of the Party branch disagreed; so the two of them simply forwarded Shi's application to the Bureau

33

Party headquarters without going through the branch committee. Guo Hongcai immediately went to Bureau Director Fang Wenxuan of the Bureau Party Committee and told him what had happened. Fang sent for Ho Ting and criticized her for her actions. Of course, this was only one of many incidents that made Guo Hongcai a thorn in the sides of Ho Ting and Luo Haitao, who were always on the lookout for a chance to fix his wagon. But he somehow managed to keep himself out of harm's way. With the sectarian dissension in the branch committee, the members began drifting toward two separate camps. He Jiabin spoke to Ho Ting about this on a number of occasions, probably because there had been so much grumbling among the comrades. He recommended that they hold an informal meeting to hash it out. In all her years as branch secretary there hadn't been a single informal gathering, and that was inexcusable.

Faced with this situation, Ho Ting finally called an informal meeting. Normally, when he was talking to Ho Ting, Luo Haitao was all over Guo Hongcai with criticisms, but once the meeting was convened, he kept his opinions to himself. Then as soon as the meeting was over and they went back to the Party headquarters to meet behind closed doors, out poured the endless criticisms. It was more than He Jiabin could take, but Shi Quanqing sat there and fueled the flames of dissension by commenting, "Watch what you're saying. Someone in the room might start spreading rumors that will affect our unity."

He Jiabin would have ignored them if this snide comment hadn't been aimed at him. "Why didn't you say any of this to Comrade Guo's face at the meeting and get it out into the open instead of running him down behind his back? You hold these meetings behind closed doors because you're afraid people might talk. Well, you can check for yourselves. During all the years I've worked here, when have I ever spread any rumors? Who's really undermining unity here?"

"I didn't mean you," Shi Quanqing said. "I was talking about Wang Mengyun."

"I don't care who you were talking about, it's still not right. Besides, Wang Mengyun was reassigned elsewhere a long time ago, so none of this has anything to do with him. What the hell are you up to?"

The dark expression on Luo Haitao's face was like a summer sky just before the outbreak of a storm. "All the office staff are here, so where do you get off accusing us of running anyone down behind his back?"

This was just the sort of quibbling response a troublemaker like him could be counted on to make. "If you won't confront someone, then you're talking behind his back. And as a section chief and a Party member, not only are you abetting Shi Quanqing's slanderous, trumped-up accusations of Comrade Guo, but you're a participant yourself, and that's wrong. I refuse to be a part of this kind of meeting." He Jiabin rose to leave.

Luo Haitao could see that He Jiabin was making sense, and since He was obviously a man of principle, Luo took a different, more defensive tack: "Thanks to you, the meeting has turned into a farce. Now how do you expect us to continue?"

"Not continuing this meeting is the best thing that could happen to you. The more meetings of this type are held, the greater the mistakes you'll be guilty of."

Incidents like this became common knowledge in a hurry, but that wasn't He Jiabin's doing. The Bureau Party Committee soon learned of the disharmony among the various unit chiefs. Feng Xiaoxian talked to several rank-and-file comrades to get a feel for the situation, and naturally, He Jiabin was among them. He made a complete report of the problems in the department.

But then Director Feng, who was responsible for political and personnel affairs, called in Ho Ting and told her everything he'd heard from He Jiabin and the others. Of course, it would have been difficult to question his motives, and if it had been a unit where political affairs were running smoothly and the political level of the person in charge was high, there wouldn't have been much of a problem working things out. But objectively speaking, the organizational issues He Jiabin wanted to discuss at the branch committee meeting had all been postponed indefinitely, ostensibly

35

because he still had too many nonproletarian tendencies and his ideas had to await further tests. Ho Ting, who had paid no attention to political study for years, made the comrades who had reported on her to Director Feng spend a week studying Chairman Mao's essay on liberalism.

Predictably, there is a deep sense of mystery and foreboding associated with room 213. Its door is always shut tightly, for this is the place where so many people's fates are determined. It is behind this door that unit and section chief assignments are made, raises in salary and promotions are given, admission to the Party is affirmed, certain people are disciplined and others reassigned . . .

All this is on He Jiabin's mind as he makes his way to room 213. With the exception of reassignment, none of these considerations has anything to do with him. Is that what lies in store for him? What else is he qualified to do? He is nearly fifty and has already used up more than twenty of those years working at the same job, without ever really accomplishing anything. Formerly a student of physics, if he'd been assigned after college graduation to a job better suited to his specialty, he might have made his mark. But why dredge up the past? There's always a need for a basic knowledge of physics here, though with the way they go about organizing construction, a graduate of a second-rate technical school could easily handle the job. And so for more than twenty years he has muddled along, ignorant of current research in physics in China, let alone the rest of the world. Worse yet, he's just about forgotten the little he once knew. He sighs over the wasted years as he walks into room 213, Feng Xiaoxian's office.

"You sent for me, Director Feng?"

Director Feng raises his massive intellectual's head from behind a huge stack of documents. Perhaps his thoughts are still on the documents he has been poring over because he looks right through He Jiabin for the longest time. "Uh, I sent for you, yes, who told you? Lao Ho?" Then he seems to remember. "Oh, right, I wanted to talk to you. Have a seat."

Feng Xiaoxian makes himself comfortable, removes his reading glasses and puts them into a case that is neither fashionable nor very fancy.

From Feng Xiaoxian's mannerisms and the way he dresses, one might assume that he is fresh from the countryside. He prefers black cloth shoes to leather ones, and he wears a Chinese tunic—at first these tunics had been gray, then they were replaced by blue twill, then blue serge, and finally blue wool.

In the summer months he keeps his tunic unbuttoned and rolls his undershirt all the way up to his armpits. He is forever rubbing his hairy chest with his hands, as though lathering himself up in a bath, keeping it reasonably free of grime. When he isn't rubbing his chest, he is rolling up his pant legs as high as they go, so he can rub his hairy legs with both hands. When winter arrives, making such activities impracticable, he removes his cloth slip-ons—he doesn't like leather shoes or any shoes with laces because putting them on and taking them off is too much trouble—and scratches between his toes; fortunately, it is too cold for him to take off his socks. These quirks of his, which only appear during meetings, like conditioned reflexes, possibly surface because he is so absorbed in the topics discussed at the meeting. At other times he gives the impression of being deep, shrewd, and unpredictable. Like now, for instance.

He Jiabin can't tell if Feng Xiaoxian is pondering what he should say, or if he simply can't recall why he sent for the man.

It is neither. No, he is trying to recall everything he knows about this He Jiabin, so he can determine how to deal with him. This fellow isn't a student of the Daqing model, nor is he a progressive worker; rather, he is a man who is forever making his generally caustic opinions known. He has some strange ideas and a flair for wrangling, whether he has a basis for his arguments or not. He is sophisticated enough in political theory to find a way to bring Marx or Engels into his arguments. And he is the one who reported to Bureau Director Fang that Feng received some local products from his hometown. Fortunately for Feng, he'd turned the matter over to Ho Ting, who explained that these gifts were an expression of thanks for local support of the construction of the power plant and that, of course, they would be shared by everyone

37

in the Ministry. Since Feng had everything he needed anyway, the loss of these gifts did not affect him. He never missed an opportunity to comment that he wanted for nothing. Eventually, Ho Ting delivered some of the walnuts and the bamboo-leaf liqueur to his house, for which he paid her, giving her something less than the market price—no, quite a bit less—as a matter of fact, little more than a symbolic gesture. But, owing to Ho Ting's lack of discretion, the incident somehow became common knowledge. A matter like this should always be handled discreetly, and only a fool like Ho Ting could mess it up so badly. So Fang seized the opportunity to make a report at a Party meeting, warning against the practice of accepting gifts from units outside the state plan in exchange for allocating to them supplies earmarked for planned construction projects. There was to be no influence peddling. Feng Xiaoxian fumed over Fang's use of a trivial matter like that to show off, but he managed to counter with a face-saving speech: "Yes, we must preserve Party integrity, traditions, and style. How many difficulties have we experienced in the past? Were they greater than those we face today or not? The War of Resistance against Japan, the War of Liberation, land reform, the War to Resist America and Aid Korea, and the three years of national trials that nearly destroyed the nation and decimated our people—we've been through it all. And for what? The prestige of the Party is high, but that has only been realized through the combined efforts of Party cadres at every level and the rank-and-file members. And yet today too many cadres have abandoned the integrity, traditions, and style of the Party, turning their backs on the masses and corrupting law and order. If this situation is allowed to continue, our national undertakings will be seriously disrupted!"

This was a case of "you attack yours and I'll attack mine," and no one at the meeting could make head or tails of what he was saying.

Feng Xiaoxian was no match for Fang in a confrontation, and whenever the two of them clashed, Feng always came out looking like a simpleton, while in fact, it was all a show. He had plenty of opportunities to settle scores with Fang since he avoided getting caught up in trivial affairs that ultimately led nowhere, like Fang did. Nor would he make the mistake of doing the dirty work himself to get even with Fang. Using his authority as director of personnel, he had already surrounded Fang with his own people, who reported to him on everything his adversary said and did; even the thoughts running through Fang's mind were the subject of inquiry and analysis by these people, who then reported the results of their systematic observations to Feng.

As for Fang, decades of revolutionary work had all been spent in vain. What talents did he have? What qualifications? After joining the revolution in 1941 he became a bureau director, two years after Feng. How did he manage that? Because he had a little taste of culture; but education can be a disadvantage since it sometimes leads to disreputable practices. . . .

Inexplicably, Feng suddenly feels that this He Jiabin is a lot like Fang. And with that thought he now knows how to proceed. "How've you been getting along lately?" he asks benignly, avoiding a frontal attack.

"Getting along in what?"

Feng Xiaoxian frowns. What kind of answer is that? Taking that kind of attitude when talking to one's superior shows an abysmal lack of respect. But he chooses not to make an issue of it. He'll just go ahead and do what he has to do; no sense making the man hate him in the process. "Well," he explains patiently, "in, uh, for instance, ideology, work, life . . ."

He Jiabin understands perfectly. There is no cadre in charge of personnel because there are no personnel duties to perform, and he is suddenly on guard, knowing that he is dealing with an invisible adversary. As he thinks back to what Ho Ting said to him just a short while ago, he assumes that this meeting comes out of his refusal to seek personal lessons from the Daqing experience and write an end-of-year summary on what he learned from Daqing. But if the man across from him doesn't bring up the subject, he certainly isn't foolish enough to do so. He answers Feng's ambiguous question with an equally ambiguous response. "No complaints, I'm getting along all right."

Okay, now we're in business. As long as he responds, we can get to the business at hand.

"All right isn't good enough. Our bureau aims to become

another Daqing within two years, which means that every one of us has to perform his duties in accordance with Daqing standards."

Here it comes, He Jiabin thinks.

"What's your personal Daqing plan?"

It is clear to He Jiabin that the other man knows he has no Daqing plan and hasn't made a summary of his Daqing experience; since Ho Ting reported this to Feng some time ago, what purpose is served by beating around the bush like this? Director Fang wouldn't handle it like this. He'd say straight out: "Comrade He Jiabin, why haven't you made up your Daqing plan or written a summary?"

If Feng Xiaoxian would come right to the point, He Jiabin might put a little more stock in the man's sincerity. That is, after all, his political function and job. He is treating He Jiabin like a three-year-old, trying to trick him into believing that Ho Ting didn't report him. What a joke! A department head is expected to report to her superior on the ideological orthodoxy of her subordinates, as long as the reports are factual and don't set out to smear or slander anyone. Why the cover-up? He hadn't tried to cover up the fact that he'd reported to the Bureau Party Committee on the problems in Ho Ting's department.

"I haven't made a Daqing plan."

"Why not? It's a matter of principle."

"Not to my way of thinking." He Jiabin laughs to himself. What would Feng do if he knew that some of the comrades in the department had simply copied their personal Daqing plans from each other?

Feng Xiaoxian puts his reading glasses back on and stares at He Jiabin as though he has suddenly turned into some strange zoo animal, which he is scrutinizing carefully. He is stuck for a response to He Jiabin. Should he pin a label on him? No, this isn't the time for that sort of thing; besides, labels have become so commonplace that nobody takes them seriously anymore. And they matter even less to someone like He Jiabin. There is also the problem of finding a suitable label, since none of those used in over twenty years of political campaigns covers this type of situation.

Should he criticize him then? How can he, since he isn't sure what the man is up to? But his cavalier attitude toward Daqing is serious enough to be criticized, since it is a harbinger of unhealthy tendencies. As a deputy bureau director responsible for personnel matters and political work, he is particularly sensitive to the serious ramifications of this issue. Daqing is a banner raised by Chairman Mao himself, and no one ever dared oppose it until now, let alone an upstart who is one of *his* own subordinates! No, that'll never do! Besides, this fellow doesn't care when or where he pops off; and if the news gets out, how will it reflect on him, a deputy bureau director in charge of political work and personnel? To hell with how it affects He Jiabin, even temporarily. So what to do? First things first—he has to make his point without any ambiguity.

"You have a very mistaken view, as I see it, and you won't get my support. You're on a dangerous course."

"I haven't expressed any view."

Just like an intellectual, always looking for a debate. But, my fine, feathered friend, where politics are concerned, you've got a few things to learn.

"Well then, now's a good time to express one. Since you refuse to make a personal plan or write a summary, you must have your reasons."

Among interrogators, this approach is known as "the lure."

"I don't have any particular view. But I do have a friend whose younger sister works in a women's oil production team at Daqing. I ran into her when she came home for a family visit a few years ago, and I asked her what she did in her spare time.

" 'Not much.'

" 'What do you mean "not much"? Don't you read?'

" 'Nope.'

" 'How about TV?'

" 'Nope.'

" 'Newspapers?'

" 'Nope.'

"I was shocked. 'So what do you do during your time off?'

" 'We don't have that much time off. We have to attend political study sessions every night except Saturday, and by the time they're

41

over, we barely have time to wash up and brush our teeth before turning in for the night. We didn't even have a bathhouse until just recently.'

"Now I ask you, do you think those girls don't want to study, or that they're not interested in understanding current affairs or bettering themselves? No, it's that they're exhausted all the time and don't have the energy. Now bathing may be a trivial matter, but don't forget they're oil field workers! Fortunately for them, they eventually got a bathhouse. All this talk about outstripping America and the Soviet Union doesn't take into consideration the fact that their oil workers have a work load much lighter than ours. So how are we going to outstrip them? On the strength of our workers? Not on your life! Only mechanization and modernization will do the trick. Sure, our workers have a high political consciousness, like all the rest of our people, and they aren't afraid of hard times or hard work. We should be treating them as a national treasure instead of squandering their vigor. Sooner or later they're going to become workers in a modernized industrial state, but they need time to expand their knowledge to handle all that sophisticated equipment and master the technology. And that's not all. Has anyone thought about their desires for marriage and family? They're human beings, not machines; but even machines are taken off the line for maintenance and repairs. I just wonder what's on their superiors' minds. Whatever it is, it's wrong. It's like putting blindfolds on the workers and making them identify parts by touch. Should a worker know what he's doing or not? Of course! That's what makes our workers so good. But in the ideological view of their superiors, that knowledge is a liability. In the midst of an electronic age, we're moving backwards, to the point where people aren't even allowed to use their eyes. Why don't we just close our eyes and grope along, and to hell with modernization! That should please everyone. I don't see any difference between that and having everyone go back to crawling around on all fours, only to be warned if they insist on walking upright: 'You people there, don't you know it's wrong to let your hands remain idle like that! If you keep it up, you'll turn into a bunch of idlers who only want to live a life of ease and forget the glories of work.

42

So mend your ways and join the rest of us diligently and conscientiously crawling along on all fours!' "

He's making it all up, Feng Xiaoxian is thinking.

"The Daqing management techniques also need looking into. I find it hard to believe that theirs is the only model available to us. Aren't Party members supposed to believe in dialectics? Why waste all our energy giving one order after another? A few material incentives, no matter how small, would easily produce results equal to those achieved by force."

He Jiabin pauses to catch his breath, giving Feng Xiaoxian an opportunity to squeeze in a comment. He has already heard enough to make his hair stand on end. "The red banner of Daqing was personally hoisted by Chairman Mao, so you'd better watch what you're saying!"

"I'm not saying that everything about Daqing is bad. It's played an important historical role. During the three hard years when we had no oil, the oil workers at Daqing saved us from running out completely. It was an enormous contribution, and every citizen of Daqing shares in the glory of that achievement. Then during the Cultural Revolution, when the Gang of Four brought China to the brink of economic collapse, Daqing withstood the challenge and never stopped producing. But nothing goes unchanged, and just because you're progressive today doesn't mean you'll be progressive tomorrow. There's always room for improvement. So what's wrong with trying to better Daqing? We shouldn't be talking about outstripping anyone or developing when we can't do anything outside of set patterns. Development is seen as chopping down a banner, as revisionism; it's called being abstract or idealistic! You just wait and see: the day will come when we outstrip Daqing. Nothing stays the same forever because life itself, in all its richness and glory, keeps moving forward."

As He Jiabin grows increasingly excited with every word, Feng Xiaoxian listens to all this talk of industrial management, abstractions, and idealism with considerable difficulty. But he isn't about to let on to He Jiabin that it is all over his head. The expression on his face is one of a bureau director who knows more than He Jiabin, though the truth of the matter is, he doesn't need to worry about things like this since his responsibilities are in personnel and political work. None of this has anything to do with his job. He is getting drowsy and has to stifle a yawn. After sifting through everything that He Jiabin has just said, he decides that the only thing worth remembering is his fundamental opposition to the red banner of Daqing. All his extravagant nonsense boils down to that and nothing else.

So what is he going to do with this man? Circumstances and political climate always determine action. Time, conditions, and location are the three major criteria in the Marxist approach to issues. Feng Xiaoxian silently congratulates himself—decades of revolutionary activity have not been wasted, and he is no neophyte where Marxism-Leninism is concerned. Expressing one's personal opinion to anyone on any subject is always risky. The political situation could change without warning, and today's hero could be tomorrow's goat. In his "Last Will and Testament" Sun Yat-sen wrote, "Store up the experiences of forty years of revolution"! It's always best to leave yourself a way out. That big head of his is filled with a hodgepodge of assorted knowledge, sort of like a general store.

It's time to wrap this up. "But, we're all responsible for our own words and deeds. If you don't make a Daqing plan or write a summary, it'll have an effect on whether or not your unit becomes a Daqing-style department, and that in turn will have an effect on the bureau. After all your years of work, you ought to know that at least! No individual should affect an entire bureau. Are you prepared to accept the responsibility if we fail to become a Daqing-style bureau because of your obstinacy?"

"It's not my responsibility to accept! Where does it say that I won't be able to perform my duties unless I study Daqing? It's always the same with this Daqing study, year in and year out—summaries, assessments, passing on valuable experience—and what's it gotten us? That time would have been better spent at good, steady work, like trying to resolve the friction in our department or dealing with problems among the cadres."

He Jiabin has more to say, including his criticisms of political work within the bureau, but he keeps his mouth shut because he knows he'd be wasting his breath. That is how the bureau works.

Feng Xiaoxian quickly senses that he can't keep arguing like this with He Jiabin, who is not a man to mince words. He might really put Feng on the spot. One of the legacies of the Cultural Revolution is that virtually everything is now open to public scrutiny, from Central Committee directives to the private lives of leaders, even such incidental matters as who treats whom to a free meal, who uses public funds to have furniture made for his private use, and more. This sort of talk fills the streets. The leaders' prestige has never been lower, as witnessed by this run-of-the-mill cadre talking back to him. People are ready to report you at the drop of a hat these days, or spread malicious rumors, anywhere and at any time, and a person who tries to eliminate such influences, no matter how tentatively, leaves himself vulnerable to accusations, attacks, and revenge. In a word, it is hard being a leader these days because in ideological terms the people are like a cake of bean curd that can't be molded no matter what you do. Before the Cultural Revolution, who would have dared to speak to the leader of his own unit like this?

There's no getting around it, the fifties were really the good old days. Lots of people miss the standard of living, the political consciousness of the people, the relations between people back then. Even Feng Xiaoxian is nostalgic for those days. If He Jiabin talked like this back in 1957, he'd have been branded a Rightist. No wonder the Party branch turned down his application. They apparently knew what they were doing. Anyone with organizational views like this would wreak havoc in the Party.

Better send him on his way and let Ho Ting deal with him.

He Jiabin has just gotten off work. He spots Wan Qun standing in the slush with what looks like a frown on her face but might only be an impression created by the deep wrinkles in her brow. She calls to He Jiabin, "Lao He, tomorrow's Sunday. Will you go to the coal yard with me and help me bring back some charcoal briquettes?" There is no need for any politeness between the two of them.

"Why not wait for them to deliver it?"

"I've been waiting. Whenever I press them they promise to send it over, but I'm still waiting. I have to go get it myself before I run out completely."

Being a single parent is hard on a woman. Why doesn't she remarry? He's given up trying to convince her. Maybe things wouldn't have turned out so badly if he hadn't urged her to marry in the first place. He Jiabin can't escape his guilt feelings.

In 1962, right after Wan Qun's graduation from college, she was assigned to a job here and immediately won the hearts of her colleagues.

Those days, if someone told her some wild story about a person with four ears, she'd cock her head and listen earnestly, as though it were somehow possible, then open her eyes wide and remark credulously, "Really?"

No matter how outlandish the joke, she'd laugh as though it were the funniest thing she'd ever heard.

Everyone loved to tease her with childish jokes and stories, for there was something irresistible about looking into those trusting eyes, like getting a glimpse of Paradise. She loved to sing the popular song "Havana Dove": "When I leave my beloved homeland, my true love croons tearfully, I'll follow you to the ends of the earth, like a dove flying over the ocean . . ."

Back then she was that dove, cooing softly wherever she went. But now her innocence and her free and easy manner have disappeared. Her eyes are sunken, and the corners of her mouth, which once arched upwards mischievously, droop from the weight of her worries and give testimony to the failure of her life. Her bangs, which once fell lightly over her forehead—where are they now? She is so thin that the veins on her exposed forehead stand out even when she isn't angry. Insensitive people would probably say that she has "the look of a widow." Well, she is a widow. In 1970, her husband, accused of being a member of the "May Sixteenth" radical element, committed suicide at one of the May Seventh cadre schools.

He Jiabin regrets having encouraged his friend to ask her to marry him back then. But he didn't have a crystal ball, and every marriage is a gamble anyway!

He met this friend in college, and even though the fellow was an

46

engineering student, he had a pretty good background in painting, music, and literature. He was a handsome, debonair young man, just right for Wan Qun.

"If you don't go after that little dove Wan Qun, sooner or later she'll wind up in someone else's nest, even though it'd be hard to find anyone worthy of her."

"Why don't you go after her yourself?"

"Not me! All I can do with women is put them on a pedestal, like a piece of artwork, where their beauty can't be tarnished. If I were to see my own wife pregnant, like a kangaroo with a bulging pouch, or nursing like any other common mammal, I'd feel like a sinner and I'd stop loving her."

"You're an aesthete!"

"Maybe."

"Then why are you trying to talk *me* into chasing after her?"

"I can't expect everyone to be like me, to live his life in accordance with my views, can I? Besides, sooner or later some man's going to come by, and I'd rather it be you than someone else."

"You're a strange man with strange ideas!"

Wan Qun was blessed with a happy marriage. However, she was disappointed in love itself, which she discovered to be nothing more than a means of satisfying one's need for possession. Then came the millstone of politics. Naturally, after her husband's case was redressed, there was no longer any talk of suicide or counter-revolutionary witch-hunts, but who would be willing to help her shoulder the burdens of life?

He Jiabin wonders if he should hold himself responsible for her tears.

"You ought to get a gas stove," he remarks casually. But he immediately wishes he'd kept quiet, for he remembers that she once told him that she didn't want to buy a gas stove because the gas bottles are so heavy she'd have to get help every time she needed a fresh one. Asking for help once or twice is all right, but every month is out of the question. Charcoal briquettes, on the other

47

hand, she can carry upstairs on her own, as long as they are delivered to her doorstep; that way she isn't indebted to anyone.

He'd momentarily forgotten how strong willed she was.

A car is honking its horn softly but persistently. They're blocking its way. He draws Wan Qun aside to where the slush isn't quite so deep.

As the car passes, they see the eternally impenetrable face of Fang Wenxuan. Calling it a cold face would not be an exaggeration.

"Okay," He Jiabin says to Wan Qun, "I'll be over tomorrow morning about nine." He discovers to his surprise that tears are glistening in her eyes.

What's going on with this neurotic woman?

Four

The block of four-story flats must have been built before 1956 when apartments had higher ceilings; they are at least a story taller than today's four-story buildings. For someone young and healthy, a four-flight climb is next to nothing. Ye Zhiqiu is healthy enough, but her hair is thinning, the wrinkles on her face are deepening, her teeth are getting loose, and her heart isn't as strong as it used to be: the toll that forty-five years of trials and tribulations has taken.

She is winded by the time she reaches the second floor, and there's a hollow sound in her chest like that of a torn bellows. As she rests against the bannister, she wonders how she'll be received by the VIP she's taking the liberty of calling on.

Sounds fill the staircase indifferent to their surroundings; proud and resolute, they announce the logic of their existence: the chopping of filling for pot stickers, the bawling of infants, piano melodies . . . another lively Sunday! A simple tune is being played on the piano—"A Maiden's Prayer." But the pianist is just a beginner, and Ye Zhiqiu would love to help the musician get the notes right. As her memory takes over, she begins fingering the notes on the bannister, as though it were a piano keyboard. She's always liked this tune, which she played often on the assembly hall piano in middle school. It was an old, beat-up piano that had really been through the wars, its varnish flaking, scarred from top to bottom, and so badly out of tune that nothing could ever put it right again.

But none of this had ever gotten in the way of Ye Zhiqiu's "prayer." Sunlight filtering through the branches of the tall poplars would slant in through the window and shine on the hardwood floor of the assembly hall. The light and sound would be filled with the power of dreams, the dreams of a young girl, of every young girl. Once she entered college, she gave up playing the piano, for there was no time for dreams during those years. What was there to dream for? Those were days of illusions, of leisure, of the malaise of the idle class. . . . After she had started working, she scrimped and saved enough to buy a piano, but then came the Cultural Revolution, and the piano slept beneath an old blanket for ten long years. She could play it now if she wanted to, but the desire was gone. A young girl, dreams, harmony . . . these belonged to a different world, a different galaxy.

That melody, so familiar yet so vague and distant because it's being played so badly, nearly brings tears to her eyes, bittersweet tears. Her heart is filled to overflowing with tears.

Bang! Bang! Bang! Someone, as though in competition with the piano, is banging away with a hammer.

Ye Zhiqiu is surprised that a vice-minister of heavy industry would be living with common folk in an ordinary apartment like this. Could He Jiabin have given her the wrong address? No, that was impossible. He said he'd been here before himself and had talked with the man.

Granted, "common folk" isn't quite right, since these living quarters are reserved for middle-ranking officials. But by ministerial standards it seems on the ordinary side. This observation alone makes Ye feel good about Vice-Minister Zheng Ziyun before she's even met him.

Here, this is the apartment, the one where the piano music and the banging are coming from.

She knocks on the door several times before the playing stops. The door opens.

The soft aura of a rainbow seeming to flood the doorway is Ye Zhiqiu's first impression of the girl. Her hair is soft and naturally curly, the dark brown that Chinese seem to favor; it is cut short, not much longer than Mo Zheng's. Now, what's she doing comparing every child she sees with Mo Zheng as though he were her own son! The girl's slightly crossed eyes, rather than detracting from her beauty, give her a special charm. She looks just slightly mischievous. Or maybe it's a willful look. Her tight, white turtleneck sweater clings to her slender figure. Ye Zhiqiu has never seen such a graceful girl before. Only her baggy trousers seem out of place.

As always, whenever she meets someone for the first time, Ye assumes that the girl is thinking, "My God, what an ugly woman!" But the girl's eyes betray something more—sympathy, maybe even pity. Ah, what a little angel! That clumsy, amateurish piano playing must have been hers. Ye Zhiqiu immediately forgives her for having ruined "A Maiden's Prayer."

"Who are you looking for?" she asks in a soft, sweet voice.

"Is Minister Zheng Ziyun in?"

"Where are you from?"

Ye Zhiqiu shows the girl her reporter's ID card and a letter of introduction. Intrigued by the ID card, the girl warmly invites Ye in, then goes into one of the rooms. The hammering stops.

The apartment is spotless, and somehow doesn't look lived in. The walls are bare and all the furniture looks as though it has come from the Ministry, with no attempt to coordinate colors or style. Even the curtains are the light blue variety so common in government offices. Not a hint anywhere as to the tastes or interests of the occupants. Ye Zhiqiu is amazed to see a similarity to her own careless, chaotic, and negligent life-style in this strange apartment.

51

"Are you looking for me?"

Ye Zhiqiu turns. His appearance takes her completely by surprise. Although casually dressed, he has the unmistakable look of an Oxford or Cambridge man. Not at all like He Jiabin described him. He's thin, but has a firm handshake.

"Why didn't you go through the duty office at the Ministry?" he asks, not very politely. "Have a seat!" He sits down first.

"I did. They're the ones who gave me the okay, and they even agreed to set up an appointment. But you're so busy I was starting to get anxious."

"Oh!" Zheng Ziyun looks up and studies Ye Zhiqiu. This woman looks as hard as a man. What does she do? Yuanyuan said she was a reporter.

Ye suddenly notices how big his eyes are, too big for his gaunt face. Inexplicably, she imagines he must have been a beautiful little boy, with closely cropped hair, wearing a white undershirt, and having bright eyes that sparkled like stars.

What's going on with her? She often lets her mind wander like this, her eyes dictating the direction of her thoughts, which leads to the most confusing associations imaginable. Like now, for example. Why is she trying to picture this aging man as a child? She shakes her head to drive these absurd images from her mind. "Something wrong?" Zheng Ziyun asks.

"I'd like to interview you, if I might . . ." she says hastily.

A guarded look suddenly appears in his eyes, as though he wants to avoid praise and notoriety at all costs. "I'm sorry, but there's nothing I can tell you that's worth printing." Journalists obviously put him on his guard. Is this a result of his familiarity with what went on in the industry, or is it tied to the news media's loss of credibility over the past ten years? Maybe he just doesn't want to become someone "in the news."

"You've got me wrong. I'm not going to write anything, I just want your advice on something. Now that we're implementing the Four Modernizations, how should we go about modernizing our industry?"

"Oh!" Zheng Ziyun's interest is piqued. "Is this an assignment for the newspaper?"

"No, for myself." She tells him about her recent conversation with Mo Zheng, and how his scathing denunciations were right on the mark, even though she hadn't considered telling him so to his face.

"Why are you so interested in this issue?"

"Because it affects the lives of a billion people. Without a material base all this stuff about scientific, cultural, and military development is nothing but empty talk. If I only knew more about it all, I'd do everything possible to try to convince people to take it seriously. All I have now is a gut feeling that we've made a shambles out of our economic development programs. Why is that? And what can be done about it? It's beyond me. Do you realize how much the people expect from the economic policy makers? Is the country really so poor that the people have to live such miserable lives? I don't think so. If we were like the Japanese, who know how to get twice the value out of every fen spent, then we wouldn't be as poor as we are. Why do we throw our money away? Never mind the big money, just look at the road I take every day on my way to work. It's been torn up three times over the last year, first to replace the sewer pipes, then to install gas pipes, and once more to upgrade the water mains. And what about the trees alongside the road? The locust trees were cut down to plant poplars, but before two years were out, they were replaced by pine trees. . . . Can't they come up with a broad-based, long-range plan and stick to it? Every time they tear up the road, just in terms of minor costs like wages, machinery, gas, asphalt, gravel, it's all down the drain. Can't this sort of thing be stopped? Everyone seems to know that these problems exist, but for some reason nothing changes."

This woman may look hard, but here she is talking with all the earnestness of a child.

"Do you recall the opening line of *The Communist Manifesto?*" Zheng Ziyun asks her.

" 'A spectre is haunting Europe—the spectre of communism. All the powers of old Europe have entered into a holy alliance to exorcise this spectre: Pope and Czar, Metternich and Guizot, French radicals and German police spies.' "

"Excellent. Now do you recall the final line?"

" 'Working men of all countries, unite!' " She says it like a schoolgirl answering the teacher's question. What is he thinking? That it's pure "stream of consciousness"?

Zheng Ziyun gets up from the sofa and begins pacing the room with his hands behind his back, his steps light but quick. After a while he asks her, "So why have you come to see me?"

"An old classmate of mine who works in the Ministry told me that among the officials at your level, you're someone who knows how to get things done, who's got the guts to do them, and who has an open mind." That sounded awful, as though she were trying to butter him up. She suddenly feels very uncomfortable.

Zheng Ziyun shares the feeling and responds with a frown.

"What's your former classmate's name? Which section is he in?"

"His name is He Jiabin, he's in—"

"I know him. But he hasn't come by for a long time."

"He's sort of eccentric."

"He's awfully cocky, but maybe that's a common failing among intellectuals. Still he's a good man."

"That's debatable," Ye Zhiqiu says with a smile.

"What do you mean by that?"

"Your director of political work certainly wouldn't agree with you."

"Why not?"

"Maybe because his ideology is extreme and unorthodox."

Zheng smiles wryly.

"He and I were editors of the first student paper on our college campus. We argued over the choice of a name till we were blue in the face. He said my suggestions sounded like names of cosmetic stores, and that journalism was not a cosmetic. He maintained that the soul of journalism is truth and recommended calling the paper *X-ray Lab*. But the others disagreed with him, arguing that people would think we were publishing a medical journal. He shouted and carried on, insisting that a newspaper was in fact a lot like a physician, at least a radiologist, who can make a diagnosis even if he can't effect a cure. The newspaper could tell society that it was sick and could name the sickness. Or it could tell it not to be

54

hypochondriacal, that it was well, that its organs were healthy, and that everything was running smoothly. Pretty naive and extreme, don't you think? I have to laugh when I think of it. But it was touching, too, and it's not everyone who can move people in such a naive way and still avoid being corrupted by life. That's what makes He Jiabin special. It's been twenty years, and his spirit hasn't flagged a bit. In time, even granite wears away. But he hasn't changed much at all; only the lines on his face reveal the effects of those years. What do you think the greatest force on earth is? Life? Time? The human spirit? Now that I've actually managed to get into journalism, into the newspaper business, I know that what he said was impractical. But we ought to speak the truth. What's there to be afraid of? Aren't we told that true followers of dialectic materialism have nothing to fear? Maybe we haven't come far enough yet. We're always talking about Party spirit in our newspapers, but does Party spirit mean only painting a rosy picture? Hasn't that caused us enough grief already? I'm not a politician, maybe not even a very competent journalist, and even though I think the way I do, I'm just an insignificant cog in the wheel. Do you know what the most fundamental characteristic of our generation has been? We don't understand the times!"

Ye picks up her cup and drinks some tea. "This is excellent tea."

Zheng Ziyun stops pacing. So she likes Dragon Well tea, too. There doesn't seem to be any similarity between her and his wife, and if there is, he can't spot it. This woman is always thinking, always asking questions. If only a billion minds all worked like hers! Now, why is he getting carried away like this? A fondness for Dragon Well tea doesn't prove anything. His heart is filled with an inexpressible anxiety. What if everyone turned out like his wife?

"Like it?"

"It's wonderful!" Ye Zhiqiu has never been a connoisseur of tea. For her, tea has always been a troublesome matter, since neither she nor Mo Zheng has ever enjoyed the guarantee of being equipped to boil water.

Zheng Ziyun resumes his pacing. Where should he begin? What could he say to help someone so unfamiliar with industry and economics gain an understanding of all the obstacles in the way of industrial reform? She is filled with enthusiasm and a desire to understand the complexities, but it's not going to be easy. Should he let her see some economic studies? Something dealing with current industrial production, management, systems reforms, and the experiences of foreign nations? Yes, he'd have his secretary or one of the comrades in the research office give her something to read. But who is she, and where does she live?

"Pardon me, but I don't know your name."

It's right there on the letter of introduction, but he's either already forgotten it or he didn't read the letter in the first place.

"It's Ye Zhiqiu."

" 'A sense of autumn,' that's a lovely name." He stands there thoughtfully for a moment. It's the perfect name for her.

"Yes, but I'm afraid it's been wasted on someone like me."

Isn't she being a little too sensitive? Maybe even a bit neurotic? Zheng Ziyun is concerned that his casual remark may have hurt her, and he respects her too much not to try to redeem himself. "Not at all," he says good-naturedly. "Take bitter gourds, for example. No matter how bitter they are, some people still like them," he says, apropos of nothing at all. He knows he isn't being very discreet. With the exception of his wife, he has always steered clear of women outside of the office. They're a mystery to him, and he doesn't know how to mix socially. But this woman is so different from the woman he's been living with all these years that he knows he mustn't patronize her the way most men do with women; she's not someone to be taken lightly. Flattery won't get him anywhere, either, even though it works with a lot of women. She's too level headed for that.

Ye surprises him by laughing good-naturedly. "I like the comparison. I could never have come up with something as appropriate as that. Bitter gourd, that's great!"

Is she really not angry, or is it just an act? No, this sort of woman wouldn't put on an act. He knows instinctively that he can trust her, and that even though they've just met, he can talk to her about anything.

A sixth sense, now is that being idealistic or scientific?

How can time pass so quickly?

They talk about society in general, about economics, philosophy, politics. . . . She, this professional woman, puts her hands on her hips when she talks, just like a man; and when she's excited about something, she paces the floor with her hands behind her back, unconcerned that she is a first-time guest in the home of a vice-minister. They pace back and forth, finally stopping in the middle of the room to talk face-to-face.

Strange how his wife has been a Party member nearly as long as he, but they've long since stopped talking about politics, or society, or economics, or philosophy. Why is that? Is it his fault? He spends most of his waking hours at the Ministry (he and his wife no longer even sleep in the same room), attending meetings all over town, or riding back and forth in his official car. Rare for him to take even a Sunday off. He generally brings work home, like a lover who can't bear to be separated from his beloved, putting it down only when he's too tired to continue. On those rare occasions when he has the time and energy to talk, his wife, Xia Zhuyun, just sits there inattentively without saying a word, until he simply loses interest. What, he often wonders, is it going to take to shake her out of her apathy?

Could her spirit have aged along with her body? Isn't there anything that can sustain a person's emotions over the long haul? There must be more to life than possessions and appearances. Even the most beautiful women grow old and wrinkled. Why do so many women devote themselves to keeping tabs on their husbands and being on guard against other women, something over which they ultimately have no control, instead of trying to sustain their own progressive spirit? They could present their husbands with a new, loving, beautiful, and altogether appealing spiritual world.

Xia Zhuyun is concerned only with fashionable clothes and adornments. She never laughs, for fear that laugh lines will appear on her face and turn into deep wrinkles. Although nearly sixty, she looks like a woman in her mid-forties. Her face, still smooth and lustrous, hasn't a flaw on it.

Why did she join him on this long, seemingly endless journey? Not a journey steeped in myth, although it leads to a palace found only in myths.

At first, she kept asking him:

"Are we nearly there?"

"How much farther?"

"How come we're not there yet?"

Later on she began to complain, as though she'd never imagined it was going to be so trying, and to act as though she had been forced to come along.

Is he really so disappointed in her? In the beginning she must at least have had a little curiosity; but at some point along the way he got into the habit of staring at her to find a spark, even one as tiny as the glimmer of a firefly.

Her curiosity turned out to be like the glow of a branding iron, whose fire is an illusion that carries no warmth and is soon cool to the touch. Has he ever given her any warmth? He can't recall. He has been irresistibly drawn toward that beautiful mythical dream, moving forward without a thought to anything else, while she has simply sat by the side of the road, unwilling to keep up with him.

As the sky deepens, everything in the room—the sofa, the TV set, the wardrobes, and the piano, as well as the occupants' faces— turns hazy, dissolving into the color of dusk. Ye Zhiqiu experiences a sense of déjà vu. Where has she seen this before? In a dream, in one of her countless fantasies? She has the feeling that in her childhood this very sofa—long, narrow, and hard as a board—was where she'd turned somersaults, read books, and listened to her grandmother tell stories. . . . She's sat on this sofa for what seems like a lifetime, and it suddenly occurs to her that she ought to leave.

Just then the lady of the house walks in.

Xia Zhuyun tosses her handbag down on the sofa, too preoccupied with her own concerns to notice that she has company. "Yuanyuan!" she shouts.

Since there is no need for her to notice others, she's never learned how to do it; it is up to them to notice and attend to her. She only pays attention to company when there is a Toyota or Mercedes-Benz parked out front.

Zheng Ziyun frowns as he makes the introductions: "Xia Zhuyun, this is Comrade Ye Zhiqiu, a journalist."

Xia Zhuyun slowly turns and nods. "Please, have a seat!" But before Ye can respond, she shouts again: "Yuanyuan!"

Ye Zhiqiu notices how Xia Zhuyun closes her eyes as she shifts her gaze from one thing to another; this plus her excessively slow movements betray her arrogance.

Yuanyuan comes out of her room, her hair disheveled as though she's been lying down.

"Have you been reading in bed again? How many times have I told you that's bad for your eyes? Eyeglasses make girls look ugly, ugly, ugly!" She has forgotten that Ye Zhiqiu is wearing glasses; either that or she looked right through her guest in the first place and is completely unaware that she wears them.

But Yuanyuan and Zheng Ziyun are horribly embarrassed, as though they are the ones guilty of this tactless comment and graceless behavior. Father and daughter stand next to one another, wondering what they can say to get past this embarrassing moment. Ye Zhiqiu comes to their rescue. "You're right," she says. "Reading in bed is bad for your eyes."

Xia Zhuyun, oblivious to the tension in the room, would be surprised to learn that her husband and daughter found it necessary to be ashamed of anything she had done. She is too used to saying what's on her mind. "I bought you a powder-blue down parka," she says to her daughter as she opens up a large paper parcel. "It's warm but light, and very popular these days among young girls."

Zheng Ziyun seems not to have heard her. "Isn't it about time for dinner?" He turns to Yuanyuan. "Ask Auntie Wu to serve dinner."

Auntie Wu, who is clever enough to know that Yuanyuan's opinion isn't the one that counts, comes rushing out of the kitchen in her apron. "Comrade Xia, shall I serve dinner now?"

Xia Zhuyun looks at her watch. "All right!" Then she adds as an afterthought, "We have company tonight, so make a little extra."

Ye Zhiqiu notices how soft and milky white the skin on her arm is. Her fine gold wristwatch seems a little tight, however, which means that she's gained weight.

Auntie Wu wipes her hands on her apron, even though they don't really need wiping. She always looks like a woman who has just finished some exhausting, dirty chore. "Since it's Sunday I prepared a little extra, just in case we had company. I bought a hen at the free market—for seven yuan."

"Seven yuan?" Xia Zhuyun blurts out.

"It cost more because it was still alive when I bought it," Auntie Wu rushes to her own defense. "I also bought some fish."

Everyone stands around listening to Auntie Wu's report.

Ye Zhiqiu looks coldly over at Zheng Ziyun. The look of sarcasm on his face has deepened, and there is a mischievous glint in his eyes; he's about to do something. But then their eyes meet, and she can tell that he has fallen into a grim, strange mood. She protests that she really ought to leave.

"Won't you stay for dinner?" he presses her. Then he adds in a sarcastic tone meant for someone else or himself, "Didn't you hear that we've got a seven-yuan live hen?"

Ye Zhiqiu feels a sudden rush of sympathy for him. Even a respected vice-minister in charge of tens of thousands of enterprises and millions of workers has his own griefs, just like everyone else. Life mocks him sometimes, too.

His mood has changed, suddenly and unpredictably. At that moment Zheng Ziyun feels like a stranger in his own home. He stares at Ye Zhiqiu, trying to figure her out. Did that interesting conversation really take place?

Just then a real guest walks in. "Set another place at the table, I'm starved," he announces as he strides into the room. "What's for dinner?"

"Minister Wang, how nice of you to come!" Even for a guest of this stature, Xia Zhuyun merely adds a shallow note of enthusiasm to her voice and quickens her movements only slightly.

Wang Fangliang takes a long look at Ye Zhiqiu. "I don't believe I've met this comrade!"

Zheng Ziyun makes the introductions. "She's a reporter."

"Oh, a reporter! Lao Zheng, we have to butter up reporters. If we don't they might lash out at us in print, and we sure don't need that!" He has the booming voice of an orator who wants to make sure everyone in the room hears him. Here's a man who knows all about giving reports, Ye Zhiqiu is thinking.

Wang Fangliang presses ahead. "Are you here to interview him? If so, you're barking up the wrong tree. He's a heretic who was criticized long ago. Now I'm going to say something that might offend you. It's obvious from your choice of interview subjects that you're still a cub reporter. Ha-ha! Say, Lao Zheng, have you tried to impress her with your theory of 'It doesn't matter if we go out and buy our Four Modernizations or create them ourselves, because if we don't succeed, our people won't even have pants to wear'?"

"Now don't try to frighten her off," Zheng says with a smile.

Xia Zhuyun quickly glances over at Ye Zhiqiu with a look that is typical of women like her when they're confronted with a conscientious, competent woman; some interpret it as jealousy, others as indifference.

Yuanyuan walks their guest downstairs. "Where do you live, Auntie Ye? I'd like to come see you sometime."

What a kind-hearted little girl.

Ye Zhiqiu senses that Yuanyuan is trying to make up for her mother's crude behavior.

Xia Zhuyun doesn't seem to lack any of those qualities that make men fall in love with women. But is this a happy family?

Wang Fangliang slouches on the sofa with his legs crossed. His socks have slipped down so far that his ankles show. He kicks off his shoes and removes his socks, complaining as he shakes them, "Look at the junk we're producing."

A seldom-seen frown appears on Xia Zhuyun's face, but only for a moment, because she cannot bear the thought of lines on her brow. "I couldn't agree more. The washing machine I recently bought broke down after I used it only a few times."

"It must be bad," Wang Fangliang shouts, "if even our Xiao Xia here is concerned about the quality of our products. Now we know the problem's serious."

"It's exactly the same with our machinery." Some might have interpreted Zheng Ziyun's comment as gloating.

"I agree a hundred percent!" Wang Fangliang says with a sigh. "Take a simple case: the problem of leakage in our generators— water, oil, and air. Is there any technical reason why that can't be taken care of? Absolutely not! But after all this time, nothing's been done. There's the problem!"

Xia Zhuyun is fidgeting on the sofa. Talk of generators interests her far less than socks and washing machines. Wang Fangliang watches her smooth out her wrinkle-free jacket and cross her legs.

An extremely bright man, Wang Fangliang has a knack for sensing what is on other people's minds, even though his conclusions are often overly critical. He knows that in the presence of others, Xia Zhuyun invariably poses, whether a painter or photographer is present or not. Being in the same room with her for even ten minutes is exhausting.

How has Zheng been able to put up with her all these years? But he feels sorry for her, too. All women seem a bit shallow, but maybe that's their appeal. Who knows, maybe it's all even in the end.

"How've you been lately?" Wang Fangliang asks with a measure of sincerity.

"Not bad," Xia replies, her tone showing that even she knows that the state of her health isn't of much interest to anyone else, certainly not to Zheng Ziyun.

Zheng Ziyun ignores their exchange. "It's a complicated issue," he continues. "Like you said, as long as we follow operating procedures, we can solve a lot of the problems of quality. So why are the problems still with us? Aren't we spending enough? We've tried strengthening our political work and we've tried bonuses, but neither has worked. Why? Is there something fundamentally wrong with those methods? Or are we not being scientific enough and need to work harder? If we stick with the old methods of ideological work, we'll have trouble getting cooperation from the workers. Are they to blame? No, we are. Over the past few years our ideological work hasn't moved beyond empty words, boasts, slogans, labels, and bludgeons. Even though we subscribe to the theory that workers are the masters of the country, how far have we actually come in improving the quality of their lives? How much do we really respect their creative spirit? And how much do we let them exercise their inalienable rights? I know that things are tough at the moment, and that we can't solve all our problems overnight, but how much do we really care about our workers? How much compassion do we have for them? During the war years the political cadres and the masses were inseparable! Being with the cadres was like being with your own family. But now things are different, and they've lost the hearts of the people. If we don't start treating the workers like the true masters of the country, they'll stop treating enterprises as their own. The most important task before us is to recapture the people's hearts and refill them with hope and enthusiasm. That's a science, and one that we absolutely must master."

"Do you mean the behavioral psychology that Professor Dai talks about?"

"It'd be more accurate to call it industrial management psychology."

Xia Zhuyun always listens to her husband spell out his views with the condescending tolerance of an intelligent, sober wife listening to the drunken babble of a weak husband who can't hold his liquor.

He can say anything he pleases, and as long as it doesn't cost him his Mandarin hat, she is willing to put up with it. She never listens to him anyway, even though she acts like she's hanging on his every word. Nothing he says ever has any effect on what she thinks is really important. She sits there attentively, so as not to give the impression that she's an empty-headed housewife; naturally, the importance of their guest has something to do with it.

"Lao Zheng's been meaning to call on the professor to look into those theories of his." She isn't sure what psychology is all about, this so-called behavioral science, but she figures that any mention of science, which is all the rage these days, can't help but make her appear more scientific. It doesn't hurt to show off a bit.

"Not really. It's just something that Lao Wang and I are interested in. We're not looking for a panacea that'll make us instant Buddhas before whom the people will prostrate themselves as loyal disciples. It's just that the painful realities of the workplace are forcing us to find solutions to these knotty problems!"

This down-to-earth comment sounds to Xia Zhuyun like a rebuke. She stands up. "All right, that's enough, we can continue this after dinner."

The meal is wonderful, though relatively simple. Xia Zhuyun takes her time over the food, savoring each bite and cleaning every chicken bone with her evenly shaped teeth.

Zheng Ziyun eats the same way he lives his life, in a very orderly fashion.

Yuanyuan rushes through the meal, absent-mindedly shoveling rice into her mouth as though it were some sort of obligation. Xia Zhuyun surveys the mess in front of her daughter with displeasure.

Wang Fangliang, on the other hand, eats with the unfettered resolve of a man at his own table. "Have some more soup," he urges Zheng Ziyun.

"No more room!"

"Then put down the beer! You're better off with soup. Eating is like fighting a battle or doing a job. You've got to set your eyes on a target!"

"It looks like everything is your target, Uncle Wang," Yuanyuan says, resting her head on her arm and giggling.

"Yuanyuan, you shouldn't be joking like that with adults," Xia Zhuyun scolds her.

"Why not?" Wang Fangliang casts an avuncular smile at Yuanyuan. "I was scheduled to visit The East Is Red Commune this morning, and I got up so late I had to rush. Well, after tripping over a basketball in the hall and a pair of sneakers in the bathroom I yelled at my sons, 'Haven't I told you kids to put your things away?' The younger one shot back, 'I just tripped over one of *your* shoes in the study, Daddy. Isn't that setting a bad example?' What could I say? We have to listen to our children sometimes. We can't let some people talk but tell others to keep their mouths shut."

"Oh, that's right. How'd your visit to The East Is Red Commune go today?" Zheng Ziyun asks with interest.

"Tian Shoucheng really put me on the spot." A pause to whet Zheng's appetite.

The East Is Red Commune had recently sent a citizen's letter to Minister Tian complaining that a tractor they'd bought was so shoddy it couldn't be used. It was like pouring money down the drain. This was only the latest in a series of complaints about the quality of products made in the Ministry's factories, but the problems were never solved. Tian Shoucheng always had a ready excuse when he made his production reports to the State Council. During the early years of the Cultural Revolution, for example, it was obstructionism by counterrevolutionary revisionists; after that, it was obstructionism by Lin Biao and his fellow conspirators; and after that it was obstructionism by the trend to overturn verdicts against the Rightists; ultimately it was obstructionism by the Gang of Four . . .

This time, however, Tian Shoucheng had reacted firmly and quickly, to the surprise of everyone, deciding to send a ministerial-rank cadre along with the factory manager to The East Is Red Commune to retrieve the defective tractor, apologize to the commune members, and guarantee them that a high-quality tractor would be sent as a replacement.

Why the sudden turnabout? Possibly because the Gang of Four had fallen from power more than three years ago and he had run out of excuses. Or perhaps the fresh winds of economic reform indicated that sweeping changes in the economic structure were inevitable.

Over the past couple of years, farsighted, knowledgeable economic theorists and experienced comrades in leadership positions had addressed this issue in their published writings and in their speeches.

Tian Shoucheng knew perfectly well that the source of these winds would not be found in economics.

Political winds in China shift constantly, if the historical experiences of the past thirty years are to be taken as the standard.

The source of this particular wind was somewhere above him, which meant that the reforms would not be restricted to the economic structure; sooner or later they would reach the political structure, the cadre structure; they would reach into every facet of life in contemporary society.

A senior official who has lost his Party spirit is liable to become an opportunist.

Tian Shoucheng couldn't help but wonder what he'd gain from these reforms. And what he'd lose.

His retrieving the defective tractor from The East Is Red Commune was unprecedented. Given the present climate, his action would probably make the newspapers and news broadcasts. It was bound to be a good bargaining chip someday. It couldn't hurt.

For the life of him, Zheng Ziyun couldn't figure out why at the Party Committee meeting Wang Fangliang had insisted on personally taking care of the problem at The East Is Red Commune. He could tell by the sly look on the man's face that there was more to it than met the eye.

"Yesterday I told my secretary to call the county committee to get their opinion on meeting with the commune secretaries, cadres, and nearby members. They agreed. But today I looked at the meeting hall and discovered that it would only hold a few hundred people. 'What about the commune members?' I asked. So many of them had shown up that there wasn't enough room for everyone to attend. So I said, 'Why don't we hold the meeting in the square?' The county Party secretary was uncomfortable with that. 'It'll be too cold.' 'I don't care how cold it is,' I told him. 'Party members can't try to pack the audience when they're boasting about their own accomplishments, then keep everyone away when they meet for self-criticism. How would that look?' So we set up some tables in the square and hooked up a loudspeaker. When that was done, I made my announcement: 'Comrades from the commune, I'm here as vice-minister to tell you how ashamed I am about selling you a defective tractor. You're the ones who suffer because of our shoddy work. We have no right to cheat you out of your hard-earned money. From now on, I want you to stop buying tractors from that factory until they turn things around. And if that doesn't happen, then I don't want you ever to buy one from them. Their tractors are the worst in the country!' People in the audience started clamoring angrily, anxiously. 'What are we supposed to do?' they shouted. 'We've already placed orders!' I told them right on the spot, 'Send them back, send them all back!' The factory manager was apoplectic, and I could tell from the look in his face that he was thinking, 'Spending all that time under lock and key during the Cultural Revolution was the best thing that could have happened to this guy! Why couldn't they have kept him locked up a few years longer?' But he didn't say a word, since he's only a factory manager and I'm a vice-minister. Sometimes rank does have its privileges, doesn't it? What really puzzles me is why no one has the guts to run up against a factory manager like that. What's the big deal? Do you mean to tell me that all he has to do is take his tractor back to make everything right? What about later on? Keep producing the same kind of tractor? How come our cadres and our factory managers have lifetime jobs whether they operate in the black or not and whether they know what they're doing or not? Cadres and factory managers like that bring disaster with them wherever they go. We've got to deal with them.

"Well, the crowd started shouting again, 'If we send them back, where will we get replacements? We need tractors badly!'

" 'Go to the Liming Tractor Works,' I said. 'Their tractors are well made and inexpensive, and they give fine service.' Competition's a good thing. The days of monopolies and eating out of a common pot are gone.

"An accountant, a real stickler, asked me, 'How can we buy a tractor without an allocation target?'

" 'Those are the old rules. Now, with the expansion of individual prerogatives in industry, factories can exercise some of their rights!'

"The crowd surged around me, not yet ready to believe I was telling the truth. So I told them how you had permitted the Liming Tractor Works to advertise in the newspaper in June, and even told them the date the ad appeared. One of the commune Party secretaries asked me, 'Do you feel that production materials should circulate freely? Marx never said anything about that.'

" 'There's a lot Marx never said anything about,' I answered him. 'Does that mean we should just roll over and play dead? We're following Marx's principles as long as we're working for socialist production, promoting the development of the national economy, and speeding up the Four Modernizations!' "

Wang Fangliang starts laughing before anyone else has a chance to say a word. He is looking very smug.

"Uncle Wang, you're really something, exactly what a minister ought to be! If people like Uncle Tian can be a minister, anyone can. He never stops long enough to get pinned down. He's always saying, 'We must take heart from our leaders.' Or, 'I agree with what the others say.' But no one knows what he plans to do."

"Yuanyuan!" Zheng Ziyun frowns angrily.

Yuanyuan pouts and rolls her eyes. "It's true!"

"Yuanyuan," Wang Fangliang teases, "how can you talk about your future father-in-law like that?"

"Who wants him for a father-in-law?"

"Now, now, it's no secret that you and his third son are pretty friendly."

Xia Zhuyun is clearly displeased. Wang Fangliang never seems to consider the effect of his words on others.

"Hah, someone like that's no friend of mine!"

"What do you mean, 'someone like this or like that'? What's wrong with him?" Xia Zhuyun scolds her daughter.

"Anyone who likes him can have him!"

"Yuanyuan, what's gotten into you, talking like that?"

Yuanyuan throws her spoon into her bowl, spilling soup all over the table, before jumping to her feet, kicking her chair away, and running into her room.

"Why did you have to mention the advertisement?" Zheng Ziyun asks, oblivious to the argument that has been raging around him.

Wang Fangliang turns serious. "Lao Zheng, I really admire your courage!" No need to do so. Having been comrades for years, they understand each other perfectly. But Wang is impressed by Zheng's having taken the responsibility for placing an ad for the Liming Tractor Works the previous summer when talk of the market, profits, and competition was just beginning. Who could guarantee that some of the things Marx hadn't talked about, as the commune Party secretary pointed out, wouldn't crop up someday? Things like that had been common enough in the past, and Zheng Ziyun was worried that if something happened now, the factory would be in real trouble. So he took the initiative of urging them to seek approval to advertise, over his signature. That way, if things turned out badly, they'd have someone to pin the blame on. Something like this may not have raised any eyebrows at one time, but over the past ten years or so, the abnormal political situation had corrupted and polluted lots of pretty good comrades, many of them, sad to say, older comrades. Wang Fangliang has always admired Zheng for the way he disregards his own personal security. He sits thoughtfully for a moment, then takes a pack of cigarettes out of his pocket and offers one to Zheng Ziyun.

Zheng waves it aside.

A glint of mockery in Wang Fangliang's eyes. "Wife's orders?"

"I smoked too much this afternoon! She and I aren't about to start minding each other's business at our age."

"If you let her mind your business but go ahead and smoke anyway, then everyone's happy. That's how I always deal with these kinds of conflicts." With a smile on his face, he reaches into another pocket and takes out a small box with a fancy lid. He looks at Zheng Ziyun, then reads, " 'Ingredients: sugar, dextrose, gum base, organic preparations, and natural preservatives. Helpful in quitting smoking, lubricates the lungs, soothes coughing, increases energy level, and eases upset stomach. Dosage: chew one stick for thirty minutes; depending upon quantity of cigarettes smoked, the effects will last for two to four hours.' Want to try a stick of this quit-smoking gum?"

Zheng Ziyun doesn't respond, knowing that Wang likes a good joke once in a while.

Wang Fangliang has a big laugh over this. "We can't go against the boss's orders. If you're hooked, you've got to smoke. Me, I smoke *and* chew the gum. That way I can keep the boss happy and treat myself well at the same time. The best of both worlds!"

That's Wang Fangliang, always managing to steer a safe course between contradictions.

But will that be enough to deal with the coming violent clash that will test the most fundamental concepts?

People were once fond of using phrases like "class struggle" and "a fight to the finish," as though violent clashes occur only between enemy camps. Did they really think that a clash of views in the same camp would necessarily be easier to resolve? Even though you never hear "a fight to the finish" anymore, that's exactly what it will be.

Now people are questioning a set of deeply ingrained views that many others and society in general consider sacrosanct.

Like a net, these views have enmeshed the people: everyone will live or die together.

And what about members of the Communist Party, the ones whose mission is to keep the wheels of history moving forward?

Five

The alarm clock on the headboard says 6:10. Time to get up. The street sounds are growing louder. As the wife of the director of an auto works, Yu Liwen is particularly alert to the sounds of cars. By now she can tell the kind and size of a vehicle by the sound of its horn and engine.

Today she's going to make a special lunch for Chen Yongming, since he's taking one of his rare days off, and they can have lunch together. She smiles at the thought, mocking herself as a foolish woman whose world rotates around her husband. When he eats with her, the food somehow tastes better. When he's with her, the room somehow seems warmer.

But she doesn't feel like getting out of bed just yet, afraid she might wake up her husband, who is sleeping beside her. She gently turns her head on the pillow and looks closely into his gaunt face.

The sleep of an exhausted man, his arms and legs spread out, a worried look on his face. His eyes are deeply sunken. Even though he's only fifty, his hair is almost completely gray; and look at the length of it, when was it last cut? He needs a shave, too. Last night, when they lay cheek to cheek, his beard scratched her painfully. "When did you last shave?" she asked him.

He just smiled without answering, and she wondered what was on his mind.

"What are you thinking?" she asked as she tapped him on the forehead.

"Nothing special. It's just that I have this nagging feeling that I've forgotten something." He reminded himself that he shouldn't be so distant, and leaned over to kiss her on the forehead. But she was sure his mind was still elsewhere. Did he really think he had to treat her like a child? There was, she felt, something troubling him so much that he'd lost interest in everything else, even when she was lying in his arms. But she knew he loved her.

They had married late in his life. If not for a case of acute hepatitis in 1962, he probably never would have found the time to fall in love and get married. Young people these days can't understand things like that and aren't willing to believe that anyone can live this way. He was thirty-seven at the time, she was twenty-three, an intern fresh from medical college.

He lay in his hospital bed for days on end, staring blankly at the door of the ward until his eyes ached. He couldn't bear the thought of missing the white-clad figure as she walked past or came cheerfully into the ward to see how he was doing.

It was then he realized that life held more than production figures, quality control, fixed capital, liquid assets, state plans, and industrial profits, which until then had absorbed his spirit, his strength, and his emotions.

Her thin, neat eyebrows, her lovely mouth, her eternally warm eyes, and her delicate motions combined to form a restful haven, an inviting place in the shade.

He courted her the same way he worked, taking her by storm, relentless and single-minded.

Some people thought it was a bad match.

What's bad about two people falling in love?

Some people reminded him that she wasn't a Party member.

Who was to blame for her not being a Party member? She'd been kept out by prejudice, but did that make her worse than those inside? When will we ever free ourselves from abstract concepts and be able to look at the innate qualities of things?

She looked at him with anxiety in her warm eyes. "Am I good enough for you? Can I make you happy?"

He held her in his arms. "Young lady, you were born for me!"

But what sort of romance had they had?

As soon as she changed out of her uniform she'd rush into his arms, without stopping for dinner. "You really haven't had dinner?" he'd ask, as though he'd forgotten that she needed to eat to live, like other people. "It's my fault. Here, hit me!" He'd hold her tiny hand to help her hit him. Then they'd go looking for a restaurant, even though she was reluctant to give up the time they had alone together just to eat, particularly since he had so little to give in the first place.

Sometimes she'd have been waiting for him on a park bench for hours when he'd angrily come running up to her, and she couldn't tell if he was mad at her or proposing marriage: "Let's get married. How long is this courtship supposed to last? I don't have the time!"

Or he'd call her from the office: "I'm sorry I can't leave. Forgive me? Here's a kiss!"

No answer.

"Why don't you say something?" He'd raise his voice.

Still no answer.

"Oh, all right, maybe I'll have a half hour at about ten o'clock. You come to the office, okay?"

Then one summer afternoon he led her by the hand to the district office to register as man and wife.

She nearly fainted, the effect of her confused emotions and the burning sun overhead.

They stood beneath a locust tree where countless caterpillars hung from the branches, spinning their cocoons. One fell onto her neck, and she cried out weakly. She rested her head on his broad shoulder, her eyes wet with tears. Chen took a crumpled handkerchief out of his pocket and mopped her sweaty brow. "What's wrong?" he asked her anxiously.

Yu Liwen detected a note of confusion in his voice that she hadn't heard before, and she knew that people like him were never confused, even in the face of disaster. Obviously, she was the most important thing in his life, but he saw no need to tell her.

Everything was new, new and complete. And yet their new home seemed empty.

Chen Yongming busied himself around the flat without getting anything done. He moved boxes from the middle of the room over to the window; then when he felt like opening the window, he moved them into a corner.

At last he spread his hands and announced to Yu Liwen, "I'm sorry, I think I ought to take a bath today."

"Would you like me to heat some water for you?" She was embarrassed, not knowing what to do. Like the furnishings piled up in the middle of the room, she didn't feel at home here yet and was trying to find a place where she belonged.

"No, thanks!" He took a long bath in the bathroom using cold tap water.

His hair was wet, his face clean and fresh; he smelled like bath soap.

"Shall we make some dinner, my little bride?" Since their things were strewn all over the place, they couldn't find the kitchen utensils.

So on their wedding night they ate biscuits.

Their marriage was a happy one.

They had to make so much of the little time they had together that their feelings for one another intensified. A kiss from Chen Yongming could put Yu Liwen on cloud nine for days. Then she would wait for as long as it took for his next expression of tenderness. He was always away on business, and the separations kept their feelings fresh.

Being Chen Yongming's wife was no bed of roses, but it made

Yu Liwen proud. In her girlhood, when she was still living in a fantasy world, she had formed a picture of her ideal husband: a strong man who could overcome difficulties. Chen fulfilled this ideal.

Ai! Anxieties, worries, heartaches . . . during the Cultural Revolution he was nearly killed. After being locked up in a dark, dank "cow shed" for months, he was so rheumatic he could barely walk. Just seeing him, a tall man used to standing ramrod straight with his chest thrust out, suddenly reduced to shuffling along completely bent over, broke Yu Liwen's heart. Day in and day out she brought herbal medicines home for him, which she heated and cured and smeared on his inflamed joints. And he always had a quip ready: "I'm going to encourage every man I know to marry a doctor."

As she smiled, her tears fell onto her husband's shoulder. When he pulled his shoulder away, she turned her head, for she was ashamed to look him in the eye. But he stubbornly reached out and turned her head to face him. "I'm doing fine, aren't I? Just wait until I'm back to normal, and I'll carry you up Mount Xiang on my back."

So he got better, although flecks of white had begun to appear in his hair, and whenever the weather turned damp, his joints ached unbearably, like a rusty, squeaky machine. He couldn't hide something like this from the eyes of a doctor.

Naturally, they never made it to Mount Xiang.

Two years earlier, Vice-Minister Zheng Ziyun had personally called on Chen with the news that he wanted to assign him as director of the Morning Light Auto Works.

"The Ministry Party Headquarters has had its eye on you, and we think you're the man for the job."

"But I've never run a huge factory like that before."

"There are plenty of problems, and there's been quite a turnover of directors. Two of the bureau directors in the Ministry have already served. So you see how things stand. I don't need an answer right away. Think it over for a few days. I'm confident you'll give me the answer I'm looking for."

Chen Yongming didn't think it over alone; his friends and

comrades helped him out. One, who knew what was going on inside the factory, said, "With a job like that, you're damned if you do and damned if you don't. You can't win." Another friend told him, "The chair at the Morning Light Auto Works is a bit too big for the butt of someone at your level."

"Do you really think you could stick it out?"

But Chen Yongming wasn't thinking about what awaited him in terms of complicated personnel issues, or a chaotic organizational structure that reminded him of a rusty machine long out of use, or red ink, or abrogated responsibilities, or even labor problems that called for emergency measures. He was examining himself to see if he was resolute and talented enough to take on the assignment.

As a Party member, his thoughts regarding the offer were beyond the understanding of the average man.

Faced with similar situations, each person deals with life in a unique way. Were it any different, there would be no history. Heroes and traitors would all be the same. In this bizarre fashion the affairs of the world come together.

Chen Yongming was like steel tempered in fire and water in an unending progression.

Who can pinpoint the moment when a lifelong belief takes hold of a man?

Where is the knot tied? Truth, truth, that most precious of life's standards. Yet it is an impossible standard to live up to from one day to the next, always and ever. What then of the future?

It was 1949: the oral exam—the final obstacle to acceptance into the Military Academy. He was standing in front of a frail young woman, probably no more than eighteen or nineteen years old, dressed in a dark blue Chinese dress. Her face had an unhealthy pallor, her eyelids were puffy, fear was written in her eyes. A bearded, probably quite tall, man in a gray uniform sat behind a table, his legs, wrapped in leggings, sticking out. A pile of forms, one for each of the examinees, was stacked on the table. He made notations on these forms after each candidate responded to his questions. He was resting his chin in his left hand, as though his head were so heavy it needed to be propped up; this heaviness was probably the cumulative effect of asking the same question over and over. The pen in his hand was a more awesome weapon than the rifle strapped across his back.

Chen Yongming listened to him ask the young woman, "Why do you want to enter the Military Academy?"

"To work," she muttered.

"Will you work wholeheartedly to serve the people?"

"Let's say halfheartedly. The other half will be to eat."

The man lowered his head and made some quick notes on the form. He didn't even look at the woman. Maybe he was too tired. And yet if he'd only raised his head and looked at the artless young woman in front of him shaking in her boots, he might not have made an X on her form. The poor flustered girl turned and walked away without daring to even steal a glance at the form to see what he had written. She nearly tripped over the feet sticking out from under the table. As simply, as arbitrarily, and abstractly as that, a person's fate was decided.

Chen Yongming's resolve to devote his energies to Party business might very well have had its beginnings in that moment.

Ten days later Chen came to Zheng Ziyun. "What exactly do you want me to do?" he asked.

"It's very simple," Zheng replied. "There are only two requirements at the beginning. First, achieve an increase in production every month until the production value is double that of last year. Second, achieve balanced production. Beyond that, we'll see when the time comes. Given the mess that place is in, you'll have your hands full just meeting these two goals. You'll need all the help you can get. Now, what do you want from us?"

"I've always had the feeling that I've never done the job I should have as a factory manager. And I think, or rather I've observed, that you haven't been doing your job as a minister either. Since you've given me this heavy responsibility, I want to make the best of it, and after thinking it over the past few days, I'm convinced that I can only achieve these goals if I'm given full managerial authority. So there's only one condition: let me exercise that authority. Not for my own sake. What good would it do me? I'm interested only in improving the factory and, ultimately, in increasing production. Now, exactly how much authority can you give me?"

"The Ministry will back you all the way and give you all the authority you'll need, within limits." He thought for a moment. "If you take on the job, the Ministry Party Headquarters will provide all the necessary leadership. So what do you say?"

"Won't there be conflicts with the current managerial system?"

"As long as you proceed in accordance with accepted economic practices, I'll back you up with all the authority at my disposal and do everything within my power. If anyone lodges a complaint, I'll take care of it." He winked.

A man of strong character, Chen Yongming had never been someone to be won over by nice words. But as their discussion came to an end, he grabbed Zheng Ziyun's bony hand in his powerful grip and shook it hard.

Whenever he spoke with Zheng Ziyun, Chen Yongming felt charged as if his heart were filled with the strains of a march that sped up his circulation and infused him with courage and power. He frequently sighed, knowing that it wasn't every cadre who had Zheng's ability to discern and judge the talents, aspirations, and ideological qualities of his subordinates, as well as the boldness to direct people toward a distant goal.

With a leader like this, all the suffering and hard work in the world couldn't dispel the joy in his subordinates' hearts.

As far as Yu Liwen was concerned, her husband's decisions were always correct. She didn't need to understand the reasons behind them since she trusted his judgment. Although middle-aged, she still viewed society, in all its complexities, through the eyes of a naive schoolgirl. This had its advantages: there was no need for her to be like a politician, always alert to risks or weighing hidden dangers in the dark recesses of life. Her being too clever in handling people and affairs would only bring added pressure and anxiety to her husband, and cooking up schemes for his benefit would only undermine his ability to make decisions.

She was concerned only about whether Chen was gaunt, whether his eyes were bloodshot, whether he was worried about something. She relied upon her knowledge of medicine and her feminine gentleness to attend to his weariness. She was a simple woman, the delicate, loving wife of Chen Yongming, and the only person who could bring peace into his life.

Yu Liwen reaches out and lovingly strokes one of Chen Yongming's graying sideburns, which is as unyielding as his character.

Someone's knocking at the door—four knocks, then four more, followed by giggles and the sounds of a playful argument. Their sons, it's their twin sons.

"Okay," Chen Yongming had said, "I'll do it if for no other reason than to save myself trouble." He had promised to take them ice-skating today, and they were so excited they got out of bed without being told to. An outing with their father is a rare treat.

Yu Liwen tries to ignore them. Let him sleep a bit longer, she thinks to herself, and the boys seem to catch on, for after a brief muffled conversation outside the door, they walk off like good kids.

But Chen Yongming wakes up anyway. His face is infused with spirit and life, almost as though the man sleeping with a frown just a moment ago was someone else. As Yu Liwen strokes his forehead, he reaches up and takes her hand. Studying it, one finger at a time, he then kisses all five. He clears his throat loudly. Their room is so dry that he wakes up every morning with a parched throat.

Just then there is a pounding on the door, which is flung open before they have time to respond. The boys dart into the room as though shot from a cannon. Chen gets out of bed and stands in the middle of the room, where he stretches out his arms and twirls like a windmill, one son hanging on each arm.

Yu Liwen finally packs them off after breakfast, seeing them out the door and on their way before she heads toward the marketplace.

As she passes some people lined up to buy fish, she spots two women, wives of the directors of the Daqing Office and the Political Department, who are engaged in a lively discussion.

When they see her, they pull her into line. "The croakers are really fresh today. Here, get in front of us, it's nearly our turn."

"I can't do that, it'll upset the people behind. I'm not shopping for fish today, anyway." They have made her feel so awkward she's blushing from embarrassment. Opposed to cutting in line, she still hates the idea of appearing ungrateful to the women. That leaves her one option—to turn and walk away.

The other two women stand there frowning. "Just like her husband, a real phony!"

"Phony? You should have seen them when he returned from Japan, standing in the middle of a crowded airport with their arms wrapped around each other, so close together you couldn't see light between them . . . *tsk-tsk*!" With an odd sneer on her face, the woman adds, "You'd think they could at least wait till they got home to carry on like that!"

"Intellectuals!"

"That's right. The world is their oyster these days. Ever since Deng Xiaoping said that intellectuals are workers too, they've got their noses up in the clouds!" she says through clenched teeth.

Those two tongues never wag beyond their immediate circle of acquaintances, and this time their speech, expressions, raised eyebrows, and the pinched corners of their mouths make it clear that there is deep resentment in their hearts. They have suffered an egregious and irretrievable loss at the hands of Chen Yongming, for his arrival signaled the overnight fall from power of their husbands, who had been feared and respected for so long; once adversaries, the two women have now become allies.

Six

Morning shift at the factory. Li Ruilin has arrived early and, with mixed feelings, stands outside the gate for a long time. His first day back on the job after more than two months, and although he is rested physically, his mind has been in a turmoil all that time. Strange how a branch secretary who has dished it out to disgruntled workers for over twenty years can suddenly fall prey to the same discontent himself. How has it come to this?

At first he was angry, as though someone had moved his memorial tablet in Heaven. But that soon turned to sorrow, a sense that the entire world had forgotten him. Then came a period of lying in bed wondering what people would think about his staying away from the job. Would they try to force him to come back? Who would they send as their spokesman? The carrot or the stick? What was behind removing the Party secretaries of all the workshops? What's this Chen Yongming up to? Ever since his appointment as factory manager, he's been up to all sorts of shenanigans. Hadn't he been bashed during the Cultural Revolution? Maybe not hard enough!

With all these thoughts running through Li Ruilin's mind, he still manages to overlook the one thing that really matters.

Worst of all, in more than two months, not a single person came by to talk things over with him. Finally, unable to hold back any longer, he went to see Chen Yongming, who put him in his place as soon as he opened his mouth: "Have you figured things out?"

"We'll talk about that later. First I need something to do!"

"Now you're on the right track. Some things take time to figure out."

He was being reasonable and decent about it, and even though Li Ruilin's problems weren't solved, at least he could get back to work knowing that things weren't going to get any worse.

Then came the bad news. "I've instructed the paymaster to hold back all but one week of your wages for the two-month absence. We'll count those seven days as a leave with pay. Lao Li, we go back a long way, and even if you haven't figured things out by now, you've no right to stay away from work. I thought you'd learned that much from all those years you were involved in ideological work." A hardness crept into Chen Yongming's eyes. The pained look on his face showed that this conversation and his decision that had led up to it caused him considerable anguish.

Chen Yongming had agonized every day of the more than two months that Li Ruilin had stayed off the job. He knew that docking Li's pay would not only upset Li, but would raise a storm of protest in that whole group and lead to even greater discontent among certain people. Worse yet, since the price of nearly everything was going up, the loss of two months' wages would be a bitter pill to swallow. But he was comfortable with his decision, for he knew he'd find a way to help Li Ruilin out after the storm had blown over. Being "ruthless" was the key to success in running a factory like this; otherwise, anyone who was upset could stay home and sulk, and nothing would ever get done. There were already plenty of people hatching schemes to get him. Whether he succeeded or not didn't concern him from the personal angle, but a voice inside kept reminding him that success or failure depended upon constant struggle: he knew that every step he took, every decision he made, even something as trivial as buying mugs for tea, would engage a silent, invisible, yet highly significant link in a chain of protracted struggle.

Li Ruilin kept a rein on his anger when he learned that his wages had been docked; blowing up never accomplished anything. So he kept his mouth shut, as a single thought kept running through his troubled mind: More than thirty years in the Party . . .

Lao Lü Tou greets him the same as always: "Secretary Li, you're quite the early bird!"

He whistles when he speaks, since his front teeth are missing. The greeting makes Li Ruilin feel even worse.

He wants to say, "You can stop calling me 'Secretary.' From now on just call me Lao Li." But he changes his mind, unable to bear the thought that from now on he'll be joining Lao Lü Tou as a gatekeeper. They say it's as easy for a Party cadre to move down as to move up, but this is the first time he's ever heard of something like this happening. By now it has become accepted that only cadres who have made a serious blunder are demoted. Who ever heard of a cadre who hadn't actually done something wrong being demoted to worker? Denying a promotion is one thing; not allowing him to keep his position is something else altogether.

It's sort of comforting to hear Lao Lü Tou greet him as "Secretary." At least there's one person who doesn't think he's guilty of any blunder worthy of demotion from cadre to worker. So he casually urges Lao Lü Tou to knock off a few minutes early and go home to get some rest.

Lao Lü Tou goes inside the bike shed and comes back out pushing a bicycle so rickety that everything on it makes noise except the bell. He's wearing an olive-drab cap lined with gray rabbit fur, probably one his son Lü Zhimin brought back from the army. The earflaps bounce as he walks. His greasy overcoat, patched from top to bottom, should have been thrown away long ago, but like old people everywhere, he is always trying to economize for the sake of his children.

Li Ruilin knows that Lao Lü and his son are constantly at odds with each other. Does that make Lü Zhimin a bad son? No, just pigheaded and irritable, argumentative, a son who makes life hard for his father. Young people these days are more trouble than they're worth.

There's no peace for the older generation anymore, and anyone with children can count on a bellyful of troubles until the day they're finally laid out.

Every family has its problems, Li Ruilin muses as he watches Lao Lü Tou's receding back.

He walks into the caretaker's room and sits for a while but is soon back on his feet, feeling he ought to be doing something instead of just sitting around. But what? This factory, lifeless for so many years, suddenly seems revitalized, and that makes him feel as awkward as a new hand. Not a good feeling.

After stoking up the charcoal stove and putting a pot of water on to boil, Li takes the broom out from behind the door and halfheartedly sweeps the asphalt path in front of the caretaker's room. An easy job, since it is seldom used and doesn't get very dirty. As he straightens up, he gazes out at the buildings that make up the auto works where he has worked ever since leaving military service more than twenty years ago. He has watched it grow, building by building, just as one watches the development of a neighbor's child, from birth through all the stages of childhood and on to school. Sometimes you wonder how a kid who has been running around in diapers could have turned into such a beautiful young woman almost overnight, now dressed in a pair of unsightly bell-bottoms that sweep along the ground like brooms as she cradles a baby in her arms.

The auto works really look good these days. The compound is already bigger than Li's hometown, and it takes a good hour just to walk around it.

There is a big circular flower garden just inside the main gate, with asphalt paths running beside it to the left and right, like a pair of muscular arms wrapped around a big basket. The paths are bordered by tall stands of white poplars whose lower branches have been roughly pruned, leaving scars like eyes that watch people as they enter and leave the compound. They are watching Li Ruilin at this very moment. The poplars stand above a row of pine trees all cut the same height. The needles show the effects of a Beijing winter; they're so filthy with soot that it's impossible to tell what color they are, sort of like Beijing itself.

The administrative offices are beyond the flower garden, and behind them a series of workshops. Off to the right is a huge parking lot filled with new trucks ready for delivery, row upon neat row, like ranks of soldiers in brand-new uniforms ready for battle. Even Li Ruilin, with his bellyful of resentment, has to acknowledge that this sort of scene would have been impossible in the old days, when the place was such a mess that all the hard work in the world wouldn't have made any difference. Back then it had been trench warfare, nothing but constant conflicts and petty jealousies, a real minefield. Li knows all there is to know about the employees in the auto works, especially their problems. This Chen Yongming is human, isn't he? There have to be times when he's troubled by things he can't share with others, so why does he always look so cheerful and unperturbed?

Clouds of steam pour out of the spout as the water begins to boil, making the lid dance and sing. Li Ruilin brews himself a glass of jasmine tea. Tea that sells for eighty fen an ounce these days can't stand up to the stuff that used to go for sixty. Nothing's as good as it used to be. He sits down, takes out his pouch of tobacco and a packet of papers, rolls a cigarette, and sits back to enjoy a leisurely smoke as he surveys the simple furnishings of the caretaker's room.

A list of neatly printed prohibitions is posted beneath the wall clock. The pendulum swings back and forth above the notice, as though pondering the words written beneath it. The motion pleases him.

ONE-YUAN FINE FOR ANY OF THESE FIVE VIOLATIONS

1. Spitting on the floor
2. Smoking in nondesignated areas
3. Littering

4. Unauthorized parking or riding of bicycles
5. Unauthorized visits by relatives

A fine of one yuan will be imposed for any violation of the above regulations

MORNING LIGHT AUTO WORKS

Making a mountain out of a molehill again. Sure, it makes sense to keep the workers' families from dropping by anytime they feel like it. But fining someone for spitting or smoking or littering or parking their bikes where they're not supposed to is going too far. The only reason they get away with it is that everyone's always so strapped for money. Something new, that's all. Ridiculous! Go for a stroll and you'll find the street covered with cigarette butts, litter, spittle, and the more people there are, or the busier the area, the bigger the mess. At places like Wangfujing or the zoo, if you don't watch your step when you walk under a tree or behind a signboard you might find yourself in the middle of a disgusting, mottled puddle of vomit. And who doesn't spit? All Chinese spit! Just listen the next time you're in a theater or at a public lecture or squeezed into a streetcar during the morning rush hour; cyclists hear an endless chorus of throat clearing and noisy spitting as they ride down the street. Spitting never hurt anyone. And you couldn't park your bicycle in the wrong place even if you wanted to, since the old ladies and youngsters who attend the parking areas yell through bullhorns at anyone who tries to get past them. Nothing in the world can save you the two fen it costs to park your bike.

It's all Chen Yongming's doing, no doubt about that. Probably a notion he brought back from his recent trip to Japan. There's talk he's even had a greenhouse built and hired a gardener. And he's going to plant lawns as soon as spring arrives! That's all well and good, but what does it accomplish? Can it make up for power outages or shortages of materials? What does he think this place is? If he wants to see grass and flowers he can go to a park. What business do we have trying to compete with foreigners? They are,

86

after all, a bunch of capitalists. We Chinese manage to get by without grass and flowers, and we still produce our trucks.

Here he goes again, finding fault with Chen Yongming.

Who's to blame for his demotion to gatekeeper?

That spring Chen Yongming attended a management-reform conference at the Ministry and came back with even more ideas and enthusiasm than when he'd first arrived at the auto works. The situation went from bad to worse, with talk of expanding industrial enterprise self-initiative, increasing the competitive base, reforms in the leadership ranks, freely elected cabinets, scrapping the Daqing Office and the Political Department, and doing away with full-time Party secretaries in the workshops—bold steps indeed!

Li Ruilin was willing to put up with a lot, but some of this was more than he could take. How could they scrap the Political Department and the Daqing Office?

When he made the announcement, Chen Yongming said, "The Political Department and the Daqing Office are just window dressing. The real problems are in the nature and quality of our work. We need to concentrate on improving the workers' situation and increasing production, not worry about a bunch of unproductive, wasteful frills!"

And what did he mean by "freely elected cabinets"? Where was this written? Who in the Central Government had ever mentioned it? Not even the Ministry's twelve points on industrial reform said anything about freely elected cabinets.

The leaders of each of the functioning technical units were to be appointed by the factory Party Committee, based on recommendations by the workers, and they were to have free rein in choosing their own subordinates. What better way to produce factionalism? Was a section chief in a better position to put together the best possible staff than the entire Party Committee? Would he be more objective? Could he know more about the cadres than the Personnel Department? How can bourgeois methods be used to organize the leadership ranks of a socialist enterprise?

"What do you mean by 'bourgeois'?" Yang Xiaodong from Workshop Number Two shot back. "Chairman Mao himself used the term when he criticized Jiang Qing, 'Don't you go forming a cabinet . . .' Didn't you even read the indictments against the Gang of Four released by the Central Committee?"

Li Ruilin was known for dozing off at meetings and study sessions. On those rare occasions when he didn't sleep, he was wholly absorbed in plucking whiskers from his cheeks with two coins held between his fingers. He'd been doing this for more than twenty years, through countless campaigns, during countless meetings, and while reading countless documents, yet his beard was as full as ever.

He didn't answer Yang Xiaodong, for fear of revealing his own ignorance. How should he know if it was in the document or not? Besides, young people these days are always looking for an argument, since they're so much better informed about new terms and new theories, and they're always ready to make their views known—reasonable or not—to scare off prospective adversaries. Who knows what Marx or Lenin did or didn't say? Where do you go to find out? Li had learned to handle these situations by affecting an aloof, unapproachable air. If he tried to go up against these people, they'd soon see the shoddy stuff of which a Party branch secretary was made.

Chen Yongming didn't mince words: "I don't care if someone chooses his own nephew or aging aunt, as long as the result is increased production. The objective is simple: I expect noticeable improvements within three months and a real breakthrough within six. Anyone who fails to meet these terms will be replaced by someone who can. There's nothing to be afraid of—we've never had to go that far yet. To get things done you need to work with someone you can get along with. The issue is compatibility, not factionalism. You have to take into consideration the personalities of the people you have working together. Nothing's accomplished by getting up on a soapbox and proclaiming 'We're all Marxists, brothers of the same class, and that's the only compatibility we need.' Li Ruilin and Shen Hongzhao are two fine comrades, one an exemplary Party branch secretary, the other head of a workshop.

But the way they go at each other tooth and nail, how can they be expected to work together? We'd be doing them both a favor by separating them, and what's wrong with that? In the past, the Personnel and Organization departments often put together people who couldn't get along, or gave jobs to good people who had seniority but who were also incompetent. How can we expect decent work from teams like that? The Organization Department must be held accountable for sloppy work in any of the departments. The technical units and workshops have now been given a great deal more say in internal matters, and it's essential that they select people capable of assuming responsibilities without creating more problems. Our opinion polls have shown that we have the personnel but that we don't know how to use them. Poor utilization is the essential problem, since it's the same thing as not having the personnel in the first place. Then there's the problem of training."

And so not only had Li Ruilin lost his position as Party branch secretary, but during the reorganization he was even stripped of his cadre status. It was a sad and unbelievable turn of events. No one wanted him, even though he hadn't made any serious blunders. Even harder to believe than Li Ruilin's fall was that of Feng Zhenmin, the head of Workshop Number Four and a former model worker.

"Why must we make officials out of model workers?" Chen Yongming asked. "Since this is an age of mechanized mass production, we need leaders who understand the technology and have the ability to organize and direct this kind of production. Lao Feng's a good man who takes on the hardest jobs and works overtime until he nearly drops from exhaustion. So where do we stand? The organization of Workshop Number Four is a mess, and it never meets its monthly quota. He can't express himself clearly and usually forgets half of what's said at one of the factory production meetings. Forgetfulness is nothing to be ashamed of, as long you take notes to report back to the workshop. But he's semiliterate, and better off as a model worker. It's wrong to select workshop heads using the same criteria as choosing model workers, since the finest model worker isn't necessarily qualified to be a cadre. 'A general's one thing, a commander in chief's another.' Isn't that right?"

"You can't blame him. His cultural level is too low! What do you expect from someone who's lived a life of suffering and poverty? You can't compare us working stiffs to a bunch of eggheads!" Li Ruilin squared his shoulders.

"Working stiffs? What's so great about working stiffs! We're not compiling an honor roll or giving out prizes. Besides, honor rolls are a thing of the past. All they prove is that the past doesn't equal the present. You could get away with talking like that right after Liberation, since we'd just come through a long war. But we've had thirty years of peace since then, and what have you been doing all that time? Playing poker!"

Naturally, he was talking about Li Ruilin, not Lao Feng. "So what if I have?" Li Ruilin said defiantly. He didn't think that playing poker meant that he was unprincipled. Instead of trying to get a handle on important matters, Chen Yongming was more interested in trivial matters like poker playing.

Everyone liked Lao Feng, and even the most unruly youngster in Workshop Number Four would give the thumbs-up whenever his name was mentioned: "The workshop head's a great guy, but he can't solve our problems."

"And Miao Zhuoling can, I suppose?"

"Who says he can't?"

"He has a bad background and a checkered past."

Chen Yongming glared at Li as though seeing him for the first time. "Since when did you start with that kind of nonsense? That sort of talk has ruined more good comrades than I care to think about. It's been the scourge of China. Do you know how much raw talent has been wasted by prejudices like that? And who suffers? We all do! How are we supposed to carry out the Four Modernizations and socialist construction without that talent? For years now we've been standing still watching others forge ahead. In the 1950s our economy was on a par with Japan. Now take a look around you; we're a good thirty years behind them."

"I don't have to take a look. They've got rats in their ghettos this big!" he said, holding his hands out so far they could frame a cat.

"Have you ever seen one?"

"Read about it in the paper!"

"Ha, ha, ha!"

The sound of a bicycle bell breaks into Li Ruilin's reflections. Wu Guodong is riding into the factory yard on a brand-new twenty-eight-inch Eternal bicycle. He sees Li Ruilin sitting in the caretaker's room, rides up, and greets him warmly. "You . . . back to work, are you?"

"Can't just sit around, can I?" He goes over to take a look at Wu Guodong's bicycle. Where did he get the money to buy a brand-new bike after being out sick all this time? It must have cost at least 170 yuan.

"I just bought it," Wu Guodong volunteers. "The factory gave those of us who live far away salary advances to buy them. That way we don't have to ride a packed bus to and from work every day. They deduct two yuan a month from our wages." He presses the bell on the handlebars, which rings out happily, a song of contentment. Even Li Ruilin smiles when he hears it. It's not easy for a poor worker to buy a bicycle.

But Wu Guodong's smile fades as he notices the gray at Li Ruilin's temples and his receding hairline. He reaches out and muffles the sound of the bell.

No one can accuse Chen Yongming of a lack of interest in the workers' welfare. Their new, nearly completed dormitory is being built exclusively by them; for the first time in more than ten years, something is actually being done about the housing problem.

Li Ruilin, who hasn't been to work for more than two months, is reminded of the old saying, "One day in Heaven is a thousand years on earth."

"Have you gotten over your hepatitis?"

"Yeah." Wu Guodong shakes his head sadly. All his suffering is expressed in this simple action.

Li Ruilin knows just what he means. He and Wu belong to the same generation, after all, and share the same feelings toward the burdens of life and society. "Be careful you don't have a relapse."

Just then Lü Zhimin rides into the factory yard, scraping his right foot lightly over the ground before putting it back on the pedal, a token gesture toward the requirement to dismount when entering and leaving the compound. He spits his cigarette butt onto the ground.

"Get off that bike!" Li Ruilin shouts. "Get off it right this minute!" Now I'm open for business. I'll fine him one yuan and see what happens.

Lü Zhimin skids his bike to a stop. "What's wrong?" he asks with a blink of amazement. "What's wrong?"

"Hand over one yuan, that's what's wrong!"

"What for?"

Li Ruilin points to the wall beside the caretaker's room. "Read the notice: One-yuan fine for any of these five violations."

Lü Zhimin just stands there looking foolish.

Li Ruilin and Wu Guodong, on the other hand, are gloating. In this, at least, they agree, happy to see this ONE-YUAN FINE FOR ANY OF THESE FIVE VIOLATIONS come up against general opinion; it couldn't be rescinded fast enough for them. They're also pleased to see a youngster like Lü Zhimin be held accountable to rules and regulations.

How enthusiastic they all were at the beginning, not realizing that fining people like this one yuan is like taking a pound of flesh. When the disbanding of the Daqing Office and the Political Department were announced at the general meeting, Li Ruilin had leapt up onto the stage and confronted Chen Yongming hatefully: "What the hell are you trying to do? Are you interested in taking the socialist road or not?" Some of the youngsters in front had roared with laughter, whistled, even applauded. It was Lü Zhimin who went up and dragged Li Ruilin from the stage. "Come on, stand aside!" he said.

"Manager Chen announced it to the entire factory, didn't he?" Wu Guodong pipes up. "You knew!"

Lü Zhimin slowly unbuttons his shirt pocket. What can he do once Chen Yongming's name is mentioned? The employees all respect Chen, and Lü sings his praises, no matter what Chen says or proposes. But he's so enraged by the smug look on Wu

Guodong's face that he wants nothing more now than to cut him down to size. He's not going to take that from him, head of the workshop or not.

But just then, the image of Lao Lü Tou flashes through Li Ruilin's mind: he's wearing a tattered coat, pushing his rickety old bike ahead of him. It's too painful. "All right, forget it! But don't you ever do it again. And pick up that cigarette butt! Put it into the trash can where it belongs."

Lü Zhimin does as he is told, then waves at Li Ruilin, glares meaningfully at Wu Guodong, jumps back onto his bike and rides off.

Wu Guodong spins around: "Lao Li, you shouldn't . . ."

"Forget it. Why start with him? No, not me, I'm going to start at the top. They're the ones who made up the rules."

Neither agreeing nor disagreeing with Li, Wu Guodong thinks that the rules should apply to everyone. He can't remember when this feeling that everything is wrong, like an invisible pest boring into his heart, took over. Day in and day out, things just don't seem right to him; his sky seems about to fall.

Ge Xinfa and Wu Bin were supposed to meet with Yang Xiaodong after lunch to discuss some important business, but Yang still hasn't shown up. Where could he be? Hasn't he finished lunch yet? They walk back to the canteen, where they find him in the doorway talking to an obviously downcast Lü Zhimin. He's wearing a pair of sunglasses that make him look like he has dark bulging eyes. He seems even more listless and sulky than usual. Yang Xiaodong, on the other hand, his bushy eyebrows jerking up and down triumphantly, is grinning broadly; is he angry or is he just having a good time with the youngster? Wu Bin is smart enough to know that they wouldn't be standing in the canteen doorway for no reason. But he doesn't let on. "First you stuff yourself, then you stand guard at the canteen door, eh!"

Yang Xiaodong takes pride in his reputation as a straight shooter, someone who's serious to the bitter end. "Lunchtime is when everyone in the factory comes together, so I brought him over to see how many other workers wear sunglasses." He turns to Lü Zhimin. "Now do you see? A grand total of three, including you. And you know who those other two are." He's serious, all right. "I'm telling you that we won't tolerate this in our team. Don't you be one of those who goes along with every fad!"

"All right, now, take those off!" Wu Bin says with a frown. "Are you trying to be an overseas Chinese, or what?" He reaches out and snatches the sunglasses from Lü Zhimin's face.

Ge Xinfa looks toward the sky and squints. The sun is still hidden behind the gray clouds and smog. "If you're going to wear them, mid-winter isn't the time."

"I made it clear when you chose me as team leader that you thirteen are all assistant team leaders, and that you're to put yourselves in my place when you do anything that involves the team. That's the only way things'll get done right. You all agreed, remember?"

"I remember," Lü Zhimin admits. He never disputes anything Yang Xiaodong says.

These men all get along perfectly; they are a team.

Lü hasn't forgotten how Yang went to bat for him the time he got into trouble with the head of the workshop for coming to work in bell-bottoms. "Just because young hooligans go around in bell-bottoms doesn't make everyone who wears them a hooligan," he argued with Wu Guodong, "any more than wearing grimy work clothes makes someone a model worker."

As for Lü Zhimin's inability to get along with his father, no one can say who is right and who is wrong.

The old man, who is certainly no intellectual, is too lax with his son, and he always runs to Yang Xiaodong complaining about the way his son talks back to him; or about how he leaves his bath water from the night before in the middle of the floor where anyone could kick it over; or how he goes out at night and doesn't come back till very late, saying that there is "factory business" (he asked Yang if his team had frequent night meetings); or how he keeps a knife under his bed, which he plans to use on his father.

Lü Zhimin had brought a new wash basin and a couple of new towels home with him the year before, and his father asked Yang

Xiaodong if he thought they might be stolen. The more the old man assumed the worst about him, the more defiant Lü Zhimin became. Everyone Lao Lü Tou met got an earful of complaints about his son, and the situation was getting worse instead of better.

Yang Xiaodong dealt with the matter fairly, not accepting everything the father told him and criticizing the son for trying to get the old man's goat. He has never been one to believe everything he hears, especially idle rumors and inflammatory accusations. He does what is appropriate to the situation, whether it is yelling at someone or talking things out. In this respect, Lü Zhimin feels he gets better treatment from Yang Xiaodong than from his own father. A leader like that, even if he is only a team leader, is worth having.

"Okay, you can confiscate them the next time I wear them," Lü Zhimin says with determination. A pair of sunglasses isn't worth getting Xiaodong mad at him.

"The next time I see you wearing them I'll smash 'em," Yang Xiaodong says bluntly.

Wu Bin stuffs the sunglasses into Lü Zhimin's pocket, then turns to Yang Xiaodong. "What did you want to talk to us about?"

Yang Xiaodong takes a piece of paper out of his pocket and hands it to Wu Bin: yesterday's straw poll to determine how to spend the fifty-yuan bonus awarded to the team for safety, sanitation, and preventative maintenance.

Wu Bin tallies the results: all but one of the fourteen team members opted for a meal at the nearby New Wind restaurant. The sole dissenting slip merely says "Moscow."

Wu Bin recalls that there had been no discussion before the voting, yet the results were nearly unanimous. They were so united it was almost scary.

"Since today's the last day of 1979, there's nothing but clean-up work this afternoon, so you and Ge Xinfa can take off and arrange a meal at the New Wind restaurant. The Moscow restaurant's too far, and it only received one vote anyway. You guys get a table and choose the menu, since you're more experienced than the others. Just don't go over fifty yuan. We'll be finished here by three o'clock, and as soon as the workshop closes up, we'll go over as a group."

"You still haven't forgotten, have you?" Ge Xinfa says.

"I remember everything that's worth remembering. All kinds of experience can be put to use someday, as long as the time and circumstances are right. And now's the time to put your restaurant experience to use."

This gets a laugh out of all of them.

Before the quarterly bonuses were distributed the last time, Yang Xiaodong told them, "They're handing out bonuses today, but don't you two spend yours at a restaurant during working hours."

It was not a casual comment. It wasn't Yang's style to say things just for the sake of saying them.

Ge Xinfa and Wu Bin, who had a reputation for gluttony, invariably blew their bonuses in restaurants the same day they received them. Yang had already cautioned them several times. "Off to a restaurant again, hm? What about putting a little of that money aside, just in case you want to get married someday."

But whenever the subject of marriage came up, Ge Xinfa expressed his misgivings: "Get married? No way! I need my freedom. Are *you* as free now as you were as a bachelor?"

Yang Xiaodong squinted as he thought for a moment. "No, I'm not as free as I was, but there's a certain beauty in this particular loss of freedom, something no bachelor can ever fathom."

Wu Bin disagreed. "Today's one thing, tomorrow's something else. Besides, we only get one or two meals like this a month."

Ge Xinfa continued, "That's right. What good is money if you don't have a place to live? Look at Lao Song, he almost had to get down on his knees and beg Wu Guodong for a place."

"If it'd been me," Wu Bin said angrily, "I'd damn well have taken my wife and bedded down in the workshop head's office. That bastard's already got himself a wife and two little brats!" Any mention of Lao Song's housing problem always set him off.

"You shouldn't talk about Wu Guodong that way," Yang cautioned him. "He's managed to increase production in his workshop

96

without going through any back doors or abusing his authority. Even when the factory sends people to the countryside for fruit, he won't buy any if it doesn't come through the state-run market. To him it's a matter of principle. We're lucky to have a cadre like that. What do you expect from a low-ranking official without any power?"

"That doesn't give him the right to always think the worst of us," Wu Bin said. "When Lao Song requested housing, he wouldn't even look him in the eye. He just sat there poring over newspaper ads while Lao Song stood off to the side waiting for an answer. Finally he asked Lao Song, 'Marriage? How old are you?' 'Twenty-seven. You asked me the same thing a few days ago.'

"You see, he'd already forgotten how old Lao Song was. Big or small, the workshop cadres are all officials, and we're their troops. He ought to know something about us as individuals and what's on our minds. Like you know us, Xiaodong. I read a novel once about a regiment of soldiers during wartime, at least a thousand men or more. You know how good the political commissar was at his job? He learned the names of every new soldier within three days, and within a week he knew something about all their families. In our workshop there aren't more than three hundred people!"

"That was a novel!" Ge Xinfa cut in.

"Don't interrupt me, there's more. Wu Guodong said to him, 'You're still pretty young. There are thirty-year-olds in the workshop who aren't married yet. Wait a couple more years. Both the Party and the government favor late marriages, and we workers are expected to do everything possible to meet the needs of the Party and the government.'

"If I'd been Lao Song, I'd have asked him then and there, 'How old were you when you got married? Don't be such a hypocrite!' But Lao Song's too nice a guy, so all he said was, 'My situation's different. I've got to get married right away.'

"You can imagine what Wu Guodong made of that. If it's bad thoughts, he's got 'em. 'Are you in trouble?' he asked Lao Song. Shit! 'Are you in trouble?' How could he not know what a terrific, beautiful thing Lao Song did? Someone like that's got no right handling ideological affairs. And he's Party secretary to boot! When have people like him ever been concerned with us or treated

97

us like human beings? At one with the people, hah! They've got to learn that we have the right to get married, to give our opinions, to ask for housing, or to eat out if we want to. They act like dictators and run herd over us. So, you're only half-right, Xiaodong. There's more to being a good workshop cadre than increasing production. They have to gain the hearts of their subordinates, like you have. Everyone's willing to work for you, no matter how tired they are, because you treat 'em right. We're human beings, after all, not animals. People need warmth, they need concern for their well-being, sympathy, words of comfort, a little care. The power these things bring can't be bought and can't be forced."

Wu Bin and Ge Xinfa had knocked off early to eat at a restaurant more than once, and Yang Xiaodong had warned them that the next time he'd report them to Wu Guodong. They ignored his warning, and when they returned to the workshop that day, he was waiting for them. "I told you not to do that again," he said, "but you went ahead anyway. That was your first mistake. Eating when you should have been working is a violation of factory discipline. That was your second mistake. Rather than waiting for me to report you, you should go admit your mistakes to Wu Guodong on your own."

But they held back, neither wanting to take the lead. So Yang Xiaodong grabbed them by the arms. "You won't go on your own? Okay, then I'll drag you over there, and while I'm there, I'll criticize myself, too. I'll confess that your going to a restaurant while you should have been working proves that I haven't been doing my job."

After admonishing their behavior, Wu Guodong docked their wages for the time they were off the job. But neither of them held a grudge against Yang Xiaodong, since he'd always been up-front with them, never attacking them behind their backs or mounting a campaign against them. Never once had he reported on anyone behind his back or used anyone to get ahead. And he never put the squeeze on anyone.

* * *

At a little after three o'clock, Wu Guodong spots Yang Xiaodong's team changing quickly out of their work clothes and washing up, shouting and carrying on as they try to hurry each other, as though it were some kind of emergency. When he discovers that Wu Bin and Ge Xinfa are missing, he goes over and rubs his hand across Wu Bin's lathe. Clean and freshly oiled. The area around the lathe has been swept. The tooled axle covers are neatly stacked on the rack; everything has been picked up, and all the tools have been returned to the toolbox and locked up. Nothing wrong here. And yet he feels it's his duty as a Party secretary to find out what's going on. "Where are you all off to?" he asks Yang Xiaodong.

"The whole team's going over to eat at the New Wind restaurant."

"Whose treat?"

"We're treating ourselves! Didn't you say we could spend our group bonus any way we wanted, without any interference from the workshop?"

Lü Zhimin, who is standing nearby, shouts, "We're off for some murder and arson!"

Wu Guodong is sure the comment is intended for him. That's going a bit too far. After all, he is a Party secretary.

He watches them walk their bikes out of the bicycle shed. The seats are raised so high the men have to lean over the handlebars and raise their rear ends as they ride out to the accompaniment of a chorus of ringing bells. They look like a swarm of locusts.

Locusts, that's what they are! To Wu Guodong, at least. All right, fine! Go ahead and squander your bonus in a restaurant if that's what you want! The very thought makes Wu Guodong's hair stand on end.

He wonders why this group of misfits has been assigned to the lathe shop. He's troubled by their unity. They do everything together, work and play. He's never witnessed a single dispute among them. Even in the distribution of wages, the touchiest business of all, no member of the team has ever come to him with a complaint about an injustice or a demand for promotion. He's seen it all with other teams—whining, arguing, disunity, even work stoppages, and all over money. And whose fault is that? No one's.

99

What can they do? They're poor. Do he and his wife ever argue about anything except money?

If a member of their team gets sick and has to take a couple of days off, which might jeopardize his bonus, his fellow team members pitch in and help him out. Wu Guodong has seen it happen. Once, when Lü Zhimin had the flu, the clinic refused to approve sick leave because he only had a fever of thirty-seven degrees centigrade. So Yang Xiaodong told him to stay home and did double duty to take up the slack.

Then there is their work record. Prior to 1978 the workshop had never met its production quota, and the blame was placed on the lathe shop for slowing everyone down. Wu Guodong had bawled them out time and again for delaying the work of the chassis shop.

They protested that the fault lay with the inexperienced head of the chassis shop, who'd only been there since 1968 and was already the shop head. They said he lacked ability, experience, and the respect of his workers. Since he was a millworker who didn't understand lathe work, he'd made a mess of everything.

When he refused to take the blame for his inability to carry out his duties, they demanded a reorganization of the production unit, separating it into a lathe shop, a benchwork shop, a milling shop, and a chassis shop; once the donkeys were separated from the horses, they'd see just who was carrying out their duties and who wasn't.

Wu Guodong took their advice and reorganized the workshop production teams.

On the day the lathe shop was set up, they held a meeting. "Now that we're an independent unit," they said, "it's up to us to do a good job. We'll show them we're not a bunch of misfits."

After the meeting they put up a notice announcing that the team had become an independent unit on the fifth of January, 1978, and was determined to do the best job possible. Everything was just fine, except for the last line: "See you at the end of the year!" Wu Guodong didn't like that one bit. Whoever heard of a notice like that? Who was that "See you at the end of the year!" intended for? Hmm? It looked like they were pumping themselves up to take on the entire workshop and him, the man in charge.

The reorganization did the job. The team met its quota for twenty-four consecutive months. In 1978 it was singled out as a progressive team, one of only eight among the twenty-two teams in the workshop. And this year it was named an all-factory progressive production unit, as well as cited by the company for the quality of its work.

What made this team so special? Was it Party spirit? Not a chance! Only two of them were Party members, and three belonged to the Communist Youth League.

Was it their leadership? Did Yang Xiaodong really have that many tricks up his sleeve? If anyone knew Yang Xiaodong's story, it was Wu Guodong. Yang's father had joined the Kuomintang, and Yang was a member of neither the Communist Party nor the Communist Youth League. In 1967 he was reprimanded for driving trucks without permission. It wasn't the driving that got him into trouble, but the way he tried to cover it up by making a lot of keys on the sly, then disengaging the odometers so that no one could tell that the trucks had been driven. He pushed the trucks out of the yard, starting them up only after he was far down the road; then, on the way back, he turned off the engines, coasted up to the factory gate, and pushed the trucks back inside. All this after working hours. Back then the general work ethic was so bad that it took a long time for either the leaders or the sentries to discover what he was doing. The entire episode showed how crafty he was. So how did he hold this bunch together? Was it like a gang of thieves, where the biggest thief is top dog?

Maybe it was concern over the team's reputation. But who would ever believe that this bunch gave a damn about their reputation? Not when they run off to a restaurant every time they get a bonus.

So what was it? Wu Guodong simply couldn't figure it out. He never let down his guard where they were concerned, even if they were the leaders of the pack. He always expected the worst from them. Even the axle covers they produced were suspect as far as he was concerned. It was as though these covers were an illusion produced by some secret elixir, and that when the power wore off, they'd turn into a pile of rubble.

101

But Wu Guodong was a practical man who knew that a factory is run on technical competence, and that a leader has to be unyielding. No matter how close he was to someone personally, if that person lacked the technical skill to do a job, Wu Guodong had no use for him. He didn't like Yang Xiaodong personally, but the man got the job done without any shenanigans or goofing off, and he gave his all as a worker. Wu Guodong knew he needed people like Yang if he was to keep production on the rise.

Then Wu Guodong discovered that Chen Yongming liked Yang Xiaodong. He frequently saw Chen passing the time of day with Yang and his bunch. They talked about all sorts of things, from ecological balance to all the overseas junkets taken by the nation's leaders, even to the inevitability of Khomeini's fall from power in Iran. Sometimes they even larded their speech with phrases in English or Japanese. What's so hot about all that stuff? People like that are hard to deal with, for the simple reason that they know too much.

Seven

The artist's face has grown flabby, wrinkled, slack jowled; yet there is a childlike, dreamy look in his eyes, which truly seem to be windows to his soul. Although his eyes differ from his paintings, which leave such lasting impressions on their viewers, for Zheng Ziyun they evoke both envy and sadness, and ultimately make him feel as though he were gazing into a splendid painting into which only one's soul is allowed entrance. But even if he could, would he have entered? Whatever the answer, by now it is already too late. Once he wanted to study anthropology, history, literature, but Fate made him an official.

The artist is a friend of Wang Fangliang, whose circle of friends includes all sorts of people, from vice-premiers to scholars of ancient scripts and famous chefs.

Zheng Ziyun once praised a painting at an exhibition to Wang: "This painting's pretty good!"

Wang Fangliang responded with a loud laugh. "Well, well!" Impossible to tell if he was approving or being sarcastic. "These are tough times for artists!" he continued in a serious tone.

"Why's that?"

"In China painting a nude means the same as taking someone to bed, and I don't mean your own wife." He laughed even harder.

Taking someone to bed?

It was a painting of enchanting nymphs, whose naked limbs were stretched out languidly. Although the canvas wasn't large, it managed somehow to reveal the eternal mysteries of life.

The figures represented not flesh-and-blood women, but the Eternal Mother. The frail figures evoked not only male protectiveness, but also a powerful sense of Man's dependence and belonging, the forces that have impelled mankind forward, that have given birth to history, that have produced genius.

"Ask him if he'd be willing to sell it to me."

Zheng Ziyun's father had once tersely characterized him as "headstrong as an ox."

The artist surprised Zheng by giving him the painting, which made him regret his impulsive request, not to mention his headstrong nature. What was he going to do with it? Hang it? What would his comrades at the Ministry think if they saw a painting of nudes hanging on his wall? If he were just another clerk, it would go unnoticed; but for cadres at his level, everything became simple and complex at the same time. Yet if he didn't hang it, that would be a denial of the artist's dedication to his work.

Whatever he decided, he certainly couldn't just take the painting as a gift. But when he proposed some sort of payment, Wang Fangliang objected. "Money means nothing to him anyway, so don't worry about it. If you try to pay him, you'll probably just offend him."

All this happened a long time ago, yet it still preys on Zheng Ziyun's mind.

That afternoon he had an idea: Why not take the artist to a restaurant where they could talk over dinner? Since he'd been in a bad mood all day anyway, the thought of going home for dinner wasn't particularly inviting. On the surface it didn't seem serious, but nothing involving high-ranking personnel is ever as simple as it seems; and no outsider can ever gauge what lies behind even the most casual comment.

A few days earlier a senior comrade in the State Economic Commission had asked the Ministry of Heavy Industry to prepare a report on its enterprise reorganization for a meeting with responsible members from each ministry. Tian Shoucheng thrust this thankless job on him, telling him to first send over a draft of the speech for approval. The completed draft was returned to him that morning by Zheng's secretary, Xiao Ji. According to Tian Shoucheng, the senior cadre wanted him to stress the importance of studying the Daqing model in the successful reorganization of their enterprises, and Tian himself complained that the draft didn't cover all that it should, specifically that the "Study Daqing" banner was not raised high enough. When he heard this, Zheng sneered and tore up the draft. "Xiao Ji," he said to his secretary, "call up the State Economic Commission and tell them I won't be giving the report."

"Not so fast!" Wang Fangliang stopped Xiao Ji. He turned to Zheng. "All you need to do is send them an outline. They don't have to know what you're going to say until you actually give the report. Don't you think you'd better go through with it?"

"There's no point in it," Zheng replied without even looking up.

"That's up to you, but Xiao Ji, when you make the call tell them that Vice-Minister Zheng can't make the report because our work is far from finished."

Zheng looked at Wang with a sneer.

Wang threw up his hands. "What's that look for? It's not worth it!"

It soon blew over. Just a superficial wound caused by a tiny dart that left no permanent scar.

The Personnel Department had assigned Ji Hengquan as Zheng Ziyun's secretary when he was given his old job back.

Zheng hadn't requested anyone in particular to be his secretary, nor did he want a personal secretary who would always be at his side, pen and notebook ready. To him that was an unnecessary, even insulting, throwback to feudal traditions. Being accustomed to doing things for himself, whether it was drafting a report, giving written instructions, debriefing others, or analyzing a situation, he didn't see the need for having anyone else. He certainly didn't expect to spend the rest of his life at this or any other job. Wherever he was assigned, he did the best job he could, and if he was removed, he could always spend his time reading. There were so many books to read! The last thing in the world he needed was to spend time and energy seeking out patrons or followers in order to gain power or consolidate his position.

For Ji Hengquan, who had previously worked as secretary to several ministers, this work was right up his alley. But he found Zheng Ziyun to be an unpredictable boss who frequently did things that were highly unconventional. That made his own job difficult. Zheng was strong willed and temperamental, which was all the proof Ji Hengquan needed that his boss would climb no higher in official circles; it was a mystery to him how he had made it this high. Ji was convinced that headstrong people were incapable of controlling their own destiny. And if by chance Zheng managed to move up, sooner or later he'd come crashing down, and hard. Xiao Ji, who saw no possibility that Zheng would finish out his career on top, observed his boss's activities as though he were a guinea pig in a scientific experiment. Who could say when Zheng's correspondence, his telephone conversations, his meetings with others, or even his list of visitors might come in handy, either to bail Zheng out of a jam or help cook his goose?

The truth of the matter was that Ji Hengquan was no different from anyone else; his attitude was a by-product of the unique nature of political life in society. In fairness, he was a competent secretary who could adapt his talents to the needs of a variety of bosses. But on the personal level, he was too conditioned by society to be a good secretary for someone like Zheng Ziyun; his great failing was not having a sense of right and wrong.

As far as Ji was concerned, it was more than merely headstrong for a vice-minister to respond to a senior comrade of the State

Economic Commission as Zheng had just done—it was downright pathetic. Zheng Ziyun obviously didn't know how to weigh the consequences of his words and actions. How did he know who might be in that particular comrade's corner? And even if the man didn't have the backing of a powerful clique, he at least represented the policies of some members of the central government. No matter what backing or inclinations the man had, boxing him into a corner was not the way to make an ally of him. Relationships among people are so delicate that friends are sometimes won and lost by a mere flick of the wrist.

Ji Hengquan decided to take Wang Fangliang's advice. Once Zheng cooled down and discovered that Ji hadn't handled the matter as he wished, he'd realize it had been for his own good and would let the matter drop. Wang Fangliang may have been the carefree one around the office, one who didn't seem concerned about anything that happened, but he was far more formidable than Zheng. He was the sort of person who only shows his true colors at critical moments. Even Minister Tian was afraid of him.

Xia Zhuyun was insistent on the other end of the telephone: "Why aren't you coming home for dinner?"

"Who are you having dinner with?"

"Who? Why don't I know him?" The painting had hung on their living-room wall for at least a month; for thirty straight days she had looked at it, never once so much as glancing at the artist's signature. Besides, why did she need to know him?

She lost her temper: "Here it is New Year's Eve and you're not coming home! This family doesn't mean a damned thing to you!"—that really stung him—"Fangfang and Peiwen are here with the baby, while you're going out to eat with some painter." She said the word painter as though she were talking about a piece of scorched meat or a discarded dress.

"I can eat anywhere I want," Zheng replied sluggishly and slammed down the receiver, terminating the diatribe coming through the phone.

The news that his eldest son-in-law had come to dinner only

strengthened his resolve not to go home. That "perfect match" of a son-in-law disgusted him. Xia Zhuyun had picked him out for their daughter, but to Zheng he had the look of a con artist. His slick demeanor reminded Zheng of the well-to-do peasants and petty merchants they'd seen so often when they entered towns back during the War of Liberation.

People like that were free to do as they liked, as far as Zheng was concerned, but it made Yuanyuan's life a misery. He wished he'd invited her to join him this afternoon, but he didn't feel like calling back and getting another earful of complaints. His daughter was his only tie to a home from which he felt so estranged. Although forty years apart in age, father and daughter had always been blessed with a common language.

The cul-de-sac is so narrow there isn't room to turn the Toyota around, and the driver has to back the car in.

The tiny compound looks as though it was once the home of a single family, filled with the trees that Beijing residents love so much—date, persimmon, pear, Chinese rose—a warm, cozy, peaceful place. But at some time in the past, several families had moved in, and tiny kitchens sprang up like mushrooms after a rainfall, stretching even to the heart of the compound, like stones on a dike moving inexorably toward the center of a river.

The compound is filled with every imaginable aroma: vinegary cabbage, oniony flat cakes, oily fish, and every imaginable sound: quarreling spouses, crying babies, blasting radios, resounding clappers. The noise ascends to the heavens. From the volume of the radio, it's obvious that the listener is hard-of-hearing, probably an old lady who is mincing meat filling. Such women switch on their radios the minute they open their eyes in the morning and leave them on all day blaring the music of *Swan Lake,* simple explanations of *Das Kapital,* and historical dramas like *The Life of Yue Fei,* not a single word of which they ever really listen to.

The artist has a studio in a tiny earthquake shelter erected after the 1976 Tangshan earthquake. It's cold and dank now, but during the summer months, the newspaper stuck on the walls must drip with moisture from the unbearable heat. The artist is so tall and the ceiling so low that he's forced to stoop when inside. But looking at the half-finished painting on the easel or the completed ones hanging on the walls is enough to make you forget the fetid odors and the din coming into the tiny room from the small compound. China's intellectuals, Zheng Ziyun thinks, must be the "objects" in the phrase "beautiful objects at low cost." As he stands there in the tiny studio, feeling a bit lost, he thinks of the technicians at the Ministry and the masses of workers in the factories, and quickly revises his view. No, it's the common man in China who is the quintessential "beautiful object at low cost."

In the car on the way over the artist suddenly blurted out, "In the thirty years since Liberation, this is the first time a minister—"

"Vice-minister," Zheng Ziyun corrected him.

"Not even a deputy bureau chief has ever been to my home. But please don't think that I'm one of those people who are over-whelmed by such honors. It's not your rank that impresses me, but your understanding of my profession and the way you deal with people and situations." The artist spoke rapidly, clutching the door handle, as though getting ready to open the door and jump out if his meaning was misunderstood.

"Here's a man who cherishes his self-respect!" Zheng Ziyun thought. But instead of saying anything, he patted the back of the artist's hand that rested on the seat between them.

Zheng Ziyun was impressed by how easily two complete strangers could hit it off, while people who had known each other for years could be separated by such vast distances. The reason was probably to be found in people's temperaments. Once again he thought of Yuanyuan, Xia Zhuyun, Tian Shoucheng, and suddenly the image of Ye Zhiqiu's homely face flashed before his eyes.

They look a little too refined for their surroundings as they sit there quietly sipping *maotai* and nibbling snacks. Their teeth are getting bad and they don't have the appetite they once had, but they're enjoying themselves smoking and talking.

109

The young men at the table to their right, their faces flushed with drink, are playing the finger-guessing drinking game:

"Skillful seven!"

"Six, six, easy as you go!"

"Five fingers at the head!"

"Four horses!"

"The works!"

"The treasure!"

They are too caught up in their noisy game to notice that they are disrupting the entire restaurant, and one of the waiters has to go over to quiet them down.

The artist frowns. "We Chinese don't know how to eat without causing a scene."

Zheng Ziyun takes a look around. "Everyone here, except for the two of us, is young. You can't blame them, eating out and having a few drinks is about the only pastime they've got. How else can they burn off some of that excess energy? Go dancing? Not on your life! It's funny, but back in the fifties, when dancing was so popular, I never heard of anyone turning into a hooligan because of it. Since there's no cultural life, how about travel? No, they can't afford it. I feel sorry for them, but what can I do? There has to be some healthy outlet for all that energy."

"You're right!" the artist remarks with feeling.

"I wonder why some people make such a fuss over the young people's needs and aspirations, why they're viewed with such contempt? It's as though thinking different thoughts is treasonous. Have they forgotten how different we were from our parents' generation? As scientific socialists and dialectical materialists, we ought to acknowledge their right to transform even the things that we approve of, so long as those changes are legal and don't interfere with the rights of others. We don't recognize anything other than things passed down by our ancestors and some foreign stuff that we and the previous generation have accepted and grown accustomed to, like classical music, early twentieth-century ballroom dancing, nineteenth-century forms of literary expression. . . . Since we were so fond of these things when we were young, we object to anyone trying to take them one step further. We've turned into apologists for these things. Life is moving too quickly for us, so we object to the fast-paced music of the young, the fast dancing, and the rapid changes in literary expression. But it's only natural for them to seek changes and search for new things, it's the way of life.

"Some authors' experiments with 'stream of consciousness' have caused a real furor. No one's forcing anyone to read their stuff or look at modern art, but like it or not, progress will continue. Things that we now consider sacrosanct will die out someday, even the things that they hold so dearly will disappear in a few decades." A thin smile appears at the corners of Zheng's mouth. "It's wrong to expect young people to share our thoughts and feelings. It's also impossible. It's just as wrong to expect them to forge the same kind of relationship with the Party that we had when we were young. Back then we were engaged in a life-and-death struggle with the old society. Young people today are demanding more opportunities to think independently and make decisions about their own lives. They have experienced more than we had at their age, and they've seen far greater changes. The realities of life have taught them to be more reflective and more decisive. We in the Party can't afford to lose confidence in progress. You can rest if you're tired, but don't hold the others back."

At a table close to Zheng's, Yang Xiaodong looks into the faces of the thirteen men seated around him. They are talking about things that have nothing to do with their celebration or the bonus that made it possible. He knows that's because things like this happen so infrequently in their lives.

For these men, victims of prejudice and distrust who are struggling to throw off their coarseness and better themselves, this event undeniably brings them hope, gives them confidence, and affirms not only their past accomplishments, but the brightness of their future as well. And this brightness comes from their own unyielding natures rather than the charity of others; the irrational ideas still permeating society only strengthen their indomitable resolve to resist and never give in.

But you won't hear them talk about things like that or show

their feelings. They are too tough for that and are not men who make a show of their emotions.

There's only the dark beer, with its white froth that pours over the bottle necks as they're opened and forces the men to quickly fill their glasses.

Yang Xiaodong opens a bottle and fills their glasses before raising his own. "We're here today because of everyone's combined efforts," he says. "Let's drink to that!" There's more he wants to say, but he feels his heartbeat quicken and can tell that his voice is quavering slightly; he's too embarrassed to go on.

They get to their feet and raise their glasses. "Not so fast," Wu Bin speaks up. "Let's get a picture of this!" He takes a camera out of his olive-drab knapsack.

Ge Xinfa is impressed: "You've thought of everything!"

"Squeeze closer together," Wu Bin directs them, "as close as possible."

"What about you?" Lü Zhimin asks. "Get someone else to take the picture."

Wu Bin turns and looks into the gaze of Zheng Ziyun at the next table. "Would you mind taking a picture of us? Make sure we're all in that little square, don't cut anyone out, then just press this button. It's an automatic camera."

Zheng Ziyun happily agrees, even though he wonders why they brought a camera along with them for an ordinary meal. Is this a bachelor party for one of them? Hardly, not with that bunch of youngsters. Well then, maybe it's a reunion of old friends. "What's the occasion?" he asks.

"It's a happy day for us," Wu Bin answers him, "a special event. We're treating ourselves to a meal from the bonus we got."

With that, they begin clinking their glasses and spilling beer all over the table, their emotions pouring from their hearts. They couldn't hold their laughter back if they tried.

Everything that Yang Xiaodong has been wanting to say is compressed into a single sentence: "I hope we can do this again next year!"

By this time Zheng Ziyun has returned to his own table, but his attention remains focused on the men at the other table. He listens to the artist with one ear, his gaze riveted on Yang Xiaodong and his men.

Wu Bin taps his plate with his chopsticks to get everyone to quiet down, then stands up and raises his glass, saying with uncharacteristic seriousness, "I say we should drink to Xiaodong. We've taken a team that was put down by everyone and turned it into a progressive unit, and it's our team leader who's made it possible. Come on, you guys, drink up!"

Yang Xiaodong brushes them off and refuses to stand up.

Zheng Ziyun's interest is greater than ever after listening to Wu Bin's toast. He casts a satisfied look at the artist, like the owner of an old, established shop who won't stoop to boasting about his store. And these youngsters sitting right next to him, well, you couldn't find another bunch like them if you scoured the city; he is as proud of them as a storekeeper would be of his own unique merchandise.

"Look, everyone's standing with their glasses ready, waiting for you. If you're too good to drink with us, we'll just have to keep standing."

Yang Xiaodong gets to his feet and clinks glasses with each of them. "But you're wrong if you think this is the work of any one man."

"What factory are you from?" Zheng Ziyun asks Wu Bin.

"Morning Light Auto Works."

Interesting. That's Chen Yongming's factory. Zheng decides to keep listening. "Who would put down a progressive unit like yours?"

"We were chosen as a progressive unit by the workers," Lü Zhimin answers him. "As far as the head of the workshop's concerned, we're a bunch of misfits. If it'd been up to him, we'd have been pushed aside instead of being named a progressive unit. He's always waiting for us to slip up."

"Why talk about him?" objects Wu Bin. "We've never done anything to be ashamed of. As workers we've given our all. I'm not working for him, the factory isn't his private concern. We get our wages and bonuses from the state!"

With a note of friendly sarcasm in his voice, the artist says to

Zheng Ziyun, "It doesn't look like officials are very popular, even minor ones. What about you?"

Zheng mulls this over for a moment before answering with a smile, "I'll bet there are people giving me hell behind my back, too." He raises his glass, takes a drink, and continues, "It's unavoidable, even the emperors knew that. What matters is who's the one giving you hell." He leans over and asks Lü Zhimin, whose chair is closest to his, "Why all the complaints about the head of the workshop?"

"No matter how hard we work, he's always saying bad things about the entire team. Take Lao Song, for instance . . ." He points with his chin to a worried-looking young man at the other end of the table and says softly, "He did a pretty terrific thing. He introduced his older brother to a girl, but after they went together for a while, his brother lost interest in her. Her family invited him to lunch on National Day, but he never showed up, even though they waited for him until three in the afternoon. Three times they went looking for him, but he was never at home, and it was clear he was avoiding them. He just let the thing go on without doing anything about it. So Lao Song decided it was up to him. 'If you want to call it off, go tell them; if you don't, then do something. If it's money you're worried about, I can lend you a couple of hundred.'

"But his brother wouldn't say anything one way or the other. Finally, the girl's family had had enough, but Lao Song felt personally responsible and offered to take his brother's place. She was a decent girl and said she wasn't sure it would work, since she was four years older than Lao Song. We didn't think it would work either. But Lao Song had made up his mind, and he eventually won her over. A few days ago he went to see Xiaodong, our team leader, the fellow over there with the crew cut.

"Xiaodong asked him if he wanted his opinion, or if he was notifying him of his decision. 'If you've already made up your mind, then I'm behind you! But if you want my opinion, I'm absolutely against it!'

"Lao Song told him, 'At first I thought I was making a sacrifice, but I knew that wouldn't work in the long run and would make our lives together miserable. But we really like each other now, and my folks are very fond of her. . . . Meanwhile, I've broken with my brother.'

"Xiaodong liked what he heard, so he called us all together and spelled out the situation, telling us that we were going to have to be ready to deal with comments from other units that Lao Song had stolen the girl from his older brother, or that Lao Song was getting a mother, not a wife. Now it's not just us who respect Lao Song, but lots of people in other teams as well. Everyone agrees that he did a pretty terrific and a very moral thing. Don't you agree?"

"Sure, but why does he look so unhappy?"

"No place to live!" Lü Zhimin shouts to Yang Xiaodong, "Xiaodong, we've still got to do something about Lao Song's housing problem."

Yang Xiaodong looks at the men as though he wants to say something, but just then Wu Bin is having some fun with Xiao Xu, one of the other men: "Have you ever seen Shakespeare? Even when a king proposes marriage, he gets down on one knee! So what's holding you back?"

Xiao Xu stammers excitedly: "N . . . Nothing's holding me back, except I don't know what to say."

"How many times have I gone over this with you?" Yang Xiaodong complains. "After you take her home, you get her phone number and address. It's up to you to figure out a reason to see her again, and to set the time and place. The reason's crucial, so you have to come up with a good one."

Xiao Xu's embarrassment is obvious; he is so eager to find a girlfriend that his face is bright red.

"Since you don't have much to do anyway," Yang Xiaodong says to him, "why don't you practice at work by talking with some of the women in the workshop? Pretty soon it'll get so easy you won't be nervous when you talk to your girlfriend."

"Take a look at nature," Wu Bin cuts in. "Flowers have beautiful petals and deer have beautiful antlers. You have to find a way to steal someone's heart."

Zheng Ziyun is moved by their talk, even a little envious; the sort of envy that a doddering, physically spent old man feels when he sees the strong, resilient legs of his grandchildren, who can run around for hours without feeling tired.

These fellows are different, all right. They know about falling in love, and they're not ashamed to talk about it. Naturally, the love in their lives lacks the literary beauty of Shakespeare's plays. And what about himself? Nothing like this ever happened in his life. He thinks back to his proposal of marriage to Xia Zhuyun, which had been about as romantic as a business meeting:

"Would you like to get married?"

"If that's what you need, it's all right with me."

Need? What sort of need? Biological? Spiritual? Looking back on their marriage now, apparently neither.

What could Xia Zhuyun have been thinking? Not once since the day they tied the knot have they talked about it. They belonged, of course, to an extraordinary time, when there was so much excitement all around that they had no opportunity to let things settle and look at them closely. Wait a minute, where's he letting his thoughts take him?

"You see," he says to the artist, "affairs of the heart are still in season."

"So? That's the way we did it when we were young."

Zheng Ziyun says nothing. He's forgotten that artists are different. They live emotional lives. Is that the way society is divided, or is it his own problem? Some people live full spiritual lives while others become officials and are caught up in intrigues. How wonderful it would be if someday relations among officials at all levels could be like a painting or a tender poem! But emotions don't play a role in politics.

While they are talking, Yang Xiaodong proposes a temporary solution to Lao Song's housing problem: first they'll partition a portion of his parents' room, which is big enough, then he and his wife can move into one of the new factory apartments as soon as they're finished. From now on, two men from each shift will carry bricks, while others cover for them at the factory. The plan is approved by acclamation.

A huge burden has been lifted from Lao Song's heart. Yang Xiaodong's proposed solution to his problem isn't the only reason; these fellows understand him and are in his corner, unlike Wu Guodong, who always thinks the worst of him.

Some people have a sort of sickness that forces them to trample, insult, and ridicule everything clean and beautiful they encounter; in their eyes all these things are withered and colorless. Destroying them gives them satisfaction.

Ever since he went to Wu Guodong to request housing after getting married, Lao Song has felt unbelievably demeaned. When Wu Guodong talked to him about his situation, his tone of voice made it sound dirty.

"You in trouble?" He caught Lao Song completely off guard.

Lao Song wondered when the day would come when people would stop playing with others' emotions.

Wu wasn't an evil person deep down; in fact, he wasn't bad at all. Nor was he a real big shot, and he hadn't really intended to hurt anyone. He just represented a certain type of will, one of the crutches of society. Standing before this will, an innocent heart appeared small, impotent, isolated, like a leaf that's fallen into a maelstrom and is about to be swallowed up.

"How does the head of your workshop do in terms of production?" Zheng Ziyun asks.

"Your neck must be sore from having to turn around to talk with us," Lü Zhimin says. "Why don't you join us?"

"What do you say?" Zheng Ziyun asks the artist. He adds under his breath, "They're workers at one of the Ministry's auto works, an interesting bunch. Let's shoot the breeze with them."

"Okay with me," the artist says with a grin. "Whatever the host says."

"What are you smiling about?" Zheng asks quizzically.

"Tell you later. Let's hear what they have to say first."

"Our workshop head does fine with production," Wu Bin says. "No complaints there."

Zheng Ziyun decides to play the devil's advocate: "He should be all right then."

Wu Bin looks him straight in the eye and isn't very impressed with what he sees, taking the fellow to be a typical bookish type who doesn't know the first thing about a factory. "So you think doing a good job with production is all there is to it, do you?" he says patronizingly. "What about the lives of the men? He treats us like workhorses or machines, but even workhorses have to eat and machines need oil!"

"Now you're talking, young fellow!" the artist blurts out emotionally. Already slightly drunk, he moves around in his seat like a fidgety child.

"Of course he is!" Ge Xinfa backs up his friend.

"This is quite a team you've got here!" There is already a soft spot in Zheng's heart for this bunch of young men, especially the crew-cut Yang Xiaodong. He looks like a man who knows what he's doing, and not just in terms of intelligence. He isn't someone to waste his or his men's emotions or energy. The tortuous road he has taken through life has left scars on his generation: he is skeptical, cool headed, bright, practical, and competent.

"We're nothing special," Yang Xiaodong says, "but we hang together."

"Xiaodong knows all about human feelings. He's got feelings for us, and we've got feelings for him," asserts Wu Bin.

"How old is he?" the artist asks.

"Thirty-one!"

"Not bad for someone that age!"

"If you think he's nothing but the leader of a small team, you're mistaken," Wu Bin says. "It takes someone special to do what he's doing in a factory like this, not like your ministers or bureau heads who don't know how to do anything except sign their names on documents. Anyone could do that."

The artist is in seventh heaven. He nudges Zheng Ziyun's leg under the table. "Did you hear that?"

"He's right," Zheng says with a straight face. "That's what my daughter's been saying."

"There's no mystery to it," Yang Xiaodong explains. "It's just a matter of trying to keep people happy. There are enough troubles in daily life as it is, and a bad work environment can only make living impossible. Since people spend a third of their lives at work, it doesn't make sense to deny them happiness and warmth at the workplace, does it?"

They seldom hear this sort of "officialese" from Yang Xiaodong, but for some reason this meal seems to be bringing out all sorts of lofty sentiments. The beer, chicken, and shrimp have something to do with that, but things are different today, as though, having found something they could believe in, these men have become willing to say things they wouldn't normally say, things they might otherwise be too embarrassed to say, things that move them.

Lü Zhimin picks up the thread of conversation: "You can laugh if you want to, gentlemen," he says, turning to Zheng Ziyun and the artist, "but even though we've never met before, I'll be honest and tell you that I'm the dumbest guy on the team, and everyone here has gotten on my case plenty of times. But I've found a home here, and I wouldn't leave it if I could. You get a good feeling here, no matter how bad things are out there—"

"You said it!" Ge Xinfa cuts him off. "Like taking the bus to work in the morning, everyone knows what that's like. This morning the driver slammed on the brakes, and the person behind me bumped me so hard I stepped on the heel of the woman in front of me. 'You're disgusting!' she said as she turned around and cut me in two with a nasty look. But I just ignored her since a man's not supposed to argue with a woman. But I was fuming. She thought she was such a beauty that everyone wanted to step on her heel."

"Right," Lü Zhimin says. "We'd love to have our own cars rather than suffer through those bus rides, or if not a car, at least a motorbike. But who can afford it on our pay? And even if we could, there aren't enough to go around. You have to line up for everything these days, even to buy a head of cabbage. Then there's the housing problem. There are six people in our family from three generations, and we've lived in one ten-square-meter room for twenty years . . ." Lü Zhimin suddenly realizes that his complaining is ruining the mood around the table. Things were so lively when they were talking about good things. He changes the subject: "We could talk about things that make us unhappy till we're blue in the face, but it won't do any good. What I mean to say is that every cloud has its silver lining, and for me, it's the team." A gleam in his eyes. Normally given to underscoring what he says by banging on a table, this time there is something different—real emotion in his voice. "As far as solving everybody's problems, whether it's housing, wages, or transportation, that's something the team can't do. But concern for us comes first in the team, and it's not just a bunch of talk either. That's what people are all about—as long as you're happy you can do anything. So if I haven't got my own place, or I don't get a raise, or you, Ge Xinfa, if you get pushed around on the bus, or if we come to work with a bellyful of anger, as soon as we look into these thirteen faces, all those problems seem to vanish."

The others sit quietly, deep in thought.

Yang Xiaodong wants that to change: "Hey, we're supposed to be having a celebration meal here! If we start singing everyone's praises that'll take all the fun out of it." He lowers his voice and says conspiratorily, "Let's not be like Minister Tian, trying to get everybody to have a revolutionary Spring Festival, a revolutionary National Day, a revolutionary New Year's. Let's be a little more down-to-earth. I'm going to eat, whether you guys want to or not." He turns to Zheng Ziyun. "What would you like?" He reaches over with his chopsticks and picks off a big piece of fish, which he puts on Zheng's plate. "Here, have some, don't let it go to waste!" Then he turns back to his friends. "Anybody who doesn't eat has only himself to blame," he says loudly. "Hurry, it's getting cold."

"Not so fast," Ge Xinfa says. "If we had another revolutionary Spring Festival, we'd get enough overtime to splurge on another meal."

"I don't agree," Wu Bin says. "It's not worth it!" He tips back his head and drains his glass, then slams it back down on the table and says scornfully, "Have you forgotten 1976, when the minister came to the factory to participate in a revolutionary Spring Festival with the working masses, and Wu Guodong begged everybody, pleaded with us, 'Men, I need your help. We've all got to turn out for him. It won't take long, I guarantee it. With the minister doing a little manual labor, it won't take long; it really won't. We can't let one of our leaders lose face.' So everyone got up at the crack of dawn on New Year's Day and showed up at the workshop. *He* finally showed up at ten, bringing a woman with him—ai! What the hell was she doing there?"

"She was the head of one of the Ministry offices," Yang Xiaodong explains.

"Some head!" Wu Bin shoots back. "They put on quite a show, those two, bragging back and forth for over an hour about how they were reinstating all the former Rightists; then they were gone like a puff of smoke. That was all well and good for them, since they had servants waiting at home to start the real celebration, not like us, who'd been looking forward to a couple of days off to get some rest and see some friends, or like the women here, who were looking forward to getting caught up on some of their neglected housework. So when it was over, the whole day was shot, when you throw in the time spent on the road. For him, that hour spent hanging around the factory worked out perfectly, since the papers made a big deal out of a minister spending a revolutionary New Year's at a factory, and he got all the credit. So what happens to a showoff like that? At the Eleventh Party Congress he was elected as an alternate to the Central Committee. It's a goddamn joke, that's what it is! People like that really know how to climb to the top. And where does that leave China? We've gotten rid of the Gang of Four, so how can things like that still happen?"

Ge Xinfa refills his glass for him. "Come on, drink up, why let yourself get down in the dumps! He's an official and you're a worker. As long as your pay envelope keeps coming, what's the difference?"

But Wu Bin isn't about to let it drop. "There's plenty of difference. How are we ever going to achieve the Four Modernizations with people like that in charge? They don't give a damn about us! I still get my pay envelope, but it never gets any fatter! If all officials are like that, what do we have to look forward to?"

The artist nudges Zheng Ziyun under the table again.

The lively expression that had adorned Zheng's face when he

first sat down has disappeared without a trace. He suddenly looks tired, old, indifferent, detached. He pours what remains of the bottle of *maotai* into the men's glasses and stands to leave. "Young comrades, I'd like to drink to all of you, what do you say?"

Lü Zhimin, glass in hand, says, "There should be some sort of toast."

"Such as?" Zheng Ziyun turns to the artist, who looks back at him with his childlike laughing eyes. How he wished he could laugh like a child, too, and never stop. "How's this: It's been a real pleasure sharing a glass or two with you, and I hope we all make a real contribution, no matter what the job. I'm sure we'll meet again. Bottoms up!"

They drain their glasses.

"Good stuff!" Wu Bin says as he smacks his lips.

As he's shaking hands with Zheng, Lü Zhimin says, "We forgot to ask what you two gentlemen do."

Zheng buttons up his olive-drab military overcoat. "He's an artist. Me, I do administrative work."

"Oh, taking care of eating, drinking, shitting, pissing, sleeping, things like that!"

"That's about it," Zheng laughs. "This has been quite a meal for you guys."

"The head of our workshop is probably fit to be tied."

"Give him a little more of the same and he may see the light."

They walk out of the restaurant into a cold wind, which revives their flagging spirits, like taking a dip in the ocean.

"What were you smiling about in there?" Zheng Ziyun asks. "You said you'd tell me later."

"I forget what it was, since I was smiling the whole time."

Zheng Ziyun walks slowly beside the artist toward the streetcar stop. The light reflected in his eyes from the streetlamps shows there are many thoughts running through his mind. He breaks the silence: "I learned a lot from dinner tonight. Thanks to Yang Xiaodong, I've found the answer to a major question—how do you get people excited about what they're doing? It's got nothing to do with studying the industrial example of Daqing, or with a bunch of empty slogans, and it's certainly not a matter of production first, living conditions second. No, it's caring for people. Do you know how I came to join the revolution? Not from reading *The Communist Manifesto* or *Das Kapital,* but from reading *Teaching Love*, written by an Italian, which taught me to believe in truth, goodness, and beauty, and to seek them out. Yang Xiaodong's quite the psychologist, isn't he? But I owe you an apology for inviting you out to dinner and making you spend the whole time listening to a lot of boring talk."

"Who said I was bored? They were saying things that are on everyone's mind, weren't they? I learned a lot myself."

"Oh?" This catches Zheng Ziyun by surprise. He stops and stares at the artist.

"I've been sizing you up, sort of observing you. One day I'd like to paint your portrait. But it won't be easy. Your thoughts and mood change too fast from one minute to the next. Each change captures an aspect of the real you, and it'd be a shame to lose even one of them. But they're too elusive to hold on to."

"I absolutely forbid it," Zheng Ziyun says gravely.

The artist's childlike eyes, always on the move, are clouded by a somber look. "You probably have your reasons," he says with a stubbornness matching Zheng Ziyun's, "but they're narrow-minded. The life and labors of every honest, hard-working laborer do not belong to him alone."

Eight

A t precisely a quarter to eight, like clockwork, Tian Shou-cheng strolls casually and confidently into the office, just as he does every working day, unlike other ministers, whose cars seldom arrive at their compounds before eight o'clock. This laudable practice is something he insists upon, and even if he engages in light banter with one of the office staff in the corridor, he never stops walking as he talks. Not a sign of being tired or rushed, as though he has a built-in buffer against such things.

As he enters his office, he casts a customary glance at the desk, which is big enough to sleep on. A pile of documents and reports awaits his attention. This is always the first activity of the day.

Tian removes his overcoat and hangs it on one of the coatrack pegs. Oops, that one's loose. He hangs it on another. He turns and smooths his neatly combed hair with both hands, as he always does, pours himself a cup of jasmine tea, and sits down at his desk, starting right in on the pile of paperwork: ciphered telexes, Central Committee directives, duty office telephone logs, requests for instructions and reports from various offices and sections, citizens' letters, and so on and so forth, all arranged by source, importance, and urgency.

Tian thought long and hard before taking on Xiao Yi as his secretary, but it has worked out beautifully. Of course he is good at his job, but more important, he had been the leader of a rebel faction during the Cultural Revolution. He'd never done anything to Tian Shoucheng personally; if he had, Tian would certainly have remembered.

Tian Shoucheng was sure that Xiao Yi knew of this ulterior motive behind his decision, but a secretary's personal feelings were not something he concerned himself with. It was trouble enough to gauge the impression this decision would make on the rebels who *had* attacked him during the Cultural Revolution, as well as the conservatives who had protected him. Tian wasn't about to waste time thinking about what was going through the mind of a minor subordinate like this; his hands were full with opponents at his own level. Xiao Yi could believe what he wanted, since he couldn't tell a soul. Besides, Tian always turned the really important matters over to his other secretary, Lin Shaotong.

Tian Shoucheng is happy to sail along with the current, signing, approving, or commenting on the documents that pass across his desk, whichever is appropriate.

His little boat suddenly bumps up against a dam in the river: a request for instructions on whether the service personnel at the Ministry guesthouse should be awarded a bonus.

A bonus? For guesthouse service personnel? Over the past couple of days, the newspapers have been filled with editorials calling for the renewal of ideological education with politics in command and demanding that individual bonuses not exceed an average of two months' wages. All the factories are lowering the number of bonuses given to workers, so what chance do service personnel have? Besides, the Ministry's guesthouse isn't under the jurisdiction of the Administrative Bureau of the State Council, nor of the

Municipal Service Bureau; they probably have regulations to cover situations like this for their own work units, but he'd better not adopt their procedures, since any problems that arise might be tough to handle. Tian Shoucheng isn't about to set any precedents. From what he's read in the papers and heard on radio broadcasts, it seems to him that bonuses might be on their way out. So he writes on the report, "Handle in accordance with higher directives."

That has a nice ring to it. Higher? Exactly where? Let the person responsible figure that one out. That's right, nice and ambiguous. If his memory is correct, there are no higher directives regarding bonuses for guesthouses attached to the various ministries.

The next item, a bulky document, makes him pause. What was the author thinking? Wasn't he aware of the established practice that the higher the level to which you report, the larger the type and the thinner the folder?

Tian frowns as he begins to read. Oh-oh, a citizen's letter passed down to him. What was Xiao Yi thinking when he put this on his desk? Just as he is about to call Xiao Yi into the office, he catches himself. Xiao Yi wouldn't have put this here if it weren't something he had to attend to personally.

So what's the problem? He glances quickly down the page and sees that the author is critical of the Politburo's figures regarding the number of steelworks, coal mines, and Daqing-type oilfields that would be in operation by the year 2000, calling it a Left-opportunist approach to capital construction on the order of the 1958 Great Leap Forward fiasco, which had come about because affairs were not handled strictly in accordance with objective laws. The letter also says that "Study Daqing," which is just another case of "whatever-ism," has become the governing philosophy in capital construction. The author cites the State Planning Commission's 1979 nationwide basic construction plan, criticizing it for including projects that don't qualify as basic construction, which can only delay work on legitimate projects and overextend the limited amount of investment capital. Tian Shoucheng's eyelids twitch slightly. His heart sinks. He takes a sip of tea.

Naturally, since the letter was put on his desk, experience tells him that it has to have been written by someone in the Ministry of Heavy Industry. But who? He flips back to the last page. Oh, *He Jiabin!* The same He Jiabin who was a notorious rebel during the Cultural Revolution, and who was in the thick of things during the Tiananmen Incident in 1976, putting a wreath at the Martyrs' Shrine and writing poems of mourning for Premier Zhou Enlai. Only the intervention of Bureau Director Fang Wenxuan had saved him from being arrested. But that worked out well for Tian also, because if he had been detained, the responsibility for that would have fallen on Tian's shoulders. He smiles. Being an official these days is no picnic.

Should he turn this over to He Jiabin's department? No, not a hot potato like this. Nothing critical of one of the Politburo's resolutions goes unrecorded, and if he simply passes it along without comment, what will he do if one of his superiors asks him about it someday?

Tian examines the routing instructions on the letter to see if there is any indication as to how it has been received by his superiors. No, only the words, "Forwarding a citizen's letter."

How should he handle it? He twirls his pencil absentmindedly, as though it were a magic wand that could turn bad luck into good.

Finally he writes on the letter, "Refer to Vice-Minister Zheng Ziyun." That should do it. Zheng has been all wrapped up these days in system reform, industrial management, and hoisting the banner of making ideological work more scientific; and he's opposed to the "Study Daqing" model. A few days earlier at the Morning Light Auto Works he conducted some sort of public opinion poll, with ridiculous questions like, "What do you like?" What do they like? Anything they can get away with, what else! "What do you care about?" Themselves, that's what they care about! "What do you despise?" Work, of course! "What do you need?" Money, they only know how to vote for their wallets. "What do you do in your spare time?" Eat, drink, and have a good time. Anyone who doesn't believe it can pop into any restaurant and take a look. "Can the Four Modernizations be realized?" You're asking them? "What is the major obstacle to carrying out the Four

Modernizations?" Take your pick. "Are you happy working at this factory?" They'd be happier if they could work in the States. How would you like to escort them?

What's he trying to prove? Does he really think that kind of ideological work is going to do anything but mess things up? Opinion surveys are a capitalist invention! There's only one way to handle things in a proletarian society: all individual interests and needs must be subordinate to those of the Party.

Zheng Ziyun and Tian Shoucheng contrasted: Tian is the goal-keeper, always on the defense and given to soft tactics; Zheng is on the attack, always ready to pounce.

Tian Shoucheng frequently stands off to the side and coolly watches Zheng Ziyun willingly squandering his energies. Tian's goalkeeping can't prevent Zheng from scoring on him every once in a while, but he isn't about to treat Zheng as a true adversary. Why waste the energy? Zheng already has plenty of adversaries anyway—nearly all of society.

The egg and the rock!

To illustrate: Tian spent 200,000 yuan of public funds to build himself a house that far exceeded standards set by the State Council, and Zheng responded by sending an open letter to every member of the Ministry Party Headquarters and a report to the Commission for Inspecting Discipline, requesting that Tian be required to make a public self-criticism in front of all the workers; demanding that Tian vacate the rooms that exceeded his allotment; and recommending punishment for the administrative cadres who are too busy fawning over the minister to worry about the housing problems of the workers. So what came of it? An investigative team was sent down, and even though they submitted a report after several days of digging around, what could anyone do? Tian didn't let it bother him, since it was a matter of principle emanating from a higher level. That's how things are in China.

When Tian was on a fact-finding mission abroad, he sent Zheng as second-in-command to attend a working meeting called by the

Central Committee. At that time, neither the cases of the so-called Sixty-one Traitors nor the issue of the 1959 Lushan Conference, where Mao had been stripped of his power, had been resolved, and the Liu Shaoqi question hadn't yet been put on the agenda. As a replacement, Zheng was expected to be seen and not heard, but no: "What cadre is immune from mistakes? From now on, anyone who makes a mistake should be criticized for that mistake, whatever its nature, but for that mistake alone. We have to make practice the criterion for truth and stop calling people traitors or special agents just because they make mistakes. Take the case of Liu Shaoqi, for example. All that material, and still no one looks at the issues. Instead, he's called a traitor, a turncoat, a renegade. To me those are the tactics of Soviet secret police. And what about comrades Peng Dehuai and Yang Shangkun, who were accused of secret dealings with foreign countries on the basis of a bunch of unfounded, unconvincing accusations. From now on, the principle of making practice the criterion for truth should be used in dealing with cadres."

Who was he gunning for? This was dangerous talk! Of course, now the injustice done to Liu Shaoqi has been righted, but he still took a big chance, and might live to regret it. He was headed for a fall. During the "Criticize Deng Xiaoping" campaign, the ever-cautious Tian Shoucheng had stayed out of the fray for as long as possible, waiting and watching; and still even he had made a careless move. The lesson he learned from that experience would carry him through a lifetime.

At the meeting, Zheng Ziyun criticized other comrades for taking the stance that the question of practice as the sole criterion for gauging objective truth was not a proper issue for this particular meeting since, as a theoretical matter, it should be debated at an unhurried pace elsewhere. "Only by delving into this issue now," he said, "will we be able to debate it with good results at later meetings. From the perspective of society at large, it's all right to have meaningful, planned discussions so the masses can gain a clearer understanding of issues. But comrades from the leading Party organizations must be of one mind. At this meeting we're here to discuss a number of important policy issues. These

129

discussions must be translated into action. Policy issues are intended, first and foremost, to give direction to ideology. Now if disagreement is expressed in some of the theoretical journals, then one of the leaders in the Central Committee voices his disagreement, and if one of the comrades says that at a previous group meeting they were given permission to put a policy into action, does that mean that at some later date they'll turn around and rescind that permission? The hardest-working comrades are afraid to do anything these days. Theorists are free to debate issues at an unhurried pace, but when we leave here and go back to our jobs, we have to put the decisions of this meeting into practice. We can't just sit back and continue the debate."

Sure, Zheng Ziyun, people can say what's on their minds; if you want to enter the fray or not, that's your business. But what good can come of offending those people, particularly with the mass media in attendance? When the winds shift, you can count on being attacked in the press, and once that happens there's nothing you can do about it.

And all that talk about "We must break out of the Gang of Four–imposed prison of taking Mao Zedong Thought as absolute gospel!"

Fortunately, his attitude toward the important question of "whatever-ism" was right on the mark. This was the crucial issue; all else was a bunch of nonsense. What, after all, is politics, if not testing the winds? Timing is everything. The rest is nonsense. Absolute nonsense! But it only happened once. It would be a long time before he'd have an opportunity to attend another meeting like that.

Tian Shoucheng walks into the outer office, where he hands Xiao Yi the draft he prepared a couple of days ago for Tian's upcoming speech to his subordinates. "Comrade Xiao Yi," he says, "I've looked it over, and there's something lacking in it, although I can't put my finger on it. Why don't you go over it again with the comrades in the research office, tighten it up, refine it, fill it out a bit. It shouldn't be too serious, but I don't want it too lively either.

130

I'd like it to sound elevated without making me look like I've got my head in the clouds. I'm afraid you're going to have to burn a little more midnight oil."

That is Tian Shoucheng, never doing things himself, never clearly and unambiguously revealing his true intentions or opinions to his subordinates. During the early days of his stint as Tian's secretary, Xiao Yi was really put through the wringer. Every speech went through one revision after another, which would have been all right if he'd only been told why and how he was to make the revisions. Every time Tian Shoucheng made a report, Xiao Yi lost several pounds. But as time passed, he learned how to deal with the situation, and now he listens attentively to Tian, constantly flipping through the draft in his hands and nodding respectfully to his boss.

As soon as Tian finishes, Xiao Yi says, "Fine, I'll get on it right away and do it the way you want," while, in fact, he is already thinking about where he can cut and paste, which words can be sacrificed and which pages can be moved around. He'll just sit on it for a few days without really changing anything, then at ten o'clock on the night before the speech is to be delivered, he'll deliver it to Tian's home, assuring him, "I've revised it just the way you wanted." It always works. Tian will return from delivering his speech and tell his secretary, "You did a fine job this time, much better than before." Xiao Yi will smile, content with the knowledge that the draft he delivered to Tian may well have been all but identical to the one he'd been told to revise. He has the procedure down pat.

"Oh, and I've looked at these documents, so you can forward them to the appropriate comrades."

Just then Lin Shaotong strolls into the office. He looks at Tian Shoucheng without saying a word. Tian turns and walks into the inner office, followed closely by Lin, who closes the door behind him.

Xiao Yi leaves the office to deliver the documents. Whatever those two have to say is never for his ears. Not that he's interested, for there is something unprincipled and unnatural about their relationship, and he wants nothing to do with it. He's had enough of that sort of thing, more than enough. Back during the Cultural Revolution, in the grip of a hysterical revolutionary craze—a blind faith that afflicted just about everyone at the time—he did lots of things that make him wonder if he was in his right mind. But now he's become so apathetic that hate and anger are totally alien to him.

The hysteria has long faded into the past, but it left its residual poisons in the marrow of the body social.

His position as secretary has afforded him the opportunity to see what goes on in the upper echelons, and it is nothing less than a microcosm of society in general: the latent power of progress sometimes gathers, sometimes disperses. Is society taking one step forward and two steps backward, or vice versa? Hard to say.

Ji Hengquan hands He Jiabin's citizen's letter to Zheng Ziyun. "This was sent over from Minister Tian's office!"

Zheng flips through it quickly before glancing over at Ji, then stuffing it into his desk drawer. "All right, consider it taken care of."

That's how Zheng always signals the end to a conversation about some matter he's working on—"Consider it taken care of." Based upon his experience of drafting speeches and reports for Zheng, Ji Hengquan knows only too well that the opinions expressed in He Jiabin's letter are shared almost to the letter by Zheng himself.

He waits until Ji has left the office before taking He's letter out of the drawer and reading it carefully, nodding in agreement as he reads along. When he finishes, he throws it onto the desk as though it has burned his fingers. A feeling of unhappiness settles over him.

The effects of a filter.

Because of that filter, he knows he could never have written such a straightforward report to his superiors, saying exactly what he felt about things without mincing words.

Of course, there's no need for someone of his rank to handle it that way. But is there more to it than rank alone? Could he, in all good conscience, say that worldly considerations haven't robbed him of the things he really treasures, the qualities that make life worth living and remove death's sting—his faith, his integrity, his humanity?

He hadn't seen He Jiabin for a long time after his return from the cadre school. While being investigated, they had been on the same labor team. With his background as a "rebel," He Jiabin came across as different from the others. He frequently took on jobs that were too much for Zheng and talked about things like Engels' *Dialectics of Nature* and why white cats with blue eyes are deaf (he considered this worthy of research, even though neither he nor the others had ever seen a white cat with blue eyes); he told Zheng that the head of their study group was nicknamed Mad Piano, while their company leader was called The Curve, owing to the way he served food: when he spotted someone in the line he wanted to please, he'd start to gradually increase the amount of food, reaching a peak when it was that person's turn, then slowly decrease it once the person had been served, until each serving was back to half a ladleful. Some people called him Half-Ladle, but to He Jiabin, that didn't seem to capture the man's unique qualities. And so on. Zheng always felt younger when he was around He Jiabin, who had a unique, surefire way to keep his spirits up: he never passed up an opportunity to crack a caustic joke, which helped peel years and many layers of suffering from the others' hearts.

But after he had returned to the Ministry and settled in along with everyone else, that feeling of intimacy vanished. He saw him once on a bus when he was on his way to the Ministry to see a movie. There were barbs in his greeting: "I see you have good taste!" The bus was packed, mostly with workers attached to the Ministry who were looking forward to the movie. Actually, there wasn't anything really offensive in the comment; Zheng's reaction stemmed from his knowledge that even innocent comments take on special meaning when spoken by He Jiabin. Honey drips from the mouths of some when they speak, but there are others, like this fellow, who have opinions on everything and never hesitate to state them.

Work, work, and more work has driven everything else out of

Zheng Ziyun's life. He ought to have a chat with He Jiabin; even if they didn't get around to talking about this citizen's letter, they could talk about The Curve or Mad Piano. Ye Zhiqiu had told him that she and He Jiabin were going to get together to write a report to publicize the courage, insight, and single-minded dedication to the Four Modernizations of factory managers like Chen Yongming. He wonders how the piece is coming along. Ye Zhiqiu impresses him as being slightly neurotic, one minute wanting to do research on economic system reform, the next minute wanting to write some news story. Your typical literary person! Always acting on impulse. But maybe that's what inspiration is all about. Zheng picks up the phone to call He Jiabin and set up a time to have a talk, but he hangs up before dialing the fourth number. Not such a good idea after all. The rules of the cadre school no longer apply. It's not so much the difference in rank that makes him feel that they are no longer on a par, but a fear that getting together like that might have adverse effects on their work. Zheng insists on keeping a proper professional distance in his dealings with everyone in the Ministry. He is afraid that any relationship that's too close might make it difficult to maintain his principles and could lead to misunderstandings.

But what about the letter? Tian Shoucheng is obviously passing the buck on this one. The situation is still very complex, part of a continuing struggle between the reformers and those who want to stick to the old ways. All the big talkers and the political sloganeers have closed ranks, top to bottom. He Jiabin certainly knows what he's talking about!

At the moment, those who oppose reform still haven't learned that practice is the sole criterion for gauging objective truth. But for some people, life and truth aren't always the same thing. No wonder they're so bent on holding on to power. And no wonder reform is so difficult to achieve.

The situation, full of contradictions, is intricate and extremely difficult, since the current struggle isn't against enemies, like a battlefield confrontation, but against comrades, good comrades, who, owing to errors in ideological approach and misguided ideas, have created enormous problems in society. Problems like rampant despair and pessimism, or personal antagonisms resulting from a minuscule raise in pay for one but not the other, and a level of poverty that normally exists only in times of war. No one can say why this poverty, which has already lasted so long and to which there is no end in sight, has settled upon them. There are no more capitalists, no more landlords, so why is everyone so poor? Where are the roots of this poverty? What's the purpose of living? If the situation continues much longer, the soul of the people will be eroded by the daily struggle to put food on the table. Poverty breeds indignation, anxiety, disgrace, humiliation. . .

No, the people must not live like this any longer. This is a socialist nation, and it's imperative that our people live like human beings. Zheng Ziyun bangs the top of his desk. It's 1976 all over again, when documents regarding Fang Wenxuan's opposition to Gang of Four leader Wang Hongwen were brought to light. If someone asks to see something, all you have to do is search for a while and then say, "I can't seem to find it anywhere." He stuffs He Jiabin's letter in the bottom drawer of his desk and locks it. Will we ever come up with a better way of handling citizens' letters? he muses angrily. Ignoring them just shows how little protection the people can count on if they point out problems; it's nothing less than an abrogation of social responsibility by those charged with that responsibility. The letters always wind up back in the sender's own unit. There simply aren't enough comrades like He Jiabin!

"Something on your mind?" Tian Shoucheng asks Lin Shaotong.

Of course there's something on his mind. Lin never talks to him unless there is something on his mind, and something not to be taken lightly. All the other odds and ends wind up on Xiao Yi's desk.

"I ran into Xiao Ji this morning. He said Vice-Minister Zheng and Vice-Minister Wang called on Professor Tai at B—— University yesterday morning."

"Oh?" The news comes as a complete shock to Tian Shoucheng. They're really going off the deep end now. How could two ministers, both of them Communist Party members, go off on a whim like that to call on a bourgeois professor, one of the most notorious Rightists in the country, who had been cleared only a short while ago? "He . . . ," his voice trails off. Wang Fangliang and Zheng Ziyun. No wonder there are rumors floating around that there are two rival camps in the Ministry these days! All that nonsense about a bourgeois camp and a proletarian camp. Nauseating talk like that makes it seem like the Cultural Revolution all over again.

"What did they talk about?"

"I'm not sure. They went alone, without their secretaries. But I wouldn't be surprised if it had something to do with the coming forum on ideological work."

"Didn't I make myself clear at the last Party Headquarters meeting that the forum was to be postponed? We need to wait a while."

Why the delay? Even he doesn't know. Simply his way of dealing with life: if you wait long enough, things have a way of taking care of themselves.

From the look of things, Wang Fangliang and Zheng Ziyun are planning on going ahead.

"According to comrades in the research office who participated in the planning session for the meeting, they're trying to figure out how to utilize some of the research achievements in sociology and psychology to make our ideological work more scientific."

Tian Shoucheng is speechless. Those two are always up to something, spending all their time yakking with professors, writers, or reporters, organizing forums, giving speeches, writing articles, and neglecting their regular duties in favor of things that bring them more visibility and attention. Writers are, to use the terms of Mendeleyev's periodic tables of elements, among the most effective activators, historically the first to stir up trouble. Tian Shoucheng feels threatened by Wang Fangliang and Zheng Ziyun's activities.

"According to them, making ideological work more scientific is an essential part of upgrading industrial management. Their goal is to determine, through the study of sociology and psychology, how to arouse the people's enthusiasm," Lin Shaotong explains.

Psychology? That was written off as a bourgeois pseudoscience long ago. Just because we're trying to raise the intellectual level of cadres doesn't mean we can go off half-cocked and follow any intellectual fad that comes along. Sure, arousing the people's enthusiasm is an important task, but that isn't the way to go about it. All society is concerned about system reform and upgrading industrial management, making it an absolute imperative. Virtually every central department, every province, every city is launching pilot projects and opening up new territory. Public confidence would surely be restored by breakthroughs in this area, and as Minister of Heavy Industry, Tian is responsible for making the strategic decisions that will point the way. But he'll be in trouble if he has a run-in with this clique of hotheads among the economic theorists. Better to take a wait-and-see attitude, get some people to study the issues, and at the very least get a team together to take some sort of posture. That will also serve to restore a measure of control over Zheng Ziyun and Wang Fangliang's activities.

"That's right," he says. "We really should be trying to get a handle on industrial management and look into ways of working toward system reform. I've been thinking of something, and although I haven't gotten everything worked out yet, I'm wondering if it might be a good idea to merge the industrial management office and the research office into an advisory committee with the responsibility of looking into ways of developing our work in this direction."

Although not stated explicitly, Lin Shaotong knows at once that Tian means to remove the research office from Wang Fangliang's control, making it an independent body that he can then turn against Wang. But Wang Fangliang isn't someone whose courage, intelligence, or background are to be taken lightly. It would be foolish to cross swords with him over a minor issue.

"I think that deserves a little more thought."

Tian looks at Lin without betraying any emotion. Lin looks into his boss's eyes with the same absence of expression. They understand each other perfectly.

"Okay, we'll put that on hold for now and see what happens." Tian lowers his eyes.

Tian Shoucheng generally deals with people fairly and gives them room to maneuver, although he did support the decision to kick Wang Fangliang out of the Party. "The decision to cancel your Party membership back then was wrong," he told him when they met recently, "but I was in no position to oppose it, because of our personal relationship." But Wang Fangliang would have none of it. "Bullshit!" he shot back, frowning deeply. "It was a matter of principle. You should have taken a stand instead of worming your way out by means of a nonexistent personal relationship!"

Toward the end of the Cultural Revolution, after both Tian and Zheng Ziyun had been reassigned to their jobs, Tian made a point of calling on Wang Fangliang over New Year's and other holidays. Wang still hadn't gotten his job back because of the "hatchet man" label that had been pinned on him. Naturally, he was still out of the Party as well. These visits were always made in secret, and Tian had impressed upon his secretary, Lin Shaotong, not to breathe a word of it to anyone. But at least it showed that he was a man with a heart. When he thought back to the seriousness of Wang's "crimes" and the atmosphere back then, he congratulated himself on doing even this much. How many other people would have done the same thing under those circumstances? Tian felt confident that Wang would not easily forget it. He'd heard that Zheng Ziyun not only never went to see him during that time, but when Wang went to ask Zheng to intercede on behalf of his wife, who had been told she had breast cancer, in order to keep her from having to undergo labor reform at one of the cadre schools, Zheng just rolled over and went back to sleep, leaving his wife, Xia Zhuyun, to send Wang packing. But every time there was a clash of opinions at one of the Party meetings, Wang Fangliang always seemed to tip the balance by siding with Zheng, though the two of them weren't on particularly close personal terms. Based on years of experience and observation, Tian concluded that Zheng was the type who had few friends. He had all the warmth and charm of a computer, fully programmed. Although he was a living, breathing, feeling human being, it was virtually impossible to guess what was on his mind. Which left but one possibility: he and Wang needed each other, not as friends but as allies. For what?

They weren't necessarily gunning for Tian, he deduced; most likely they were cooking up some novel scheme.

"That reporter, Comrade Ye Zhiqiu, is on the phone," Ji Hengquan announces to Zheng Ziyun.

Zheng frowns. She's going overboard with her constant phone calls and calling him Lao Zheng instead of Comrade Zheng Ziyun. There are probably a dozen people listening in on his calls, not to mention those on her end. Is she trying to show off or what? She doesn't seem the type. As if that weren't enough, she keeps sending him informal notes of one kind or another, nothing significant, just her views on social issues or follow-ups and additions to earlier conversations or debates. She has a light and airy, natural and unrestrained writing style, and reading her letters always brings him pleasure. But doesn't she realize what sort of a society this is? In China, with its long history of feudalism, anything involving women is a sensitive issue that piques everyone's interest. Your reputation can be destroyed if you let down your guard for even a moment. Zheng never forgets this in his dealings with women.

Every piece of mail that Zheng receives goes first to Ji Hengquan, who takes appropriate action before sending it on to him. Envelopes with "Personal" or "Name of sender enclosed" or "For addressee's eyes only" written on them are treated like all the rest. The same holds true for phone calls. They all go through Ji Hengquan, who determines, on the basis of the callers' rank and the nature of the business, whether or not to put them through to Zheng himself. All these casual, unnecessary phone calls and letters from Ye Zhiqiu are bound to lead to misunderstandings and could cause problems. Was there anything special in Ji's voice when he announced that she was on the phone? He seemed to be giving him a signal that even though he knows exactly what is going on between Zheng and Ye Zhiqiu, he can be trusted to keep the information to himself. Zheng can rest easy on that score. It was all more than Zheng could take!

There was that so-called postage-stamp incident. Ji Hengquan had received a letter from Ye Zhiqiu with the canceled stamp torn off. Without opening the envelope, he took it around complaining, "Okay, who took the stamp off this envelope? What am I supposed to say to the vice-minister?" As a result, everyone knew that Ye had written to Zheng, and they got the impression that there was something fishy about the relationship. Otherwise, why was even Zheng's secretary afraid to open the envelope?

Who knows, maybe Ji himself removed the stamp and had turned it into a publicity stunt.

When, Zheng wondered, would people finally be able to live without these constant masquerades? Certainly not in his lifetime. He had long since gotten used to how things were.

Should he tell Ye Zhiqiu to write him at home from now on? No! That would surely remove any doubt that there was something going on between them. Besides, he could see that Ye Zhiqiu was not favorably impressed by Xia Zhuyun, and he didn't want to make it any worse. Xia Zhuyun was, after all, his wife, and everything concerning her reflected in some way or another on him. They were considered a "model couple," and it was imperative that Zheng always be above suspicion.

He picks up the phone. "Hello!" he says with strained politeness. "This is Zheng Ziyun."

His tone of voice is wasted on Ye Zhiqiu, who blurts out, "I have some bad news. That piece you wrote on making ideological work more scientific won't be published the day after tomorrow as planned!"

"Why not? Your editor promised it would." Zheng is understandably upset. He's not just another person out there who makes his living writing manuscripts. In fact, they sent someone over expressly to ask him to write the piece.

"Orders from above, I'm told. They want you to consider making a few revisions."

"Along what lines? Be specific."

"Well, the part about 'group consciousness,' for example. We normally use the term 'collectivism.' But if you ask me," she says with a laugh, "I think 'group consciousness' might be better received than 'collectivism,' since it has more of a united front feel to it. It's the same as using 'human nature' instead of 'proletarian feelings' to get broader acceptance, since arousing enthusiasm includes all the people, not just so-called progressives like the martyr Lei Feng. I think you ought to stick with your term and not give in. Our political work department doesn't have a clear enough picture of the significance of making our ideological work more scientific. They can't break free of the old ideas. They still oppose theories of psychology, sociology, social psychology, and anthropology, and they feel that placing patterns of human behavior determined by behavioral sciences in the service of industrial management reforms is just another example of promoting the study of bourgeois pseudosciences. As far as I'm concerned, it's only a difference in methodology, but one plus one equals two for capitalists and the proletariat alike. Did you see the piece on the Toyota Auto Works in *Information News* the other day? I think they do a better job with their employees than we do. If one dies, the family is given funeral expenses. Their birthdays are acknowledged with a gift . . . that's what psychology is all about. Sure, they do it to increase profits for their capitalist bosses, but why can't we use the same methods to benefit socialism?"

She was talking as though the article were hers and she was trying to bring people around to her way of thinking. Or maybe she sensed a lack of conviction on his part.

Pursuit, there's always a cost. Zheng Ziyun was not an ambitious man—if the word "ambitious" can even be used. Having reached the age of sixty-five, he finds the many aspirations of his youth have been telescoped into a single hope: he'd be satisfied if, on the strength of his own successes and failures in the economic realm over all these years, he could introduce some industrial management techniques that would work in this new historical age of socialism. He chose this time to begin setting some of his thoughts down on paper. He knew there might be inaccuracies in his ideas, but as long as people were willing to debate them over the next twenty years or so, eventually adopting even a portion of them, he would feel vindicated. Making ideological work more scientific was the first of many, and it had already run into trouble. Should he consider their recommendations? Could he possibly be jumping the gun? Twenty years of debate was all well and good, but was it suitable for someone in his position? And just what was his position? A vice-minister . . . but if he didn't make any revisions, the piece might not get into print at all. Everyone has to compromise once in a while to get his way and make the bulk of his ideas available to others.

Zheng Ziyun doesn't want to answer until he's thought things over carefully. And he knows he shouldn't be saying too much to Ye Zhiqiu.

Ye Zhiqiu lowers her voice, as though disappointed in Zheng's reaction. "There is one thing you ought to know. There are times when both sides refuse to budge, so the paper agrees to publish a piece as it is, but when it actually appears you wouldn't recognize it. They'll say that the editor on duty made changes as the article was going to print, without being properly informed. Be sure to get their assurance in this regard. And if they won't publish it, why not send a copy directly to the Central Committee? You have important things to say in this article."

"Thank you. We'll talk about it later." He hangs up quickly, as though the telephone were suddenly too hot to handle. No one in the Ministry dared to talk to him like that, unconcerned about overstepping bounds.

These bounds, in one form or another, permeate every layer of society; we seek their protection, since they help us avoid confronting things we haven't the courage to face squarely, and they give us an excuse to put our intuitive knowledge in deep freeze.

The bright sunlight outside nearly blinds Zheng. He leans back in his chair, but even when he closes his eyes, that blazing fireball remains beneath his lids, that and the image of the windowpanes.

It has been a relatively easy day, with none of those marathon meetings filled with confrontations and little substance. But Zheng is weary, not from work but from a troubled heart.

This sort of dejection comes upon him every time he stands back and looks at his own wavering or when he struggles over the pros and cons of some worldly concept. Lacking the courage to be self-sacrificing, he is like someone struck by his own ugly image in a mirror. He has never told anyone about these feelings, nor has anyone sensed them, not even his wife. Maybe this is the source of his misanthropy.

All right, maybe compromise is the answer—give in a bit! Faced with a reality he is powerless to change, he realizes how infinitesimal he is in relation to the enormous social machinery.

He may also have hung up so abruptly to avoid Ye Zhiqiu's reproach for not sticking to his principles. She'd never actually say anything like that, but what about deep down in her heart?

A man's sentiments and character don't always correspond to his position. Zheng Ziyun always feels vaguely inadequate when he is with Ye Zhiqiu, for she has a strange power that makes people want to show their best side whenever she's around.

Nine

Total exhaustion. Chen Yongming's ears feel like they're stuffed with cotton; the sounds of gongs and cymbals, the shouts of people, the popping of firecrackers seem so far away.

The families that had been allocated new apartments all wanted to treat Chen to some pot stickers. But that seemed excessive, so someone recommended that each family contribute some pot stickers and send someone over to the Capital Construction Team to cook them in the communal pot. When Chen Yongming showed up, everyone would eat together.

Everyone crowds around the steaming pot, pushing and shoving and making Chen Yongming very uneasy. He knows he can't interfere with their enjoyment just because he doesn't appreciate that type of "fun," so he's forced to stand there a bit longer. He has a responsibility toward the general happiness, even if that enjoyment generates no more warmth than the flickering end of a lit cigarette. What can he do?

For several days now he has had almost no sleep. If only he could pass on some strength to Lü Zhimin as he fights for his life!

Xiao Lü had fallen from a scaffold while painting a drainpipe: an accident that could have been avoided, a careless loss of concentration when the work was nearly finished.

"He should have been more careful!" someone said.

No, Chen Yongming was responsible since he was in charge. He should have realized that the men would get careless as the work neared completion. He isn't just another impetuous youngster like Lü Zhimin, so why didn't he warn them to be on their guard against just this sort of possibility?

He sat on the bench outside the operating room for what seemed like years, but couldn't have been more than a few hours. His heart skipped a beat every time someone in a white surgical gown came out. His nerves were so frayed that even when Yu Liwen walked up and sat beside him on the bench, he wouldn't look at her. No one was going to lessen his preoccupying sense of remorse over Lü Zhimin's accident. "How's he doing?" he asked, avoiding her eyes. "I have to know."

"He's in critical condition, a ruptured liver . . ."

"Will he make it?"

"We're doing our best . . ."

"Okay. Keep at it."

Not until he'd been assured that Lü Zhimin was out of danger did he finally lay his head on Yu Liwen's soft shoulder without a word.

The red silk banner flaps noisily in the wind. There are tears in Chen Yongming's eyes. That shouldn't be. Why tears? Maybe they're for Lü Zhimin, who is lying in a hospital bed after just coming off the critical list; or maybe they're for all these people, so happy, so grateful even for the little they've been given.

Who should be grateful to whom? These decent people are being forced to live in a topsy-turvy world.

These rows of simple, crude flats, embarrassingly shabby, are the nests for which they've waited so patiently, so longingly for years.

Chen Yongming recalls what Lü Zhimin said from his hospital bed to his friend: "Xiao Song, since we're good friends, I want you to move in first. So what if the room is earmarked for me; I'm telling you I want you to have it . . . no, don't argue with me. The factory manager said he's going to keep building, so sooner or later I'll get my place; it's just a matter of time!"

What would all those people sitting in their high-rises paying lip service to camaraderie think if they could hear one of their workers express true camaraderie even at the brink of death, or if they could see the workers' expressions of gratitude for being assigned a shabby room? Probably nothing.

The differences in people's expectations and desires are determined by material possessions.

When the first batch of pot stickers is ready, Li Ruilin elbows his way through the crowd and reaches out to take them. "This bowl's for Lao Chen, and I'm going to give it to him." The uncompromising look in his eyes precludes any arguments.

Li Ruilin feels it's his right.

Some time ago, Chen had given Li the responsibility for constructing a fish-breeding pond. A long-term project for the benefit of the workers and their families, it would materially improve the quality of all their lives. Before beginning the work, Chen told him to flatten the earth around the pond site with a steamroller and make the cofferdam with stones under a layer of sand. At the time, Li Ruilin still hadn't forgiven Chen for what he'd done to him, and didn't take well to Chen's advice. So he built the first section of the cofferdam without following Chen's instructions, filling it with water and putting in the hatchlings. When the first freeze came, the wall cracked, and both hatchlings and water were lost. It didn't take Li long to realize the seriousness of what he had done. How was he going to face the workers? Chen Yongming wouldn't be much of a problem, he'd just chew him out. But the workers

Feng Xiaoxian has always struck Zheng Ziyun as a plodder, someone who will never achieve much, but will never really slip up either. There are plenty of cadres like him, people who get by on their wits alone. Political departments, operating under the mistaken belief that since they lack technological skills they won't get taken in the way of the real work, are packed with them. But what sort of "political" work can be expected from someone who has a "get-by" attitude toward his social responsibilities and obligations, or who only quotes Party dogma when making a report or giving a speech? Most of them have probably forgotten what political work is all about.

After reading the letter, Zheng realized that he had underestimated Feng Xiaoxian. There was more to the fellow than he had imagined, including some facets apparent only under special circumstances.

On the basis of this letter, the Bureau Party Headquarters had decided against commending Chen Yongming. Nonsense! Why get involved at all? If someone wants to write a piece about Chen, and they've found someone to publish it, what business is it of the Ministry? The issue isn't whether or not a certain person can be written about, but whether or not the circumstances referred to in the letter should be investigated to see if the accusations are fair. If that's how they're going to do things, anyone could write an accusing letter, and instead of an investigation or any sort of follow-up, the accused would stand guilty as charged. That's no way to treat comrades, who are, after all, human beings, not dumb animals.

So hard to get anything done these days—you can't criticize and you can't commend. If there was only a way to harness all that wasted effort, just think how much work could be done!

Zheng Ziyun goes first to the dining hall, where he knows he'll find things he can't find in the imposing buildings at the front of the compound. He sees that the cooks put a good deal of care into their work; even the cabbage is salted and pickled to give it a special taste. They clearly take pride in their work and are happy,

had such high hopes for the poultry farm and the fishpond. Food prices were rising so fast that the workers were looking forward to the relief these projects would bring them. Li Ruilin was so distraught he broke down and cried in the manager's office. Chen Yongming kept his anger in check. "Don't let it get you down, Lao Li. I'll help you rebuild it."

"It's my fault, so give me what I deserve."

"There's nothing to be gained by chewing you out, Lao Li! Your tears show how bad you feel about what happened, and I can see that you still have a strong sense of responsibility. That's worth treasuring."

Having someone see into your heart makes life worth living. In that instant, all the resentment Li had harbored toward Chen Yongming for having demoted him to gatekeeper disappeared as surely and completely as had the water through the breached wall. He began to view Chen Yongming's activities in a new light.

As Li walks up with the bowl in his hands, the smell of the pot stickers nauseates Chen. He has a bad taste in his mouth, no appetite at all, and he doesn't think he can force a bite of food down. What he needs is rest, a good, long sleep. But that's out of the question. He has heard that a forum on ideological work has been called, for which all participants are to prepare reports. Depression has settled upon him; always tired and grumpy these days, he can't help but look at the dark side of things.

What's more, Vice-Minister Zheng called to say he'll be visiting the factory the next day, Sunday, when the Ministry is closed. He wants Chen to pick him up so he can give his driver the day off. Did he deliberately choose the one day when he would have to make the visit alone? If it were any day but Sunday, his secretary would be making all the arrangements, and he'd be accompanied by bureau directors, department heads, engineers, technicians, secretaries, a whole gang of people. What's he coming for?

Chen frequently feels that he is more than just one person. As he accepts the bowl of pot stickers from the somber Li Ruilin, an exuberant, fresh Chen Yongming is born in a moment of intense emotion. For someone who has lived a lifetime of misery, this sort of excitement comes all too seldom. That's what makes this tender moment so special. He finds himself wishing that someone would complain to him about something or be critical of him. Lü Zhimin is lying in the hospital at that very minute, and all these fervent eyes seem to be avoiding him somehow, like people of breeding who cannot bring themselves to look at a beggar. "Thank you," Chen mumbles, picking up his chopsticks to eat. "Thank you all." But his hand is shaking so much he can barely pick up the food. He raises his head to look at the people standing around him. The firecrackers, the cymbals and drums, the shouting—all are stilled as the people watch him in silence. Chen feels as though something solid were closing around him. He has turned into an enclosed embryo that is gaining strength. He spots the rheumy eyes of Lao Lü Tou. His unshaven chin is quivering. Chen spears a pot sticker and holds it up to Lao Lü's mouth. "I let you down," he says to the old man.

Tears stream down Lao Lü Tou's face as he chews the pot sticker Chen has given him. "Lao Chen, please don't talk like that!"

The silence is broken only by the sound of his sobs.

"Beat the drums!" Chen shouts. "Come on, beat them!"

An unnerving tattoo of drumbeats shatters the stillness.

Word leaked out that it was Zheng Ziyun who recommended Chen Yongming for the directorship of Morning Light Auto Works. That was why Feng Xiaoxian wrote Zheng a letter. Naturally, there was another, far less obvious, reason as well—envy, and a smug pleasure in seeing him sweat. Feng had once been the manager of Morning Light Auto Works himself. Of course that was when the Gang of Four was in power, and he wasn't entirely to blame for the poor work record. There was no excuse for Zheng's bad-mouthing him and making things difficult, whether he meant to or not. Viewed in retrospect, the letter was a bad idea from the very beginning—why was he getting involved? Anyone in the factory who had a complaint could communicate it directly to the Ministry. In order to respond to the letter, Zheng would have to visit the factory and see for himself. How much of the information in Feng's letter corresponded with fact? It certainly had the tone of authority.

148

Dear Comrade Ziyun:

Greetings! Yesterday I received a letter from two mid-level cadres from the Morning Light Auto Works with a complaint th[ey] want me to take to Minister Tian the next time I see him. They'r[e] disturbed by news that the Ministry and a certain newspaper are going to publish reports that commend the factory leadership. They're dead-set against this. According to them, even though there's been some progress at the auto works, there are still plenty of problems. They say that mid-level cadres and the workers are disgruntled, that production has remained static, and that the factory is heavily in debt and terribly overstaffed. They report that the leaders are using welfare benefits to win the hearts of the workers, are paying more attention to living conditions than to production, and are using illicit means to get building materials to construct living quarters. According to them, a serious accident occurred as a result of using the factory workers as a labor force. They say that shady accounting practices have been used to charge these costs to a capital account. There are also quality control problems in production, as well as managerial problems, some in the realm of fundamental direction and basic line; this includes the abolition of the Political Department and the Daqing Office. They say that mid-level cadres aren't happy working there. With dissatisfied cadres and disgruntled workers, singing the praises of the factory leadership now would be counterproductive and add to the workers' discontent. The letter also refers to a newspaper article praising a certain comrade, which has sparked some rumors. If these matters aren't dealt with carefully, the writers feel, even greater discontent among the workers can be expected.

I don't know the actual situation, so I can't make any specific recommendations, but since they asked me to forward their report to Minister Tian, that's what I'll have to do. We'll see what he says. Please report to Minister Tian on the situation when you have a chance.

Respectfully,

Feng Xiaoxian

149

unlike so many dining-hall workers who boil the cabbage as though they were preparing pig swill.

The factory day-care center is completely up to standards. Zheng notices that there are animal figures above each bed: Mama Panda cooking over a stove in a pink apron, a little white rabbit holding a big carrot in a light blue vest, a red fox stealing grapes. Each drawing reminds him of a fairy tale he read as a child. Any child sleeping in one of those beds is sure to have sweet dreams. What wonderful little beds and chairs. He's too tall for the beds, but how about one of the chairs? Why not! He smiles and sits down, his knees sticking straight up. Very uncomfortable. Not such a good idea, after all. Unlike water, which can be reduced to its original state—hydrogen and oxygen—people can't get smaller and they can't go back in time, either in body or in spirit. Zheng shakes his head.

Chen Yongming stares at Zheng Ziyun with bloodshot eyes, as though he's seeing something he doesn't like. Zheng pats him on the shoulder. "It's nothing, you're tired. If you got more sleep, you wouldn't be so edgy."

Chen grits his teeth; his cheeks grow taut.

From the dining hall they go to the newly built dormitories. Time has really flown. The place looks as though the inhabitants have been living there a hundred years. The tiny balconies are covered with tattered but still colorful bedding and clothes, and are piled high with cast-off stovepipes and junk left over from the earthquake: broken bamboo poles, pieces of wood, planks, bricks. All this is a footnote to the attempt by China's fatalistic masses to gloss over their poverty.

Zheng turns and looks at Chen Yongming, then quickly looks away, feeling uneasy, as though this ramshackle appearance somehow has something to do with him.

Zheng Ziyun, who has visited a great many factories, frequently has the feeling that getting to know a factory is very much the same as getting to know a person: hearsay is never enough. He can feel the pulse of the factory as he walks through the workshops. He is impressed by the way Chen reels off the constantly changing figures on things like output, profits, and realized quotas without

151

a notebook, relying solely on his memory. A rare breed among factory managers.

There is a palpable, stimulating rhythm in the workshop activity. No one is goldbricking, or reading the newspaper, or walking around, or dozing off behind the tool boxes. Zheng's attention is caught by a lathe worker and a millworker carefully checking a part against some sort of form. He walks over. It is a mimeographed check list. "Do they use these all the time?" he asks Chen.

"It's all part of balanced and planned production. It's not just at the factory level that we have production quotas; each workshop, each team, even each individual has them. These include monthly, weekly, and daily quotas, and we keep meticulous records. These quotas carry the force of orders, which must be followed. If one level sends down a hundred parts they must be accounted and signed for by the next level; if only ninety-nine are received at, say, the third level, we check to see what happened to the missing part. That way we maintain strict accounting from the time the raw materials enter the factory all the way through to the finished product, and there's no room for any funny business. We have accurate figures on the number of finished products, rejects, and ratios. This procedure not only increases the individual's sense of responsibility, but also gives him a way of determining whether or not he's done his job that day."

Zheng Ziyun nods. "How do you handle bonuses here?" he asks.

"The way we see it, the fair distribution of bonuses is basically a management problem. The initial reaction to the July 1978 announcement that bonuses could be distributed was very positive. But problems cropped up soon after that. Bonuses have to be approved, which introduces the issue of fairness. But since management was in such a shambles back then, and there were no standards of production—quantity or quality—and no figures, everything was done by subjective impressions. That led to disputes, breakdowns in unity, and resentment. 'If you get a first-class bonus but I only get a second-class one, show me why you deserve it. I want to know the reasons!' The team heads were really put through the mill over those monthly bonuses. This forced us to implement management changes: the team heads had to have a

152

way to decide who were the better workers and why. After coming up with a set of standards, we posted the figures at the end of each month. Everyone could see whether or not they deserved a bonus that month. The figures spoke for themselves. That eliminated the approval procedure, the need for meetings, and the possibility of disputes."

"What about the workers who didn't care about earning bonuses?"

"At first there were some whose financial situations were good enough that they didn't need bonuses and didn't see any reason for busting a gut just for an extra five yuan. We made some changes in the bonus system to deal with this. If someone didn't meet his quota, he not only missed out on a bonus but even took a cut in pay. It was decided that anyone who fell short of his quota without good reason, such as inadequate tools, problems with materials, or ill health, would take a pay cut of five percent, ten if the shortage affected the rest of the team and fifteen if it affected the whole workshop."

"And no one griped?"

"Oh, sure. 'You can't punish me,' some of them complained. 'Where does it say you can do that?' My answer was, 'Where does it say you can fail to meet your quota?' "

"And the factory approved?" Zheng Ziyun is amazed by the boldness of Chen's approach.

There is so much more that Zheng wants to ask, but he can see from Chen's chapped lips that the man is completely worn out.

A ball comes sailing over from the basketball court and hits Zheng Ziyun in the heel, nearly tripping him. Several apologetic shouts of "Uh-oh!" Over the past few years, words like "excuse me" have disappeared from these men's vocabulary. There are also some snickers, probably over Zheng's inability to get out of the way. He turns around just in time to meet the gaze of Wu Bin, who is running over to retrieve the ball. Wu freezes in his tracks, his mouth open. A quick glance at Chen's demeanor tells him that the man is no common visitor.

Zheng smiles and reaches out his hand. "Hi, remember me?"

Wu Bin shakes his hand with his own greasy, sweaty hand. "I sure do." He turns and whistles to his friends on the court, who come running over. They are the young men he met at the New Wind restaurant.

"You know each other?" Chen is surprised.

After briefly explaining how they met, Zheng turns to Yang Xiaodong. "What a coincidence, you're just the man I was looking for."

"Me?" What could this man possibly want with me? he thinks.

"That's right. There's going to be a forum on ideological work at the Ministry in a few days, and I'd like you to be there to talk about some of your experiences."

Chen Yongming laughs. "You've sure got the right man!"

"You must be joking," Yang says anxiously. "I'm not even a Party member, so how am I supposed to talk about ideological work? Why don't you invite our workshop head, Wu Guodong?"

"You mean the workshop head you were bad-mouthing the other day?"

"That's right," Wu Bin answers him. "That's the type you want at a meeting. He attended the first meeting held by the Ministry to study the industrial example of the progressive Daqing model and even gave a report at the Capital Gymnasium on what he learned from that meeting. He was treated to a big meal, stayed in a first-class guesthouse, met members of the Central Committee, and did a lot of bragging about our factory. He always knows just what to say, so you won't have to worry about him slipping up at your meeting."

Zheng Ziyun turns to Chen Yongming. "Hear that? They're criticizing you."

"They're also criticizing the Ministry, aren't they?" Chen replies, not to be outdone.

"I wouldn't know what to say," Yang Xiaodong complains.

"Just repeat what you said the other day in the restaurant. You can have Wu Guodong come along, too." He looks back at Chen Yongming. "The head of each household!"

Zheng turns and walks toward a row of new trucks in the

parking lot, with Yang Xiaodong and his men following on his heels. Since they've already met, they don't feel like strangers. Their impressions of each other are already good, so the young men aren't particularly awed by his rank and position.

Zheng opens the door of the first truck in line and rubs his finger across the driver's seat, leaving a streak through a fine layer of dust. "It's not airtight. How about fuel consumption?" he asks Chen Yongming.

"Fifteen to sixteen liters per hundred kilometers."

"It's only twelve or thirteen for similar Japanese trucks." Not so much a criticism as a lament. No one needs to tell him that the source of this problem isn't Chen Yongming's auto works. Not all the parts used in the trucks are made here; many come from a host of subcontractors.

But for Chen the comment once again evokes his dream of a unified auto works that includes all the feeder factories under one roof. A unified system of management would iron out the wrinkles and inject new life and healthy competition into their operations, which are currently hit-or-miss at best. With a system like that, nothing could hold them back. They might even be able to outdo Japan! So why isn't it being done?

Zheng Ziyun climbs into the driver's seat. "Climb in if you don't fear for your lives," he announces.

Having heard that Zheng knows how to drive, Chen doesn't try to stop him. He knows that in some of the outlying areas where traffic control is more lax, Zheng is in the habit of sometimes taking over for the drivers.

Wu Bin jumps in. He likes this man, Zheng Ziyun. He has good sense, is down to earth, and doesn't spend all his time sitting at his desk signing papers. Wu Bin feels a slight self-reproach in his heart. Maybe I've been too arbitrary in condemning people at Zheng's level! He also wants to be on the scene just in case the old guy runs into something he can't handle.

Wu Bin glances over as Zheng steps on the accelerator. The engine turns over. "Okay, he knows what he's doing." Wu Bin looks out as Zheng backs the truck out, turns the wheel, drives out of the parking lot, and heads down the asphalt drive.

"I didn't see that young fellow Lü," Zheng says to Wu Bin.

"He had an accident while we were putting up the housing. He's still in the hospital!"

"Oh! How did people feel about that?"

Wu Bin steals a glance at Zheng Ziyun without answering him right away. Zheng senses that his comment has put Wu Bin on guard. He smiles at the man's loyalty to the factory manager. Zheng knows how the people feel about the incident without Wu Bin having to tell him.

"Different ways," Wu Bin finally says. "Some gloated, mainly the bureaucrats. Most people understood perfectly."

"This truck doesn't accelerate fast enough," Zheng says to change the subject.

Night has fallen by the time Chen drives Zheng back into town. They're too tired to talk, and the mood inside the car is heavy. Chen puts a cassette into the tape deck on the dashboard.

Zheng recognizes the music. "Chopin's Second Piano Concerto in F Minor," he comments.

"When I was in middle school," Chen says dreamily without taking his eyes off the darkness ahead, "I was all caught up in playing the violin. I love music. It's the jewel in the crown of art. I also wanted to get a Ph.D. in physics . . . but I wound up as a factory manager!" There is a certain bitterness in his soft laugh.

Zheng Ziyun doesn't make a sound.

A picture of their lives flashes through his mind. An unending procession of failures . . . like Sisyphus.

Chen abruptly pulls over to the side of the road and stops. He opens the door, letting in the unmistakable scent of spring, of trees beginning to bud and grass sprouting from the earth; insects are awakening from their winter sleep. It won't be long before thunder and rain come.

Chen and Zheng climb out of the car and look wordlessly up at the sky. A moonless night, pitch black.

"The stars always seem farther away in the winter," Chen says. "They're closer in the summer, and much brighter. You can't see the stars when the moon's out, and you can't see the moon when the stars are out."

"Which do you like better, the moon or the stars?"

"Even the most evil things look gentle and soft in the moon-light, and that gives me a vaguely mysterious feeling. But the stars make me feel lonely. I can't help but feel that I'm part of that vast canopy of sky."

Zheng realizes that people aren't afraid of getting hurt as much as they're afraid of the dreary loneliness that follows. And what about himself: how many times has he looked up at the cold, lonely, star-filled sky and shared that feeling? . . .

"There are some people gunning for me," Chen says with a frosty, stubborn tone of voice. "They say I went too far by using some of the profits earmarked for the state to build housing for the workers, a chicken farm, and a fishpond instead. Would I have done that if I didn't know what was going on? The factory books were a mess before I came. Not one of my predecessors had ever audited them. Well, I did, and I found that there were three funds that had never been drawn on. No one in the Ministry knows this, not even the Finance Department. The new state policy allows for consolidating these funds for use by the factory, doesn't it? But let's back up a bit. So what if I built housing for the workers? While the others threw hundreds of millions down the drain, I used two million yuan to put up housing for the workers. No one claimed financial responsibility for wasting hundreds of millions over those Model 1700 rolling mills. If they want to take me to court, they can. I don't think they have a case."

Zheng Ziyun doesn't say a word. He knows that people like Chen need understanding and support, not sympathy or pity. There is no need to be too concerned about people like him, because they can be counted on to stick to their principles.

Chen continues pleading his own case. "They've accused me of trying to win over the workers. They call me the social benefits manager. That makes me proud. The people who say those things are indescribably stupid. Anyone in this country who thinks he can increase production without attending to the workers' living conditions is dreaming! Everything I've done so far has been to

157

increase production!" He flings his lit cigarette to the ground. Tiny sparks fly from it into the dark. When the anger has passed, he says to Zheng, "You've been standing here just listening to me gripe. You must be famished. Come to my place and have something to eat. We can top it off with some good *Daqu* liquor from Luzhou."

"Go ahead and gripe. We all have to do it sometimes. Otherwise we make things too hard on ourselves. But I want you to know, Lao Chen, that I'll back you up all the way, even though I don't have much clout and spend a lot of time banging my head against a wall. I've got plenty of things to get off my chest, too. As long as you're aware of that, everything's okay."

As Chen opens the door to his flat, they can hear the sounds of frying—either flat cakes or pot stickers.

Zheng follows the factory manager into the room. He hears a woman's voice gently reproach Chen: "Late again!" Then he sees an arm in a green sweater reach out and pull Chen's face down. He stops in the entryway. He can hear the sound of a kiss being planted on someone's cheek. He smiles inwardly. A factory manager here in China with Western habits like that! But is there really any difference between Chinese and Westerners behind closed doors? These two must have a good marriage, and Chen doesn't seem to try to disguise it. These days so many people feel constrained, having grown used to the idea that expressing natural human feelings is somehow crude. Particularly at this social level. Even when men talk about their own wives they assume a puritanical attitude, as though all those kids somehow just appeared. Naturally, there's not a hint about the happiness of their home life.

As Chen Yongming steps aside, the light falls on Zheng Ziyun. Yu Liwen quickly covers her face with her flour-covered hands. "Oh, no," she blurts out in embarrassment, throwing a reproachful look at her husband for not warning her that he's brought someone home with him.

To save her further embarrassment, Zheng Ziyun pats Chen lightly on the back as a sign not to let on who he is. "Call me Lao Zheng," he introduces himself.

Along with the liquor that night, they snack on some deep-fried peanuts and pine nuts until the flat cakes are ready. The flat cakes are wonderfully fragrant, all crisp and yellow around the edges and piping hot inside, too hot to eat for a moment. Afterward they have bowls of millet porridge. It's been a long time since Zheng last tasted millet porridge. The meal warms him up. Every inch of the tiny, two-room flat is put to use, and it has a cozy, lived-in look unlike the cold, empty flat he lives in. Just looking at Yu Liwen's smooth brow and watching her delicate movements takes the edge off the most complex, disturbing problems and makes everything seem so simple.

It's after eight o'clock by the time Zheng gets home. There is a dull pain in his chest, and he's so exhausted he's ready to fall. But he takes out a sheet of stationery and writes his response to Feng Xiaoxian:

Dear Comrade Feng Xiaoxian:

I was pleased to receive your letter and to read the opinions expressed by the two comrades from the Morning Light Auto Works.

In all the years Comrade Chen Yongming has worked in the Ministry of Heavy Industry, particularly during the savage reign of the Gang of Four, he has had the courage to stress the importance of management and reform, a stance that made him a bitter enemy of the Gang of Four. He has set the standard for industrial reform in the Ministry. Since being assigned to the Morning Light Auto Works, he has boldly taken on the toughest jobs and seen them through without worrying about the difficulties.

The problems of indebtedness, overstaffing, and quality control at the Morning Light Auto Works are a legacy of the Gang of Four era, not something caused by Comrade Chen Yongming.

Solving these problems to everyone's satisfaction is going to take time, and patience is called for.

I hope you will correct any errors in this report and will share

159

this letter with the two comrades at Morning Light Auto Works. If they disagree with my findings, please have them write to me directly, and we can try to work out our differences.

Respectfully yours,

Zheng Ziyun

A sharp pain in his back. His heart is acting up again. He needs to be strong and healthy. There are still battles to be fought, and it's up to him to give the younger generation more time to prepare themselves for what's coming.

But if his heart keeps acting up . . . there's still so much to do . . .

The watch beneath his pillow ticks so loudly it reminds him of the rhythmic chugging of a passing train. He pulls it out and tosses it under the bed.

Ten

Early summer—the weather is warming up. The noon break has been extended, but Mo Zheng is not pleased. The mornings are easy to get through, and all he needs is enough time to eat lunch and rest a little before going back to work. But he'd be happier with a shorter noon break and the chance to go home earlier in the evening. He always looks forward to returning home. It's a lonely little room, but he never feels lonesome there, because so many of his friends—his music and his books—are there with him. It doesn't bother him that he's not very good at the piano, since he's not going to make a career of it: every chord seems to loosen a knot in his heart. In *Jean-Christophe* Romain Rolland writes, "Music, you soothed my agonized soul, you restored peace to my heart. . . ." How true that is! Writers seem to know everything. Just knowing that there are writers in the world is enough to drive away Mo Zheng's loneliness. He feels intimate with all those people from other places and times; he can see into the depths of their souls. He's always wondered why the characters in the books he reads, and the lives they lead, are so familiar to him. Why are they like his closest friends, while the real people he knows are little more than strangers?

Ideals and reality each have their own logic. In the real world, people use different standards in their thinking, their reasoning, and the way they understand and make judgments about life.

Once Team Leader Su lost his wallet. Since even he wasn't sure where he lost it, why did the team members look at Mo Zheng suspiciously and whisper behind his back? They would stop talking when he walked up, but as soon as he moved off, they'd start up again. Whispering campaigns like that had been the death of many good people. Some of the team members gave hair-raising accounts of other robberies, and venomously said that the culprit would be caught sooner or later, no matter how clever he was. These comments, directed at Mo Zheng, were accompanied by menacing looks that said, We know you stole it. Just you wait, we'll prove it soon enough.

Mo Zheng endured it, waiting for one of them to accuse him to his face so he could answer the insult with his fists. You don't use kid gloves on people like this.

The wallet eventually turned up in Team Leader Su's room. Everyone just laughed and called Su scatterbrained. Not a word of apology or sympathy for Mo Zheng. He was waiting, fists clenched, for one of them to open his mouth.

Sure, he'd stolen before, but these people knew the reasons and the circumstances. And it had happened a long time ago.

As he sits on the grass fiddling with his pruning shears, Mo Zheng is thinking about all the sweat and hard work people put into caring for a tree—trimming its branches, loosening the soil around it, watering and fertilizing it, ridding it of pests, but no one has ever invested that much care and attention in him, a living human being. In some ways, human beings are more fragile than plants. Ye Zhiqiu cares about him, but no matter how broad and strong her shoulders, she can't carry the burdens of social prejudice that weigh so heavily on him. How could a crooked tree like him be put to the task of straightening out others?

Zheng Yuanyuan has pruning shears that would work on him. He forces a smile. All that keeps his spirit balanced in the face of social pressure is the support of two women. Life has forced him into a corner and made him little more than a charity case. How can he call himself a man! Men are supposed to be the strong ones. Rubbish! The strong one is society—a rat that nibbles away at people's humanity—a society totally corrupted during the ten years of the Cultural Revolution.

Mo Zheng sighs and lays down the shears. He takes off his jacket, spreads it out on the ground in the shade of the tree, and lies down on his back.

The foliage above is thick and the damp ground around him gives off a cool, moist, refreshing scent. When he rolls his head to the side, tender blades of grass like gentle fingers caress his coarse, sunburned cheeks and chapped lips.

Gentle! Only the grass and the sunlight are good to him, giving him the same fragrance, tenderness, and warmth they give others.

White clouds drift slowly across the soft blue sky. Off in the distance a sparrow hawk flies through the air, spreading its wings occasionally, like a sunbather on the beach, as it soars on the wind currents.

A cool breeze brushes against his face. His mind drifts with the wind and clouds, as though he were that distant sparrow hawk or a cloud afloat. He falls asleep.

He has gotten too little sleep for too long, in part because he has been reading a chapter of *Les Misérables* every night before going to sleep so he can tell Zheng Yuanyuan what happens to Jean Valjean as he grows old and what becomes of Cosette, his daughter. This was Ye Zhiqiu's idea. She said it was for Yuanyuan's benefit, but she was really interested in finding a way for him to brush up on his French after all these years.

"What for?" he objected. "I'm not taking the college boards."

"Does that mean you can just sit around all day eating and sleeping?"

"What else is there to do?"

"You ought to educate yourself. If you found a way to enrich your spirit, your life wouldn't be such a mess."

That was how she got by—she turned to literature when things weren't going well in the outside world.

It all seemed childish to Mo Zheng, and he wasn't buying it. It was like trying to fix a broken bone with iodine; and if it hadn't been for something Yuanyuan said, he'd never have taken on the responsibility.

He had just come home from work one day when he heard a strange voice inside. The voice seemed totally out of place in the barrackslike quarters he shared with Ye Zhiqiu. So dainty, so feminine. He just stood there for the longest time, not daring to enter, afraid that the slightest sound might frighten that lovely voice away.

". . . How could a strict idealist like Bishop Myriel refuse to judge Jean Valjean on the basis of a sheet of paper? All these people here who call themselves materialists and disciples of Marx are so narrow-minded. Maybe it's not narrow-mindedness at all, but another kind of idealism. It's a shame the translation of Hugo's novel was never finished. I'd really like to know how it ends."

There was a comforting honesty in that voice. Strange how a voice heard for the first time can unlock a heart that has been sealed tight for so many years. People often try to pinpoint what makes a person change, assuming that a major, even traumatic event is at the center of it. But for someone at life's crossroads, a single sentence can mean the difference between life and death; someone dragged to death's door by hunger can be brought back to the path of life by a single bowl of porridge; hope can be renewed for someone who has always been treated as an inferior creature when someone sees his human worth.

Mo Zheng heard Ye Zhiqiu say, "I can ask Mo Zheng to read it for you. He has a copy of *Les Misérables* in French, which he can summarize for you. The only problem is, he's gotten lazy, and all my urging to brush up on his French has fallen on deaf ears. Nothing interests him. I haven't any idea how he passes the time in that little room of his."

How? Usually lying in bed and counting the white insulators on the wires in the ceiling: one, two, three . . . there are eighteen altogether.

"Who's Mo Zheng? Your son?"

Mo Zheng thought he detected an edge in Ye Zhiqiu's voice. "I don't have any children. He's a young friend of mine." Neither of them said anything more until Ye Zhiqiu broke the silence: "Is he home? I thought I heard something. Mo Zheng!"

He panicked. He wanted desperately to see what this kind-hearted person looked like, but he didn't know what to say to her or what he should do.

Well, she wasn't a raving beauty; her looks were like a stream of spring water that slowly made its way deep into the mountains. He wasn't stunned by her appearance, but found himself suddenly thrown off balance, overcome by a feeling that saddened him. He had the fatalistic conviction that he was standing before someone he would long for but never possess.

All his trepidations disappeared as though they'd never existed when she thrust out her hand and said, "I'm Zheng Yuanyuan. It's not much of a name, I know, but I can't come up with a better one."

Her hand was so small he was afraid to take it, for fear that he might hurt her.

Zheng Yuanyuan sat down on the stool Ye Zhiqiu had told Mo Zheng to throw away. It wobbled. Yuanyuan shrieked as she fell backwards. Mo Zheng quickly caught her before she hit the floor.

"I told you to throw that away," Ye Zhiqiu complained, "but no. Now you see what almost happened!"

Yuanyuan patted her chest to calm down. "You must be a pretty good volleyball player."

Mo Zheng just stood there dazed, broken stool in hand, without saying a word.

"Would you be willing to tell me the rest of the story of Jean Valjean?" She gazed up at him willfully.

There is nothing more irresistible to a man than a willful look in the eyes of a woman he cares for. "I might disappoint you," Mo Zheng answered, just to say something.

"I'll come over every night at seven-thirty." Yuanyuan was

surprised by the way she was ordering around this man she had only just met, by her impetuousness and coquettishness. God! Why had she done that? She'd never acted like that with a boy before. Something special was happening here. She had given him a right of sorts, something that set him apart from everyone else. Why him? What about his self-respect, his dignity? She could still feel his strong hand on her hip where he had caught her just before she fell. Damn! Damn it anyway! Was she being frivolous? With a stern look and a cold edge to her voice, she turned her back on Mo Zheng and said to Ye Zhiqiu, "Auntie Ye, I'd better be going."

The warmth in the room seemed to leave with her. Mo Zheng took the broken stool into his room, where he sat down and stared at it. Had that lovely, petite girl really sat on this very stool? Petite—she barely came up to his shoulder.

Mo Zheng paced the floor of his room late into the night, until Ye Zhiqiu shouted at him from the next room, "Mo Zheng, don't you think you ought to get some sleep? If you don't feel like sleeping, at least take off your boots. That constant clomp, clomp, clomp sounds like a tank coming down the hall."

How long since he had last thrown himself into any task, let alone looking up words and phrases in a dictionary? He wished he were a writer or a translator, so he could keep those willful eyes riveted expectantly on him forever.

What luck that he'd decided, halfheartedly, to hold on to this book. Why, he wondered, after his parents' names had been cleared and their possessions returned to him, had he kept only this copy of *Les Misérables*? Maybe it had something to do with the deep impression it had made on him as a child when his mother read it to him. How he loved the heart of Jean Valjean, so filled with love for humankind, in spite of being so badly scarred. That love even embraced Inspector Javert at the end. Maybe it was because he saw so much of himself in Jean Valjean.

He searched Yuanyuan's face for a reaction when he read passages from the novel or summarized it for her. Did she love Jean Valjean like he did, or did she merely feel sorry for him? What difference could it make to him one way or the other? Why was it so important for him to know? Did she know about his past? Ye Zhiqiu wouldn't have told her, of course. What would she think of him if she did know? Jean Valjean, after all, is a character in a novel; fiction and real life are two completely different things. His past experiences would surely alarm a girl who had grown up in a conventional environment.

Mo Zheng began to envy Hugo, a man who lived more than a hundred years earlier, but whose work was still able to bring precious tears to those lovely eyes. Could Mo Zheng find a way to catch those tears, string them together, and wear them around his neck? He had to stop thinking crazy thoughts like that; they frightened him. He was falling into a bottomless pit. For someone like him, from whom society had taken everything, if love, the only thing left to him, was lost, he'd have no more reason to live.

None of this escaped Ye Zhiqiu's sharp eyes. She had never been a mother, but her maternal instincts made her worry about Mo Zheng. She blamed herself for what was happening and fretted over the tragedy she saw coming. Although Yuanyuan's father, with his incorruptibility and progressiveness, was a rarity in his circles, a girl from that sort of family, whose mother worried only about worldly things, could not help being influenced by class distinctions. Even if she turned her back on all this, it still wouldn't work. Was she strong enough to defy her family? Ye Zhiqiu knew she must put a stop to their relationship for both their sakes. Having never been in love herself, it was inevitable that she'd oversimplify things. "Yuanyuan," she said, "do you know who Mo Zheng is like?"

"Who he's like?" A smart kid. By not answering the question, she kept her feelings hidden.

"Jean Valjean. And I don't mean in a literary sense."

"Oh!" Yuanyuan responded. Nothing more. Impossible to tell if it represented surprise, disagreement, or regret.

"Do you know what I'm getting at?"

"What you're getting at?" Another non-answer.

"What I'm getting at is that dreams of love are not for him."

"Is that right?" Yuanyuan kept her eyes lowered as she flipped through the magazine in her hands. She was so mortified she had to busy herself to keep from bursting into tears. There was no mistaking Ye Zhiqiu's meaning: she was accusing Yuanyuan of flirting with Mo Zheng. This cut her to the quick. She had more suitors than she could count.

Once outside, Yuanyuan regained her emotional bearings. Jean Valjean . . . no dreams of love. He probably had no dreams at all. Poor Mo Zheng. Her heart ached for him. Tears came, but not because she felt humiliated. She dried her eyes. Why was she crying? She had never understood her own feelings before, but now she did, thanks to Ye Zhiqiu. Just like a painter's canvas, on which forms begin to take shape as the artist applies the paint. Did she love him? She didn't know. But she liked the idea of having him do her bidding. That wasn't love; it was possession. But maybe possession is what love is all about. What is there about Mo Zheng worthy of love? He'd never get into a university French department, he'd never be rich, and he'd never be a Party member. He didn't know how to say things that people liked to hear. And yet, when Granny Wang upstairs had a stroke, he was the one who went with her to the hospital and stayed until her son returned from Xinjiang. The doctors and nurses thought he was her grandson. One time, he released a beautiful bird that had accidentally flown into his room. What else was there? Nothing. It all probably meant nothing to other people, especially something as trivial as releasing a bird, but to Yuanyuan it meant a lot. Ai, who knows what love is all about?

What a foolish girl!

Fangfang's husband, Peiwen, was a graduate student in economics. Yuanyuan had read his thesis. It was filled with quotes from Marx, Engels, Lenin, Stalin, Mao Zedong; but as for his own ideas, well, sorry, there didn't seem to be any. He could quote from any work by Marx or Engels at random without looking. Papa once said, "Just like when we were kids, memorizing all the classics." She couldn't tell if he was being sarcastic or approving. It was laughable watching Fangfang listen to a tape recording of her husband quoting the scriptures, her mouth open in awe. His achievements in economics were limited to taking petty advantage

of others, having an opportunistic cleverness, and an unwilling-
ness to let go of anything. Even Mama, with all her astuteness, was
no match for him, probably because she never studied economics.
Ridiculous! Did they really expect Yuanyuan to look for a husband
like this? Disgusting!

Papa and Mama were well off financially, but were they happy?
When had Papa last sat Mama down and had a heart-to-heart talk
with her? When was the last time the two of them had stood in
front of a window watching leaves rustle in the rain or branches
bend under the weight of snow? When had they last watched a pair
of doves cooing at one another and smiled knowingly at each other?
They lived in the same house but spent their time making life
miserable for each other. What had happened to them?

As for Party membership, Yuanyuan was less prejudiced than
most people her age, who reacted scornfully to any suggestion of
applying for membership: "Join *that* thing?" But she saw no reason
to use that as the sole basis for judging someone.

The question remained: was it love, or was it pity? And what if
it was just pity? Love isn't a charitable emotion, and it's not as
though life wouldn't be worth living without that certain someone. She had to know if she really needed him—for her to be in
love it must be she who needed him and not he who needed her;
that would make it pity. Ye Zhiqiu was right: letting him fall in
love with her if she knew it wouldn't work out might kill him.

She tortured herself for days on end.

Ye Zhiqiu noticed that Mo Zheng was losing weight and had
little to say to anyone. He stopped reading and playing the piano.
But she still felt she'd done the right thing, that he'd snap out of it
soon enough. At the same time she was disappointed in Zheng
Yuanyuan. Like father, like daughter. That article of his, why did
he delete all the scientific arguments that would have infuriated
the so-called experts, with all their arrogance and self-importance?
What was he afraid of?

But this time Ye Zhiqiu was wrong. Mo Zheng was too far gone
to cure.

Every night he went straight to his room after dinner, where he
listened for footsteps on the stairs—closer, coming closer, then

moving on, up to the next floor. His torment seemed endless—anticipation, disappointment, up and down. He passed every minute, every second like that until ten o'clock, when it was too late for her to come, and would begin looking forward to the next day, when it would start all over again. Disappointment was no stranger, so why was it so painfully hard to deal with this time?

Given the differences between them, Mo Zheng couldn't go to see her; all he could do was wait. If he hadn't been cast in the role of Jean Valjean, he'd have fought for her, no matter what it took. With his strength and courage, he could make her love him. But as it stood, he could only wonder if she was toying with him. He doubted it. She wasn't the type. More than once she had confessed to him, "There I go, lying again."

"Lying?" He couldn't keep up with her changing moods. No matter how clever the man, a woman's thoughts are always more than he can fathom.

"Lying." She nodded solemnly. "Mama confronted me: 'You've been going out every night—what sort of monkey business are you up to?' She gave me a serious look and emphasized the words 'monkey business.' I said, 'I'm studying French.' Hurry up and teach me a couple of phrases I can use when I get home."

Mo Zheng taught her a silly French phrase, which she pronounced with a strong nasal accent. The words "monkey business" hurt Mo Zheng. He frowned, then quickly forced a smile.

Was this a secret pact? A love pact?

She knew, she had to know. In their relationship he had no rights except the ones she gave him. He could only accept her love, born not out of pity but compassion and respect for his pride, which had taken such a beating throughout his life. It seemed she wasn't even aware of that. Because of this lack of awareness, Mo Zheng was able to see a hidden side of her. What was her heart made of? As a child, he had often heard his mother pray to the Virgin Mary. For him there was no Virgin Mary, only Yuanyuan.

But did she know everything, including the fact that he was a Jean Valjean?

Despair . . .

*　*　*

Mo Zheng hasn't heard the knocking at the door.

Yuanyuan's recent torment is written all over her face, dejection has settled on it like a layer of dust. The mere sight disturbs Ye Zhiqiu deeply. She's too young for that. But then, what does she know, having never been in love herself? Time for her to go to her room. She has mixed feelings, is happy though worried, as she wonders what's going to happen now.

Save for what they say with their eyes, nothing happens.

Yuanyuan angrily turns her back to Mo Zheng. The lovely fine hair at the nape of her neck is so close to his lips. No, he has to tell her first. "I want you to know . . ."

"No!" Yuanyuan spins around and cuts him off. "Don't say anything!" She's upset. "You're so selfish, you think only of yourself!"

Just that one sentence. Buried in her words is the loving, sweet, commanding tone of a woman talking to a man who belongs to her.

But her anger is genuine. Whatever she feels for Mo Zheng, she resents having to come to him. Since she considers him her equal, she expects a great deal from him, like all women in love.

What has made her think he's selfish? He doesn't understand, but if Yuanyuan says so, it must be true. He's worried. "Do you want me, want me . . ." He doesn't finish, but there's no doubt that he nearly said, Do you want me to get down on my knees? Do you want me to die for you? Clichés by now, after so many people all over the world have said them, are saying them even now. But for people in love they will always be new.

Mo Zheng hasn't said them because he's too busy treasuring every second with her.

Yuanyuan sits down on the sofa and says softly, "I want something to eat. I'm hungry, and I'm thirsty." No need to explain that she's had no appetite for several days. It has suddenly returned.

It couldn't have come at a worse time. Where did he put that tin of pastries? He looks right past it.

"Stupid!" Yuanyuan blurts out with a stamp of her foot. "It's right there on the bookcase!"

He scalds the back of his hand while he's making coffee. Yuanyuan jumps up and takes his hand in hers. "Does it hurt?"

No one has ever showed that kind of concern for those hands of his!

Mo Zheng's eyes mist over, and the lines in her face appear softer. He feels like he's melting, like when he listens to music, a sensation that brings a mild pain to his heart.

"Yes, it hurts," he says softly as he looks into her eyes. "Right here." He places her hand over his heart.

"Oh!" she sighs. "It's all my fault." She lowers her eyes.

"No, I'm grateful."

Yuanyuan can feel his hot breath on her hair and is afraid to raise her head. She stares at the black button of his jacket and the blue threads used to sew it on. Those blue threads say everything there is to be said about his lonely, frustrating life. She slowly withdraws her hand from his and fingers the black button. What's he waiting for? she wonders, somewhat fearfully. For her to say something? What will he do?

He takes her hand in his again, presses it to his lips, and kisses it before letting it go. He picks up the cup of hot coffee, stirs it, and blows on it before handing it to her. "Careful, it's hot." As though nothing has happened.

Yuanyuan feels that something has been lost. When she takes the cup from him, she looks up into his eyes. The guarded look that's always been there, just beneath the surface, ready to serve him in any situation, where is it now? His unyielding nature, where is it now? She can see that his dark eyes now have a new master.

Mo Zheng knows it's only a dream. He often has bad dreams like this, and he wishes he could wake up at once. He struggles to open his eyes, but it's no use. He's lying in the road with cars and bicycles bearing down on him, honking their horns and ringing their bells angrily, threateningly: "If you don't hurry and wake up, we'll run you down."

"Get up!" the policeman shouts. "You useless drunk, I'm going to run you in!"

He tries to stand up and defend himself: "I'm not useless, I'm not drunk. I don't know why I'm lying here." But his legs won't move and he can't speak. The people begin to spit and curse. His heart is breaking. Finally he screams and wakes himself up.

The engine of a motorbike roars past him. He turns to look. Above a low hedge he sees Yuanyuan's smiling face and her willful eyes behind a pair of tinted goggles; she looks more coquettish than ever.

A girl riding a motorbike! How many other girls do that? But she could ride down the street on the back of a donkey and Mo Zheng wouldn't be surprised. He scrambles to his feet. There are blades of grass stuck in his hair, his burly, tanned chest shows beneath his unbuttoned shirt, his eyes are heavy with sleep. He is like a sprite that has emerged from the ground, as fresh as the grass itself.

"What were you dreaming about?" She hopes it was her.

"I can't remember!" He doesn't want her to know.

"You can never remember anything!" Obviously it wasn't about her!

"All I can remember is a young woman in tinted goggles riding a red motorbike." He might have been talking about someone a million miles away.

"What's she like?"

"She has a terrible temper."

"That's no good, you ought to toss her aside."

"Yes, that's probably the best way to handle it."

"I dare you!" She suddenly looks very serious. Pouting, she steps down on the starter and turns the engine over.

Mo Zheng leaps over the hedge and grabs the handlebars. "Yuanyuan!"

She turns and looks away. Her short hair blows gently in the wind. Mo Zheng doesn't know what to do. "Yuanyuan!" He pleads. His bright, sunny day has suddenly turned bleak.

"Hm?" Yuanyuan is yielding.

"Where are you going?"

"To see Papa. He's chairing a meeting on political work at the Ministry."

"Isn't he supposed to be home resting?"

"The meeting was Uncle Tian's idea, but when he heard some of the talk going around, he wanted to postpone it until things cleared up. Papa felt strongly that postponing it was a bad idea and that it should go on as scheduled. Well, Uncle Tian refused to chair the meeting, and even tore up the speech he'd prepared. So Papa had to take over. The meeting's this afternoon. He didn't even have time to write a speech. I'm worried that the excitement will be too much for his weak heart. He urged me to go and listen. He's always complaining that I don't know enough. He says I ought to be taking advantage of my youth, while my memory is still keen, and gain a better understanding of society."

Mo Zheng hasn't met Zheng Ziyun, and he's not particularly interested in the kinds of things Yuanyuan is talking about. But he wonders if his perspective might be too one-sided. He is like the earth itself: a cold outer crust around a fiery core. Even from the little Yuanyuan has told him, he begins to realize that all kinds of people are working hard for the betterment of society. It's wrong to point the finger at a certain class of people and accuse them of resting on their laurels and blocking development in production. There are hard workers and slackers everywhere, among high-level cadres, mid-level cadres, and rank-and-file workers.

Yuanyuan once told him that she loved her father the most. He thinks about his own father—that weak, fearful, unhappy intellectual. A mere shake of the head or sigh of disapproval was enough to drive him into hiding amid his bookshelves, where he would let go, almost imperceptibly.

Eleven

Some people treat literature as though it were of no more value than toilet paper. And then there are those who go through life without ever reading a novel.

But sometimes literature becomes a feast for young and old to fight over. Crime and immorality, inflation, profiteering, late trains, traffic jams, housing shortages, static wages, even bed-wetting, all ills are laid at the writer's doorstep. How could something like this come about in a society with such a long and proud literary tradition?

The piece on Chen Yongming's work as manager of the Morning Light Auto Works, coauthored by Ye Zhiqiu and He Jiabin, finally appeared in print. It was an event that not only turned them into targets of public criticism, but even dragged Zheng Ziyun into the fray because of his letter to Feng Xiaoxian, the man who had set his sights on Chen Yongming; his repudiation of the Ministry Party Headquarter's decision not to commend Chen Yongming; and his statement regarding the article: "Publish it! If there are problems, I'll take the responsibility."

Those who opposed the article knew that this was a tempest in a teapot, and that the real issue was the way Zheng Ziyun handled things—by adding a twist that invariably baffled people. He never did anything illegal or unconstitutional or even in direct disobedience of the twelve laws of Party membership. And yet, in their minds, he was always breaking unwritten rules, for which, even though he might not be held strictly accountable, he would someday have to answer.

Zheng's advocacy of the article, which was in direct opposition to Tian Shoucheng, came as no surprise, and it secretly pleased Tian. Instead of blowing up, he knew that if he gave Zheng enough rope, he'd hang himself sooner or later.

So when Feng Xiaoxian and Bureau Director Song Ke, who had both served as managers of the Morning Light Auto Works, came to Tian to find out whether the publication of the article could be considered a direct attack on them, he hedged by telling them, "I don't know what's going on here. It was published without the approval of the Ministry Party Headquarters."

What especially rankled Feng and Song was the part about the former managers of the auto works who, when people were besieged during the reign of the Gang of Four, beat a hasty retreat instead of meeting the challenge. They were considered by some to be deserters. According to the article, one of these men, a bureau director in the Ministry, had an extremely poor record as manager of the Morning Light Auto Works, but when he was reassigned to the Ministry, he was even named a member of the Party Headquarters. Anyone who knew the situation at the Ministry didn't have to be told that this referred to Song Ke.

The claptrap of a bunch of bookish intellectuals! A strong arm is no match for a powerful thigh. Back then even the Political Department couldn't get anything done with all the interference by the Gang of Four; did people expect an insignificant bureau director to liberate all of humanity?

Commending Chen Yongming was one thing (assuming he was everything they said), but what was served by all that other stuff? That fellow He Jiabin is on the Ministry of Heavy Industry payroll and under the direct supervision of Feng Xiaoxian, so if that hasn't occurred to him, he has a lot to learn. Intellectuals are strange birds. But it was, after all, a "literary" work, not a Central Committee directive, so there was no requirement that it be comprehensive. And even Central Committee directives aren't logically formulated like mathematical equations. People usually have a more reasonable view of things that don't affect them directly, but Feng Xiaoxian and Song Ke weren't about to drop the matter and move on. Everyone agrees that criticism and self-criticism are fine Party traditions, but if they go unchecked, people begin to think they can get away with anything and no one can touch them.

"I hear that Bureau Director Song has sent someone to investigate He Jiabin's dossier already," Lin Shaotong says to Tian Shoucheng, drawing out the word "someone" as a reminder to Tian that Song Ke's wife is a section chief in the Personnel Department in charge of cadre records.

Tian voices his disapproval: "Lao Song isn't being discreet enough in this matter, and we don't need the notoriety. The people are already bridling over this dossier-investigation business. Besides, He Jiabin is just a comrade who works in the trenches."

Lin continues: "There's word that Vice-Minister Zheng was seen at Jingshan Park in the company of that female reporter."

Tian quickly lowers his eyes, as though this were something he shouldn't have heard. "What does that prove? They weren't caught in bed together." Tian knows Zheng Ziyun well, having worked with him for many years, and is confident that he is incapable of something like this. How nice if he weren't. That would solve everything. Tian knows that nothing brings a man down quicker than something like this. Tian's awareness is the legacy of Confucius, whose thoughts on such subjects have been passed down through the two millennia of China's feudal history, and are still imbedded in the consciousness of all Chinese. But Tian, a practical man, never rests his hopes on things that haven't happened yet. "As I see it," he says to Lin Shaotong, "if this is how Comrade Feng Xiaoxian and the others feel, why don't you check around the Ministry for reactions to the article. We can bring this up for discussion at one of the Party Headquarters meetings when the time's right." He doesn't say what sort of reactions he's looking for—no need for that. Lin Shaotong knows what's expected of him and is already working out the details in his head.

The forum on political work at the Ministry, which was held on schedule, made Tian eager to have a showdown with Zheng.

Zheng's speech at the forum put him squarely in opposition to the slogan "foster proletarian ideology, eliminate bourgeois ideology," which had recently become popular again. Having received tacit approval from those above, the speech was cited and printed in both public and restricted periodicals, but that merely served to boost his reputation, deservedly or not. Of greater significance . . .

A short time before, one of the leaders on the State Council had added Zheng's name to the list of participants sent by Tian Shoucheng for a meeting to discuss work in the Ministry of Heavy Industry. It didn't take Tian long to figure out that this was a point against him, since it must have appeared that he was trying to squeeze Zheng out.

When he took his customary seat in the front row, where the leading cadres from each ministry normally sat, the State Council member asked loudly, "Zheng Ziyun, is Zheng Ziyun here?"

Tian's sensitive ears picked up something in his tone of voice. Appreciation? Smugness? Esteem? If not, why say it so loudly? There weren't that many people there, and a quick glance would have told him what he needed to know, particularly since he knew the man he was looking for.

"Here," Zheng Ziyun answered simply, almost complacently. Things had gone pretty well for him since the fall of the Gang of Four. Of course, not having been in a leadership role during the Cultural Revolution spared him the necessity of taking a stance and making his position clear. Those damned stances and positions spelled doom for lots of people, who bore the scars of countless attacks. Zheng was in the hospital during several months of the campaign against Deng Xiaoping, although no one knew if he was really sick. His star was clearly on the rise—he couldn't have picked a better time to get sick. "Getting sick" is one of civilized man's great discoveries.

The same State Council member had once asked him playfully, "Comrade Tian, everyone else spends some time in the hospital. What keeps you so healthy?" Something strange in that smile.

Tian was feeling resentful, but even worse was the sense of regret that he could only keep bottled up inside. Back when Jiang Qing had participated in an industrial exhibition at the Ministry of Heavy Industry, he ordered a specially made stainless-steel toilet from one of his factories, which was installed at the Ministry for her use. Whether she used it or not, his intentions were clear. Then later, in July 1976, when the Central Committee held a forum on national planning, he instigated an attack on the State Council for holding a meeting that dealt with ideological matters. No one had forced him to do any of this, and he couldn't talk his way out of it. No one mentioned these things anymore, but they hadn't been forgotten. Sure, they were relatively trivial matters, but, God, they could be his ruination, especially that toilet!

The State Council member waved to Zheng Ziyun. "Come over here," he said. "Sit up front!" He added with a satisfied air, "Things have really been moving ahead in the Ministry of Heavy Industry these days!"

It was not a casual comment. Tian Shoucheng knew all about political life in the upper strata. Every word, every gesture is a sign. In this case, the sign said that Zheng Ziyun was on his way up the promotion ladder. At the moment, there was little likelihood that Zheng would actually replace him. As long as his benefactor up there remained in his corner, his position was probably secure. Besides, Zheng would never be party to something like that. The demotion of a high-ranking official to kitchen worker could never happen in China like it does in the West. Not that Tian Shoucheng was favored by society, but something like that would send ripples throughout the cadre ranks and jeopardize the privileges of an entire class. Tian knew that as well as anyone. As long as he didn't commit a major political blunder—and there was little chance of that for someone as cautious as he—the position should be his for life.

But Zheng still represented a threat, since he was going somewhere and would certainly continue to work in heavy industry. Zheng wasn't the type to play dirty tricks, and there had never been any bad blood between them; but he knew what was going on in the Ministry, and someday he might get carried away and do something rash. And with all his dreams of reform, God knows he might catch the fancy of someone high up. If that happened there'd be hell to pay.

Tian knew that the dispute over the article had not been a real test of strength within the Ministry. Clearly the time for getting everything out in the open hadn't arrived. He must keep himself under control. Confident that he had a better grasp of politics than Zheng, he was sure that sooner or later someone would put an end to this current atmosphere of openness. As long as Tian sat tight, Zheng Ziyun would get what was coming to him, and Tian would be the beneficiary.

Decades of faith in dialectic materialism could not have been spent in vain.

Tian Shoucheng checks his watch as the Party Headquarters meeting is coming to an end—11:30. Now to bring up He Jiabin's article—there's enough time to talk about it, but not so much that it could go on too long. No need to say too much; just sort of get it started.

"Since there's still a little time left," he says, "there's something I think we should talk about." Seeing that he hasn't gotten their attention, he waits until the room quiets down. Random discussions have broken out, and it will take a moment to regain their attention. The individual shades of color that emerged during the meeting will be replaced by a new, uniform, yet indescribable shade—at most meetings, boredom reigns. Now the only problem is Wang Fangliang, sitting there noisily flicking the cigarette lighter someone brought back for him from an overseas trip.

"Over the past couple of years," Tian goes on, "the literary scene has been pretty lively, with lots of writers raising the issue of intervening in life. We've produced a writer in our own ministry, who's written a piece about Comrade Chen Yongming of the Morning Light Auto Works. I guess that counts as intervention in the life of the Ministry of Heavy Industry! Yes, we've got some talent in our ministry! Ha, ha!" He laughs even though he fears that any organization that "boasts" of a novelist in its ranks is in for real trouble, since every conversation, every incident might be turned into material for a novel. Even if a person who recognizes himself in a work of fiction doesn't come out and admit it, people in the know will surely talk behind his back. There he is, that's the one! Since novels wind up on bookstore shelves all over the country, there is always the possibility that someone will recommend the book to a vice-premier or some big shot in the Organization Department of the Central Committee or the Commission for Inspecting Discipline . . .

Zheng Ziyun lights a cigarette. But instead of smoking it, he cocks his head and squints, watching the glowing tip.

"I don't know much about literature," Tian continues, "but back in the Yan'an days, I was privileged to hear Chairman Mao's instructions that literature should serve the workers, peasants, and soldiers, that it should serve the political goals of the proletariat. Uh . . ."

"Is that what the Chairman's 'Talks' say?" Wang Fangliang interrupts. "Haven't you read the papers recently? Ha, ha!" He looks around smugly.

Tian is well aware of Wang's tendency to needle people. He doesn't respect a single member of Party Headquarters. Ever since a recent suggestion of his regarding commercial reforms in the exportation of machine products caught the fancy of one of the leading comrades in the Central Government, he's become nearly insufferable. What did he mean by that comment? Did Tian say something wrong? No way to tell from the expressions on the faces around him. Some are just being polite; others, familiar with Andersen's "The Emperor's New Clothes," have learned their lessons well. Being laughed at by Wang Fangliang makes him uneasy, so he decides to stop beating around the bush. "He Jiabin published that article without the approval of the Party Headquarters. He was supported in his decision by Comrade Zheng Ziyun, and that has led to a lot of talk. Comrade Zheng may not have understood why the Party Headquarters withheld its approval, since he was home sick at the time——"

"I understood perfectly!" Zheng Ziyun chimes in. "But let's hear what you have to say."

"There were four points that brought us together on this issue. Number one: the article shows a disregard for historical facts. Number two: Chen Yongming promotes himself by attacking others. Number three: he takes credit for other people's accomplishments. And number four: he's politically unreliable. In sum, the effects of this article have been to undermine stability and unity."

"He couldn't have made a go of things under the Gang of Four," Song Ke volunteers. "The way things are now, I could do as good a job as he's doing. I had trouble because I did my job in accordance with Party principles. If he's doing a three-hundred-yuan job on a hundred-yuan salary, there's something we don't know about."

People always find ways to justify their actions. The majority of those present are happy to accept Song's rationale.

When surrounded by abnormality, normal conduct appears an aberration, a mistake. Majority opinion often carries more weight than the truth.

Tian Shoucheng doesn't say anything. He remains modest and amiable even in the face of the two comments that have made him look so bad. You have to be willing to sympathize with and show understanding for even the most despicable elements of society, since you never know when your time might come and there'll be someone looking down at you. The ups and downs of society are kaleidoscopic.

Tian can see agitation spreading like wildfire, and several graying heads grow animated at this dramatic moment.

Vice-Minister Kong Xiang is the first to speak. "What it all comes down to is that ours is a collective leadership, and our successes and contributions should be credited to the Party committees. Singling out any one individual is wrong!"

Like all Sichuanese, Kong has a booming voice that brings authority to virtually everything he says. The eyes behind his glasses are steely, cold, and unfathomable.

Kong Xiang has a bellyful of anger. He doesn't like the way things are being done these days. All these cultural workers getting involved in politics don't know their ass from a hole in the ground! What's needed is another anti-Rightist campaign, so we can pin a Rightist label on each and every one of them and send them out for some labor reform. Either that or shoot a couple of them. Kong Xiang has always put a lot of faith in the barrel of a gun. He joined up with the Red Army at the age of fourteen, participated in the Long March, and fought in one battle after another—he has the scars to prove it—and now this bunch of cultural workers is trying to take charge. Nonsense! Like hell they will! Point a gun at them and watch them shit in their pants.

Ever since Zheng Ziyun gave his report at the forum on ideological work at the Ministry several months earlier, Kong has grown more and more infuriated at Zheng's mannerisms and appearance: his starched, white collars; the way he smooths the creases in his trousers every time he sits down; and his "ladies first" chivalry. But the only thing he can sink his teeth into is the fact that Zheng is an intellectual. Kong has gotten into the habit—an occupational hazard—of finding something in everyone that he can sink his teeth into. The one sure way to a perfect life is to be a puppeteer holding everyone's strings.

Zheng Ziyun's report really stuck in his gullet, like a fishbone. There was nothing he could point to as being wide of the mark, particularly since he'd barely understood it. But instinct told him that it somehow threatened him, although not in the immediate future—probably, in fact, not until he and Zheng Ziyun had both turned to dust. But it was Kong Xiang's hope that, dust or not, he would always be respected.

Openly opposing Zheng Ziyun wasn't the answer, since Zheng outranked him. Besides, he couldn't—or was too lazy to—come up with a set of reasoned arguments to refute Zheng's position. Even the dusty old clichés of the Cultural Revolution were more than he could manage now, although he had heard them day in and day out during all those years he was under attack. But he hadn't shit in *his* pants out of fright when they'd pointed the gun at him, not even when he was being attacked, and that's the truth. The only lasting effect was a slight impairment in memory.

Great! Kong has hit the nail right on the head. The first volley against Zheng Ziyun. It makes Song Ke's comment look pathetic, and puts the issue on the table without referring to it directly. But no one's inclined to follow it up. People have become too cautious lately. All they talk about in private is how we have to open up, but in front of others, they just yawn or beat around the bush, afraid to offend anyone!

The only sounds in the spacious conference room are the snapping of fans and the hum of the electric fan up front.

Someone has turned the electric fan on full blast, and it is making Zheng Ziyun very uncomfortable in his front-row seat. He gets up and moves to an armchair next to the door. Although he is sitting across from the windows, his view is blocked by a row of poplars that let in a bit of the summer sun and a few patches of blue sky. Knowing that the sky beyond the trees is a deep blue lightens his mood and dispels the depression created by the gray chairs, the yellowing walls, the crummy ashtrays badly designed—like so many of the things produced by the Ministry factories—and the faces of the men in the room: some tired, some blank, others experienced and astute; some indifferent, still others angry and aggressive.

He ought to take a trip to the countryside some Sunday, even though it isn't the right time of year. Late September is the time to go to the West Hills, spring for Cherry Ravine. The Summer Palace is out because it's too crowded. Of course there's always Tanzhe Monastery. During the Cultural Revolution he had once taken Yuanyuan there to go hunting. His hunting rifle, which had been confiscated during one of the house searches, had recently been returned, but it was all rusty, just like him, old and rusty.

Song Ke notices the faraway look on Zheng's face and is angry. He's never been able to figure out what's on that man's mind.

184

The room is so hot and stuffy that the underarms of Song Ke's shirt are soaked. He unbuttons his shirt, exposing his round pot belly under his T-shirt. He's not very happy with the way the meeting is progressing, though it isn't much different from any other meeting, the way everyone skirts the controversial issues by keeping their mouths shut. But his hands are tied; the less he says the better, since he's personally involved. He doesn't want anyone to think he's letting subjective feelings sway him. He is jealous of Chen Yongming. It's because of Chen Yongming that his own name was removed from the list of candidates for vice-minister. Where did he come from all of a sudden? It's all Zheng Ziyun's doing. No wonder he hates Zheng so much. If only he weren't Chen Yongming's promoter! Even if he is, why Morning Light Auto Works, if not to show up Song Ke?

Seeing Chen and Zheng fail is his fondest hope. He opposes them at every turn, whether there is anything in it for him or not. He looks with anticipation into the faces of each of the people in the room, wondering who will speak up. After working alongside these people for years, he has learned what to expect from each one of them. But his observation disappoints him. What difference will it make anyway? Personal opinions, Party Headquarters opinions, the reactions of the Ministry rank-and-file, what effect does any of this have on Zheng Ziyun? You wouldn't get a reaction out of him even if you put his head on the chopping block.

It's all a smoke screen; otherwise, Zheng wouldn't be sitting there indifferently. Song Ke grinds out his barely smoked cigarette in the ashtray. He pours tea into the ashtray to drown the cigarette, but it sloshes onto the light blue tablecloth, shreds of tobacco, matchsticks, dark ash, and all.

"There's talk that the woman reporter who coauthored that article with He Jiabin has been divorced twice!" Kong Xiang volunteers. He shoots a warning glance at Zheng Ziyun. He said the word "divorce" as though he were saying "whorehouse" or "syphilis."

Everyone turns to look at Kong Xiang.

Zheng sneers inwardly. If Ye Zhiqiu could get married twice, she'd feel like a real woman! Since divorce is permitted, why do people like Kong Xiang treat it as though it's a crime? He can play around all he wants, but others have no right to divorce! Things move so slowly in this country; even the ways of committing murder are the same as in antiquity.

Wang Fangliang sits up in his armchair and says, "I thought this was supposed to be a Party Headquarters meeting!" What he means is that they should stop acting like it's a backroom gossip session and deal with the issues seriously, instead of disgracing themselves with all this mudslinging. Kong Xiang is the vice-minister in charge of the Political Department, and the people under him are always giving Wang a hard time. Not that he is afraid of them, but if he keeps giving them opportunities to cause trouble, more time and energy will be wasted. The less of that, the better.

His caution is well founded. Once, when he tried to help out an old comrade-in-arms by having his daughter transferred from a factory to the Ministry, not only did Kong Xiang hold up the process for more than a month, he reported the case to the Ministry's Commission for Inspecting Discipline, which then made a mountain out of a molehill by calling Wang Fangliang on the carpet. Who the hell did Kong think he was! Carrying on as though he and the others were paragons of virtue. He gave Kong an earful in front of his subordinates, recounting for everyone how many privileges he'd wangled, which of his relatives had good jobs in the Ministry, the month and year when he'd been seen at a restaurant in the company of a certain woman. They haven't spoken since.

Wang Fangliang is a happy-go-lucky sort, as long as no one has him in his sights. But once he gets his hackles up, he is a formidable adversary.

"I asked the author himself," he says, "and he told me that Chen Yongming didn't read it before it appeared in print, didn't even know it was in the works. So how can you say he's politically unreliable? I personally called him on the phone and asked, 'Did you see that article before it was published?' He said, 'No.' I told him that the reaction in the Ministry had been intense, and asked him, 'What do you think of it?' He said, 'As I see it, in China you can only write up people who are dead, not those who are still living!'

"I agree with him completely. There are simply too many people in China, too many people with nothing to do. Sometimes, before a movie can be shown in a theater it has to be cleared by the Politburo; and now one little article has turned the entire Ministry of Heavy Industry upside down, to the point where we members of the Party Headquarters have to get together to discuss it. What does that make us worth? One municipal Party committee held three separate discussions on the topic of whether women can have their hair permed. No wonder we can't get any major work finished. We're too busy wasting our time on a lot of piddling matters."

Tian Shoucheng feels even more uneasy after listening to Wang Fangliang. Even the dullest person in the room must be thinking that Tian Shoucheng didn't ask these questions himself not because they didn't occur to him, but through conscious omission.

Tian quickly gathers in the net he had thrown out: "In that case, Chen Yongming can't be held responsible for the fact that the article was inaccurate and ill conceived."

Tian watches Kong Xiang's and Song Ke's faces fall. Quickly running a mental check on his account of favors owed and owing, he knows that he's safe in calling one in.

It's tough being leader of the pack. Each of the worthies in the room has his own resources, but Tian Shoucheng alone, as the leader of the pack, is the master of every situation.

"Do you mean to say that it's the authors' responsibility?" Zheng Ziyun asks. "That's no way to close the issue. Let's just go ahead and verify every so-called error of fact in the article. I'll assign someone to it, then we can draw our own conclusions. That the Party Headquarters did not approve publication needs looking into, too. If I remember correctly, I wasn't the only comrade not in attendance at the Party Headquarters meeting that day." He looks straight at Tian Shoucheng, but doesn't give him a chance to speak. "That's number one," he continues. "Number two: when they were debating at the Party Headquarters meeting whether or not to permit publication, some of the comrades hadn't even had a chance to read the article. They didn't even see it until after it was published. Number three: only a minority of the comrades present actually opposed publication. All the others didn't vote one way or the other." He pauses to blow the ashes off his cigarette, as though he has finished. But after a brief silence, he laughs and continues, "What are we, a bunch of literary critics? If I weren't in this business, I'll tell you the truth, I'd write a novel. As it is, I'm going to write a critique in support of this particular article. Comrade Tian brought up the subject of effects just a moment ago, and I agree that it's an important consideration. But when we're talking about effects, there are some things to take into account, such as the criteria for measuring them and who establishes the criteria, the leaders or the readers, and whether it's short-term or long-term effects that really count. Some writing serves to mold character, and though it might not have any direct impact, it exerts a subtle influence on society.

"As far as I'm concerned, the effects of this article aren't bad. Sure, there are problems in structure, language, and technique, and the authors didn't paint a completely accurate picture of Chen Yongming, but we have to give them credit for having the courage to show their readers a new brand of hero for this new age."

Tian decides then and there to let the matter drop. As in a game of chess, you don't try to make up losses by adding to them. Besides, there will be plenty of opportunities later. He quickly adjourns the meeting.

Zheng Ziyun wakes from his nap feeling limp. There is a bitter taste in his mouth. After getting out of bed, he brews some tea and stands by the window looking out onto the street.

Some young people on their way home from swimming ride by on their bikes, their colorful swimsuits draped over the handlebars, flapping in the wind like banners. A girl with short hair sitting sidesaddle on the back of one of the bikes looks like Yuanyuan, her arms folded in front of her, her long, tanned legs crossed. Not a care in the world and no fear of falling off.

Yuanyuan and her mother argued again. It's too small a family to be so unsettled. From society at large down to the family unit, these days the call is for stability and unity. How simple it would be if people's aspirations could be cultivated like garden vegetables. You just plant what you want. Yuanyuan's tongue is getting sharper by the day, like her father's. No respect at all for her mother: "Are you trying to put me up on the block again? You ought to be running a stud farm!"

Wow!

Lately she's been especially sensitive to the marriage issue, and flatly refuses to discuss it with her parents. "Everyone has their secrets," she says, "even you!"

Does he? Maybe he'd be better off if he did, instead of looking back on a life that has been as ordered as geometry, with no unexpected curves. There should be many supports in a man's life, so that if one gives out, there are others to take its place.

Outside there are trees, and people walking by, but under the blazing sun everything seems listless. Except for the old woman defiantly selling popsicles in the shade across the street: "Popsicles, chocolate popsicles!" Zheng Ziyun often sees her out there. She is about his age, but looks in better shape. A short woman, with a wizened face so deeply tanned it resembles a weathered mask. The marks of a hard life. Yet there is a strength in her still resilient voice that shows she's not ready to give up yet. He, on the other hand, feels as though he already has one foot in the grave. Nannies, secretaries, offices, private cars . . . he's grown soft over the years. Modern life has played havoc with his body. A by-product of modernization is the body's growing inability to adapt to nature, combined with increased emotional vulnerability.

He is troubled. Why? The harassment at the recent Party Headquarters meeting couldn't compare with some of the things he's been through, like the 1942 rectification campaign, the "paper tiger" struggles of 1952, the anti-Rightist campaign of 1959, the Cultural Revolution; these were walls he could scale.

He longs to see communication, understanding, mutual support among people. "What kind of foolish talk is that?" Yuanyuan said to him. "Look around you, don't you realize what times these are?"

Look around? No, she's wrong. Just another one of the extreme views of her generation.

He's lonely. Terribly lonely. The steamy, sun-baked street reminds him of the Sahara desert.

He wishes someone would drop by. Or call on the phone. He needs to talk to someone, about anything.

The phone rings in the next room. He smiles. Good timing!

Xia Zhuyun lets it ring for a long time before answering. He can tell by the way she's talking—treating every word as though it were worth a thousand yuan—that it's someone she doesn't like, but he does.

"Lao Zheng!" she calls from the other room. "Phone call for you. It's that reporter Ye again!"

She says it so loudly that Ye Zhiqiu can't help but hear. Xia Zhuyun still doesn't seem to understand how rude it is to ask who's calling if it's a phone call for him.

"Hello, Zheng Ziyun here."

A note of hysteria in Ye Zhiqiu's voice. "The editorial department forwarded an anonymous letter to me."

"What does it say?"

Xia Zhuyun stops fanning herself and pricks up her ears.

"It says my article shouldn't have been published and that I am an immoral woman. It says things like I've been sleeping with the coauthor and seducing the man we wrote about, as well as a certain vice-minister, meaning you."

"What do you plan to do?"

"I'm sure this is the work of someone in the Ministry. I've still got some ink here; maybe I'll do a portrait of the whole bunch."

"I'm really sorry!" As though he had personally insulted her.

"Does it surprise you? It's nothing new."

"Is there anything I can do?"

Bang! Xia Zhuyun smacks her fan against the tea table. Zheng tightens his grip on the telephone in case she tries to snatch it away from him.

"No, nothing, but thank you. I only told you to put you on your guard. Goodbye."

"Goodbye."

They've gone too far this time.

There've been a lot of unhappy things in the past, but he hasn't had to fuss over them. Yet not fussing wasn't the same as not making his presence felt.

This time they're trying to smear a woman who is powerless to defend herself. They are too timid and cowardly to deal with real evils, but when it comes to a frail woman, they attack with all the force they can muster. What a tragedy!

"You're sorry!" Xia Zhuyun explodes. "For what? What do you plan to do for her?" She sounds like a prosecutor. What could she possibly be thinking?

He just glares at her.

She is wearing off-white house slippers on her alluringly tiny feet, like those so passionately alluded to in Pushkin's poems. Her ankles are sheathed in imported nylon stockings. She has on a white satin housecoat, embroidered with a pair of maroon phoenixes. Her red, silver-flecked silk fan is lying on her ample thigh.

Delicate. Elegantly simple. The essence of contemporary material culture. Including her black, permed hair.

She looks out of place on the worn sofa.

The whole scene is ridiculously incongruous.

In this living room, simply furnished as though everything has just been thrown together as the need arose, she looks alien, unreal.

Married for forty years, he feels more estranged every time he looks at her.

"Maybe you ought to see a doctor."

"Don't you talk to me like that!" Xia Zhuyun fires back as she smacks the arm of the sofa with her fan.

"You've become so morbidly suspicious, keeping tabs on every woman except yourself. What happened to your self-respect? You're so bitchy all the time! I don't understand some women, the way they run around on Women's Day demanding liberation, but when they go home they're just like any other wife who's totally dependent on her husband. As far as I'm concerned, women's liberation means more than political or economic equality. It means relying on your own strength, not on . . ." He pauses and looks at Xia Zhuyun's hairdo and her attire. "A woman should strive to improve herself so her husband will respect her character, her spirit, her dedication, and not treat her like some lovely flower . . ."

He keeps himself from telling her that by draping herself around her husband's neck she is living passively, devoid of ambition. A woman's reliance on laws and social pressures to force a man and wife to stay together only proves her lack of independence. The fact is, love cannot exist or prevail in any society that has no consistency in enterprise and ideals. Engels said, "Marriage doesn't just determine one's physical life, but one's spiritual life as well." Love is founded upon knowledge and common interests.

He knows she won't understand him and will assume that he's having an affair and wants a divorce.

Besides, he sees humor in a sixty-five-year-old man analyzing the foundation of love on sudden impulse. In the end, what does any of this have to do with his daily life or his ministerial duties?

Chekhov wrote, "Love is currently in retreat, a mere vestige of something that once was great; either that, or it is the seed of something that will be great one day in the future. But at present, it does not satisfy, and it provides far less than people expect of it."

Does that mean that people should not wish for it?

Maybe he's the one who should see a doctor. Maybe he's the one going just a bit mad. Who can say!

His only hope now is that his advocacy of making political work more scientific will someday help it to be understood and accepted by greater numbers of people. Perhaps in fifty years or so people might actually establish a scientific and comprehensive system of theory and practice. But why be so pessimistic? Why fifty years and not twenty?

He hopes for greater honesty in life, for more people like Chen Yongming, for an absence of the need to expend so much energy and use such unfair means to bring an inspirational article and its authors to grief.

Zheng Ziyun has lots of small hopes, all far more practical than love.

Everything has its own place. Love belongs to sociologists and to the future.

Xia Zhuyun's anger and jealousy slowly give way to fear. What's he up to? He's talking like someone giving a strange woman a lesson on how to hold on to her husband.

What does it mean when a woman's husband calmly tells her how to be appealing to him?

Xia Zhuyun realizes she lost Zheng, spiritually and emotionally, long ago. Now, and for who knows how long, what she has had is an empty shell. No, not even that, just an illusion. Why try so hard to hold on to it? What is she afraid of losing? Nothing except the vain seductiveness so many women don't know how to give up.

She begins to sob.

A woman's tears are a powerful weapon that defies reason and assures final victory.

Zheng Ziyun says nothing. He begins to feel fidgety. He can't just walk away. Crying is a sign of weakness. Besides, she's a woman, and a man simply doesn't treat a woman that way.

A knock at the door. It's 3:30, time for Xiao Ji to bring the day's documents, newspapers, and correspondence. With an enormous sense of relief, Zheng walks to the door. Xia Zhuyun stops sobbing and goes to her own room. Zheng is grateful: at least she knows how to handle herself in situations like this and doesn't make him lose face in public.

Ji Hengquan would make a good KGB agent. He senses at once that something is wrong, and he takes a quick look around the room. No one else has been there—no teacups on the table. Everything is just where it's supposed to be, so no one has blown up and thrown anything. But something's wrong. The way Zheng is flipping through the documents, not really seeing anything, is a sure sign. It is a common subconscious way of calming oneself down.

Zheng puts down the documents. "Has the inspection team for the Morning Light Auto Works been chosen?"

"Yes." Ji Hengquan never says more to Zheng Ziyun than he has to. He'd rather keep him guessing.

"Who's in charge?"

"Department Head Zhu Yiping."

Not even a bureau director! They are obviously out to show Chen Yongming up. The Ministry always sends a bureau director to a factory of this size, if not a vice-minister. He detects Song Ke's hand in this.

"Anyone from the Enterprise Management Bureau?"

"No."

They clearly don't want anything to go wrong. Hasn't the storm over that article blown over by now? Is something like that really worth remembering forever? No factory has ever been inspected without a representative from the Enterprise Management Bureau. That's their job. They're supposed to handle enterprise reform!

Does Tian Shoucheng know? If he does, he'll pretend he doesn't.

"Is there anything else?" Ji Hengquan refuses to have anything to do with Zheng Ziyun that isn't work related. And there's no need to try to get on his good side, since it won't work anyway. The best way to deal with Zheng is the same way you write a report to any higher-up: no attribution, dull, stiff, point one . . . point two . . . point three . . .

"No, that's all. Thanks."

Thanks for what? It's my job. Zheng is always thanking people. In working relationships where no one gives any more than required and no one owes anyone anything, thanks are superfluous and meaningless.

Why are people so tightfisted even when it comes to charity? In his anger, Zheng is tempted to head the inspection team himself. But this is a time to maintain a cool head. He can't always have his own way, particularly in an environment where the simplest matters are made as complicated as possible. He has to be on his guard at all times. Does that mean he's being crafty? Or combative? Does necessity dictate all human behavior, and is it necessary to complicate even the simplest matters and simplify the most complex? It's all backwards. Conceptually speaking, Zheng feels that colors are much richer than the words used to describe them, there is a remarkable gradation from deep to pale, as in the blue sky beyond the window, whose farthest reaches are lightest in color, seeming to turn to gray.

Chen Yongming can count on being lonely again. It will be like the loneliness they experienced that earlier spring night in the countryside when they gazed up at the star-filled sky.

But what about Yang Xiaodong and his men? People should hold on to hope.

How will the workers at the factory feel? Like stepchildren, probably. Doused with cold water. Thousands of workers. How could they not care that they are hurting so many people? And all because of one sentence in an article that mentioned no one by name and benefited no one!

And Zheng Ziyun, Vice-Minister Zheng Ziyun, is insignificant and helpless, just like Chen Yongming.

The old lady standing in the shade across the street selling her popsicles shouts again, "Popsicles . . . chocolate popsicles!" Maybe he should be like her, maybe he should put on a white cap and apron and start selling popsicles.

He sighs and shakes his head, then sits down at the desk and takes out his stationery. But he just sits there thoughtfully for a moment. All he can do is write a few words that will solve absolutely nothing.

Dear Comrade Chen Yongming:

The management reorganization of the Morning Light Auto Works over the past year has been very effective. I won't be able to participate in the coming inspection owing to my poor health, but I hope everything goes smoothly.

Respectfully,

Zheng Ziyun

Right, poor health! People have learned over the past few years how to use poor health as a pretext for avoiding unpleasant matters.

Twelve

Ye Zhiqiu's hand shakes as she stuffs coins into the pay-phone slot. The attendant watches her closely, just in case she tries to get away without paying. Ye Zhiqiu wonders what it is that makes her so interesting to this woman. Maybe she overheard her conversation with Zheng Ziyun. Even in a big telecommunications office like this, they don't have a phone booth for local calls. True "public" telephones! Everything is public these days: public secretaries, public emotions; nothing is off limits. How come you take a bath every day? How come you like sweets so much, but not spicy foods? That sort of stuff.

"Why'd you have to tell him so much over the phone?" He Jiabin chides her.

"What could I do? I can't go to the Ministry at a time like this. That would really give the rumormongers something to talk about. And his wife is unbearable whenever I go to his home."

"What I mean is, why tell him at all?"

"He has to know. Don't you think he has to be on guard against those people?"

"Feminine logic!"

They walk out of the building together. The streets are jammed with people, all taking casual strolls. It makes you wonder how many people are actually working on any given day in China. As though every day were a holiday. The easygoing Chinese!

Only the noise never takes a holiday!

Vehicles sound their horns to show off.

A motorbike starts up with a proud *putt-putt*. They are very fashionable these days.

A little girl is hopping around, bawling, "I want a popsicle, I want a popsicle!" Her father is dragging her down the street by her pudgy arm, as though he were holding a chicken. "If you don't stop crying," he threatens her, "I'll give you a real spanking. You've had eight already, and if you eat any more you'll get worms!"

A young street vendor is hawking his wares: "Here, buy it here, freshly baked buttery bread!"

"Paper, paper here, entertainment news, Li Guyi sings in spite of illness, Su Xiaoming sings 'Country Road'!"

From the police box at the intersection, a traffic cop shouts through his bullhorn at a reckless driver: "Hey, you in the jeep, what kind of turn is that? Hey! I'm talking to you, license 31-04889! Where do you think you're going? Did you hear me? You stop right there!"

The jeep pulls over and stops as timidly and hesitantly as a little donkey that knows it has done something wrong. Apparently, the driver stopped where he shouldn't have. Panic, probably.

"Now look!" the policeman bellows. "Where the hell do you think you're parking?"

Every single speaker in an electronics shop blares "Apollo God of Music." Nothing—not a riot, nothing—can stop the rhythm of "Apollo God of Music."

Rhythm!
The faster the beat,
The shorter the sleeves,
The larger the collar,
The wider the cuffs,
The brighter the colors . . .
Rings,
Necklaces,
Earrings . . .
Bold,
Blunt,
Rude . . .

He Jiabin even takes a bit of satisfaction in the turn of events. "Zhiqiu, we're all going to die someday, whether we want to or not. And the people who take over after us will be far more direct than we. All the worries and anxieties we brood over will be a lot simpler in their hands!"

"Jiabin," Ye Zhiqiu says in a pleading voice. "I can't take all this bustle. I've had my foot stepped on twice already."

Everything, including He Jiabin's comments and the colorful street scenes, seem to be out to get her; it all comes rushing at her, making her feel as though she were being brutalized. People pass her by without a word or so much as a glance, as though she were a winter fur hat lying in a shop window in the heart of summer.

She suddenly feels overwhelmingly lonely.

Tired, so tired!

Even if she is a haggard, lackluster professional woman, there are still times when she needs to air some grievances and hear a few comforting words.

But people have gotten used to treating her like a sexless, emotionless robot. Including He Jiabin.

She shakes her head. That wasn't always the case. Take that anonymous letter, for example. Apparently, at least some people recognize her as a woman when they spread their slanderous rumors. *That's* when her gender makes a difference.

A heavy sigh emerges from deep down in her chest.

He Jiabin turns to look at her. She seems different.

He searches her eyes behind the thick lenses of her eyeglasses. They say that eyes are windows to the soul.

Like frosted windowpanes, the lenses make everything behind them dim and shadowy, keeping the observer from getting a true picture.

But he finally spots a look of worry. Though normally placid, she is in turmoil. Women's nerves are, all in all, more shatterable and sensitive than men's. It's particularly painful to see slanderous rumors directed at such a homely woman. A woman whose life will never blossom and never produce fruit.

He Jiabin reaches out and takes her arm. They turn and walk east down Changan Boulevard.

A green leaf, totally out of place on this midsummer day, floats over and lands on Ye Zhiqiu's bony shoulder. A merciful green leaf. Touching as a poem. Instead of brushing it off, He Jiabin lets it lie there. People need to be comforted.

Up ahead a pregnant woman hobbles along the shady street. Her broad frame is covered by a baggy man's shirt, and she is eating a popsicle. Unconsciously, He Jiabin picks up the pace. As they pass her by, Ye Zhiqiu sighs deeply. What must it feel like to bear the child of the man you love? she wonders.

But she's not one to cry. Tears are beautiful, a luxury reserved for women who are loved.

"Sorry you did it?"

"No, just upset."

"Don't let it get you down. What does it matter? Even the emperors were slandered behind their backs. We made what little contribution we could. No matter what you do, you pay the price. Some pay with their lives. . . . You, me, Chen Yongming, Zheng Ziyun, Feng Xiaoxian, none of us are going to live forever, but a person's spirit will outlive him."

"This time the price was too high. All over such a trivial incident. Ai!"

"Is your reputation really that important to you?"

"Isn't yours?"

"No, what I mean is, if someone is really out to get you, what can you do? Roll over and die? You can't let these rumors put you at their mercy, because if you do, you're lost. If you ask me, it's like property, nothing but a worldly possession."

"Then why are you so eager to join the Party?" She laughs. Score one for her.

"Certainly not to make a name for myself. I believe in Marxism. I want to study it, put it into practice, use it to reform this Party of ours in which some members still have a small peasant mentality and don't know how to apply scientific Marxism."

Ye Zhiqiu takes a quick look around. Has he lost his mind? If she hadn't known He Jiabin since elementary school, she'd wonder if he'd gone completely off the deep end. "Not so loud," she warns him. "Keep your voice down!" She's afraid someone might overhear them and take something out of context.

"What have I said? Why should I keep my voice down? I haven't said anything that's counterrevolutionary!" He raises his voice even louder. Who would want to twist his words? "We should be studying Marxism as a body of scientific knowledge, and then put it into practice, not worship it."

Ye Zhiqiu shakes her head and waves him off. "Now you're going too far!" she exclaims anxiously. "You're going to get yourself in trouble going around talking like that." She glares at him. "I'm surprised your Party branch passed you," she says as she twirls her handbag nervously, as though He Jiabin's dangerous comments had found their way into it and she was determined to pour them all out.

Instead of easing her worries, as he had planned, he's made her feel worse.

In the more than twenty years since they left college, there has never been a shortage of things for them to argue about, and it's hard to say who has moved ahead and who has stood still. Maybe neither of them has moved ahead; maybe society has passed them by.

He Jiabin, who usually backs down when they argue, stands in front of Ye Zhiqiu, his legs spread and his arms outstretched. "You tell me why I'm not fit to join the Party. I'd like to know how much less of a sense of social responsibility I have than people like Feng Xiaoxian and Ho Ting. Okay, okay, Zhiqiu, I understand what's bothering you, and I'll be more careful from now on." He tries to sound conciliatory.

A self-mocking smile spreads across her face. "I was teaching you how to be sneaky!"

"Can't be done. You, of course, are a realist. If it wasn't for Bureau Director Fang Wenxuan, this time I never would have passed. Certainly not if it had been up to Ho Ting. She spread all kinds of rumors and created all sorts of obstacles. They view the Party as their private domain. The door is theirs, to open or close as they see fit, and they can turn away anyone they please. I've made enough mistakes for them to use to their own advantage, because I talk too much for my own good."

"Such as?"

"They say I've got an ideological problem, that I support the bourgeois trend toward the weakening of the family unit, things like that. Why shouldn't the family be weakened? When the system of private ownership finally dies out, the death of the family unit is inevitable. By that time, people will be living communally, and their lives will no longer be restricted by laws . . . so, they've come to the conclusion that I'm an advocate of free love! They're a bunch of morons! After all these years since Liberation, we still pay attention only to Marxist theories of class struggle. And, excuse me, but even these have been distorted—damn few people think about Marxist aesthetics, ethics, or moral issues like love and marriage."

This strikes Ye Zhiqiu as funny. "You're talking about centuries from now," she says, "too far in the future to worry about. So what if no one talks about them now? You have to take into account the majority, the spiritual level of ninety percent of the people."

"You're wrong. If we don't look into these things now, we'll never raise our spiritual level to a point where it's worthy of the name socialism." Another argument is brewing. He Jiabin doesn't want to see a frown on Ye's brow just when she's finally stopped worrying. "Next," he continues, "Ho Ting was critical of my stance. So I told her, 'Be specific. No false accusations, please.'

"So she said, 'You once said that if everyone's wages were

increased five grades, it still wouldn't pay the debt the nation owes its people. What kind of stance would you call that?'

"I told her, 'I don't recall saying that everyone's wages should go up five grades, but I do believe that everyone's wages should be increased, and if they aren't, then the nation owes them a debt.'

" 'The country's got its problems,' she says, 'don't you know that?'

"Well, I told her, 'I'm not saying that the country should be forced to raise every worker's wages, but that these problems could have been avoided, and we should be figuring out the reasons for their existence. We can't keep forcing things down the people's throats in the name of objectivity. As individuals, we have to do our utmost to reduce the country's problems as much as possible, and as far as I'm concerned, you haven't really shown any concern for the country's problems.'

" 'Me?' She thought she'd be pinning a label on me. The last thing she expected was that I'd throw it right back at her. She had no idea what I was talking about. Her eyebrows were arched high. 'What am I supposed to do? I'm not the premier!'

" 'Simple. You can do a better job where raising wages is concerned. Based on regulations, Luo Haitao shouldn't have gotten a raise, since he wasn't nominated by the masses. Xiao Wen should have gotten a raise, since his nomination was unanimous. But you threw Xiao Wen's nomination out and gave the raise to Luo Haitao instead. The people complained, but you said everyone had agreed. By creating a situation where comrades are complaining about adjustment of wages, aren't you just contributing to the country's problems?'

"There was fire in her eyes. She pounded the table and shouted, 'We're considering whether or not you're fit to join the Party!'

" 'Don't threaten me with that,' I told her. 'I'm going to make a note of this. You can't pound the table and intimidate me like that. Who are you to pound the table in front of me? I'm not your personal servant, I'm a public servant.'

"Well, she reported me to Feng Xiaoxian, who criticized me: 'It's wrong for you to be taking any notes on your department head. You have no right to argue with Ho Ting or talk back to her, since she's the boss even if she's wrong. That's insubordination.'

"You see, it's more than a problem of my stance. I've also got a problem with my attitude toward the organization. I wonder when we'll finally be able to separate the organization from the individual.

"Lastly, she said my life-style is a problem. I'm sure that's because I spend a lot of time worrying about Wan Qun. Am I supposed to just ignore her and leave her on her own—a widow with a child?"

"She really ought to get married again." Ye Zhiqiu always simplifies other people's marital problems.

"Get married? To whom? The man she loves won't have her."

"You mean Fang Wenxuan?"

Fang Wenxuan is worthy of He Jiabin's respect, though a weak man.

But in fairness, everyone has his troubles. So what are his? He Jiabin has no idea. Viewed even with the most outmoded moral concepts, he still seems, at best, quaint. During the Cultural Revolution he was removed from his post, and when he was kicked out of the Party, his wife filed for divorce and handed over several of his diaries to the authorities to show that her break with him was complete. Some of the entries showed a dissatisfaction with certain policies, and if it hadn't been for those diaries, Fang might not have suffered so badly for so long, including a broken rib from a beating. His wife claimed all their belongings for herself and then disappeared without a word.

Fang was cleared in 1970 while he was at the cadre school, where Wan Qun's husband, who had been their company leader, killed himself. He Jiabin never forgave her husband for this selfishness, for solving his own problems but leaving her and a month-old child to fend for themselves.

What incredible pressure!

Whether by design or chance, the cadre school was located in a onetime labor-reform camp. No one knew where the former inmates had been sent. Naturally, during those days, the intellectuals, those "stinking old ninths," were treated no better than criminals undergoing labor reform. They were given one day off in ten, in labor-reform-camp tradition. The way it's always been, they said.

Wan Qun was assigned space in the kitchen of a family of labor-reform workers. The ceiling was so low that He Jiabin nearly scraped his head on it when he stood upright.

Her room was dark and dank, the corners and other hard-to-reach spots filled with cobwebs. A great place to ferment bean curd. Mildew grew on everything but the tenant. It was freezing in winter, when cadre-school "warriors" went up into the mountains to burn wood and make charcoal, which the people then had to carry down on their backs. Winter brought the rains, sometimes for days on end, making the mountain roads so slippery and treacherous that even agile young men, with or without sacks of charcoal on their backs, were covered with mud when they reached the foot of the mountain.

It was still dark that morning when the whistle sounded for everyone to line up outside. There were shouts back and forth telling people what to take for the climb. Wan Qun sat up in bed, feeling almost as though she were in a different world. The noise outside had nothing to do with her; she might as well have disappeared from the face of the earth. She heard the people setting off toward the mountain to fetch charcoal, then silence returned.

She knew she should join the others, but she hadn't an ounce of energy left. She tried to crawl out of bed, but her body wouldn't respond. All she could manage now were her thoughts.

She reached out to feel the baby's hot-water bottle—it was cold. It should be filled with hot water. The diapers hanging overhead were still dripping wet. She hoped the baby wouldn't wet himself for a while, since there were no more dry diapers. She longed for a bowl of steaming, soft noodles. . . . As a child she'd hated noodles.

She had to make a fire to dry the diapers, boil some water, cook some noodles. Where was she going to get the charcoal? She'd always hated asking favors, and now that was really impossible. Wife of a counterrevolutionary! That was her husband's legacy to her and the child. Cry? No, not she. No reason to. Not everyone cries when troubles come. The power to adapt to suffering is stronger than the imagination. But when one lives with the label of wife of a counterrevolutionary and has lost a husband who never had a sense of responsibility, the two are about equal.

Self-pity and regret wouldn't help matters. It was up to her, weak as she was, to raise this child alone, to become a fierce she-wolf.

Why had he been born in the first place? He wasn't a love child, but a product of the Cultural Revolution, when having children was about all that was left to her. His face was marked by sadness from the day he was born.

For many people motherly love is a reservoir whose water spills out when the gates are opened. Maybe she was an exception, for what she discovered was not motherly love, but greater responsibilities.

Her husband, rotten to the core though physically attractive, made a big show of family harmony after they were married. Now paying the price for the falseness of her marriage, she had to accept the accusing looks, the dark, dank room, and the struggle to take care of herself and her month-old baby. All she wanted was for time to pass quickly, so that all her pain and suffering would become nothing but unhappy memories.

As the charcoal began to crackle in other damp, dingy rooms, people acted as though it were New Year's, gathering round earthen charcoal burners, drinking strong wine to keep warm, and talking happily about their mountain experiences: one had had to crawl along on all fours, like a monkey, another made his way down the mountain like a kid on a slide in the children's playground at Beihai Park.

Wan Qun's door was open, but they ignored her. Fang Wenxuan and He Jiabin walked in with gunnysacks filled with charcoal over their shoulders. They were both soaked to the skin, having spent the entire day out in the rain. It would have been hard to imagine two worse-looking human beings, and no one would have believed that one of them had once been a bureau director, the other a brilliant student from a top university. Now they were just two charcoal bearers, beaten down by cold, hunger, and exhausting labor, yet filled with compassion for a wretched, helpless woman.

205

It was getting dangerously close to the point where all they would have left was an instinct for survival.

Fang Wenxuan's thinning gray hair was plastered down by the water, accentuating his broad, square forehead. His full lips had turned blue from the cold. The wrinkles around his eyes and on his cheeks glistened with sweat and rainwater. The sharp edge of a mountain bamboo had ripped one of his rainboots. His faded blue jacket hung limply on his thin frame. His whole body showed the stress of his exhausting struggles.

Inexplicably, the sight of these two men and the scene around her made Wan Qun think of Christmas Eve and Santa Claus, of the New Year's Eve fancy-dress balls at college, of the gifts the boys piled up in the girls' dormitory windows each year on Women's Day. But that was all fun and games, while this was a result of harsh, complex, serious moral concepts.

The look on Fang's face said: There is no cadre school, there's been no suicide, you're not the wife of a counterrevolutionary, there's no rain, no slippery mountain path, no charcoal to carry, as though they had just come from his comfortable Beijing home where he'd been enjoying a cup of tea and a casual conversation, or he had just run into her at Wangfujing. "Where's your charcoal stove?" he asked her.

He Jiabin reached under the bed and found the stove amid piles of junk.

"Is there any kindling?" Fang asked.

He Jiabin rummaged through one pile. "No."

Fang walked outside and returned in a few moments with a piece of fir and an ax. He Jiabin chopped it into kindling and lit a fire.

Fang looked around him: the smoke-blackened ceiling, water seeping under the door, an empty water barrel in the corner, the unwashed bowl and chopsticks and several mostly empty bottles on top of the wooden trunk, one of them with a little salt in it.

It was an impoverished, remote village; it was the rainy season. Wan Qun had no one but herself to blame . . . this sort of thing happened all the time. And yet Fang Wenxuan, a member of the Communist Party, heard the voice of his conscience: This is inhumane! He blamed himself. There was a dark corner in his heart, too. Why couldn't he be more like He Jiabin? Why hadn't he been there for her on the day she lost her husband, when she really needed someone? He'd been afraid! Afraid of losing his newly regained freedom. Freedom isn't normally associated with cowardly passivity, for that would subvert its meaning. Now he had profaned the word that had once been written on the glorious banner of revolution.

As he was leaving he said, "Let me know if you have any problems. You won't be asking favors, but exercising your rights, the rights of all people. You have obligations to the future."

What a difference a fire in the stove made. The room seemed to come alive, like a patient coming out of a coma.

He Jiabin filled the water barrel, washed the dishes, and straightened up the bottles on the chest.

Every so often he looked over at Wan Qun, who was sitting motionless on the bed, careful not to disturb her.

He put some of the rice the canteen had sent over into the pot, adding some salt and water, then put the pot on the stove. Once it began to boil, he tossed in a handful of greens. Pointing to a can of lard, he explained, "Lao Fang got you this from the canteen."

Wan Qun suddenly realized that they were waiting on her, and she wasn't moving a finger. She hadn't even said thanks. No need to thank He Jiabin, of course, but what about Fang Wenxuan?

She took the bowl of steaming rice soup He Jiabin handed her. Just as she was starting to eat, she heard him say, "Rice porridge with greens has always been my favorite." Her spoon froze in midair. He was being so careful to avoid saying anything to hurt her. Tears began streaming down her cheeks; it was that easy. So that's all there is to it!

Her door stood open in the rain.

When they slaughtered a pig for the canteen, she was given one of the feet and some of the liver; when the driver went into town he brought back powdered milk for her; people began dropping by. The difference between a decent man and a heroic one is the difference between timidity and a disregard for one's own safety. As long as someone takes the first step, the rest, who are waiting, will follow.

He Jiabin noticed how sparingly Wan Qun used the charcoal Fang had carried down the mountain in his gunnysack. When she had to use some, she carefully picked up all the precious splinters that had fallen to the floor, as though each had a life of its own. As soon as the fire was lit, she stood close to the burner, not willing to leave for even a moment and lose its (or his) warmth.

Fang's compassion and sense of responsibility had ignited a spark in her. Damn! She was acting like a schoolgirl.

He Jiabin sensed that Wan Qun's feelings would come to naught.

She was being foolish. She had no understanding of the circumstances under which Fang had lived all these years, how his goals, his feelings, had been formed. And even if he loved her, what he had become would overpower that love, and he would ultimately give her up. She would then sink into despair again. He Jiabin was powerless to do anything about it. Who had the heart to wrest away a straw clutched in the hand of a drowning person? Who could convince someone not in her right mind that what she thought she saw was only a mirage?

But it was touching to see Wan Qun and Fang Wenxuan together. He Jiabin couldn't help but notice that there was feeling in Fang's eyes, which normally seemed to be shielded by a mask. And Wan Qun, well she'd become a cooing dove again, this time a little more experienced.

For a while, He Jiabin began to believe that he might have been wrong, that his fears had been unwarranted; he even forgot about Wan Qun's "wife of a counterrevolutionary" label. Maybe they'd get married after all. Wan Qun was a widow, and even though Fang wasn't officially divorced, he had no wife, and the formalities could always be taken care of later.

But the illusion was short lived. Maybe Wan Qun's life was truly as ephemeral as a delicate flower. When they left the cadre school and returned to Beijing, Fang resumed his duties, his wife rejoined him, and that was that.

The pain of dashed emotions is something everyone knows. Fang shouldn't have allowed these emotions in the first place. They were not included in the mold that had been used to shape him and the tens of thousands like him. What was he thinking of when he crossed that boundary? He got what he deserved.

He couldn't shake the feelings of guilt over the way he'd treated Wan Qun. Day and night his conscience reminded him, "You let her down, you really let her down!"

He couldn't escape that inner voice, just as he couldn't break free from his own confinement. His life had been one big, irreparable mistake, although he couldn't say just what sort of mistake it was. He became gloomier than ever, even more of an introvert, more unreasonable, even fickle. People who didn't understand the pain in his heart assumed that he had taken on the airs of a typical bureau director as soon as he was back in his official automobile.

His past relationship with Wan Qun was common knowledge around the office, and feelings that had been understandable and legitimate back then were now neither. If he and Wan Qun so much as glanced at each other in the corridor, people started whispering behind their backs. Naturally, most people felt sorry for them or were curious to see what would happen next. Fang couldn't blame them, particularly since it involved an alleged affair.

For someone like Feng Xiaoxian, who was always looking for a chink in Fang Wenxuan's armor, every time they had a disagreement at the office, he ran to Vice-Minister Kong Xiang to report these rumors, adding another nail to Fang's coffin. Of course, no one said anything to his face. And through it all, his and Wan Qun's actions were irreproachable. It was a matter of "to catch a thief you must have the loot, to catch a traitor you must have an accomplice." Something like this would come to light only after he had fallen completely from favor. At that time he'd be denied the right to defend himself, whether there was any hard evidence or not. How could he not feel the injustice of it all? Sometimes he felt like saying to hell with it all and stealing a kiss from the woman he loved. Far more frequent were thoughts of leaving and going far away. But he knew he couldn't leave. He couldn't just take off because he felt like it. He did what he was told to do. Like a statue cast in iron, he was powerless to shout or move.

When He Jiabin and Ye Zhiqiu reach Southern Pond, he looks at his watch. It's already after four o'clock. "I'll walk you home, okay?"

"No, I have to go to the office. There's been an abuse of authority in one of the provinces, and the newspaper is sending me and some others to look into it. We're going to be briefed before we leave." The worry in her voice is gone without a trace. She is a robot again, and He Jiabin can almost hear her click and whir. Well-oiled and running smoothly, the robot is in good working order, the epitome of efficiency.

"Another assignment that makes enemies," He Jiabin reminds her.

"It has its benefits." That's more like it. She's back on track.

"But I think if you keep going out into the provinces, pretty soon you'll have been to all twenty-nine, and then where can you go?" Even someone like Ye Zhiqiu, with a pleasing, almost fault-less personality, will wear out her welcome sooner or later; all those people constantly on their guard against her, their hearts filled with hate. He doesn't know whether to laugh or cry.

"Then someone else will take my place." Her casual answer makes him feel worse. Noticing his silence, she asks him, "What's wrong, you don't think they will?"

"No, of course they will. After all, society keeps moving forward."

He is given to bookish talk, but somehow it doesn't sound so dry or lifeless coming from him. Everything in his life, whether beautiful or ugly, commonplace or unusual, is invested with his profound emotions, and all sorts of people are drawn to him.

"What about you, heading back to the Ministry?"

"Not me! With this year's cuts in capital construction, there's nothing to do there. I'd rather be out walking around than chewing the fat at the office."

Ye Zhiqiu stops walking. "Can't you find something to do?"

"Like what? I found something to do when we wrote that piece on Chen Yongming, and look at the trouble that caused."

"Why didn't you tell me?"

"Why should I? The worst Feng Xiaoxian can do is keep me out of the Party. There were already disagreements in the branch committee."

"It'd be a shame."

"It's up to them. It's just the difference between form and substance."

"You're just rationalizing."

"No I'm not. Well, see you later."

The bus doors snap shut. Ye Zhiqiu waves to He Jiabin again. He just nods. She can see him, tall and thin, through the rear window of the bus, as she walks with a sway toward the setting sun. Where's he going? She knows that, like her, he is constantly rushing around in the service of others. But like the setting sun, their rushing about is nearing its end. They have no regrets over the time and energy they've expended, for that's what has given their lives meaning. A bottle of medicine that is unnecessarily difficult to get; the case of an innocent victim; getting some kind of certificate . . . God, how much of our lives is wasted on those endless certificates, whose titles alone would fill a book! If they served a reasonable need, then the time spent getting them would be worthwhile. Value is always relative.

He Jiabin walks into a provisions shop. "What have you got for dysentery?" he asks the shopkeeper.

Wan Qun's son, who'd had a case of toxic dysentery, has just been released from the hospital.

The clerk, her face caked with powder, her eyebrows heavily penciled, answers curtly, "Furazolidone."

He Jiabin thanks her politely, like a gentleman talking to a spoiled little girl.

After buying a decorated cake, a bottle of orange soda, and a bag of glucose, he walks out of the store with his head held high.

Not even rush hour and the bus is already crowded.

A stocky woman getting on ahead of him has two traveling bags packed nearly to bursting over each shoulder, a net bag filled with a thermos and several snack tins and shoeboxes in her left hand, and a paper shopping bag in her right.

It's not a woman, it's a human moving truck.

"Come on," the ticket taker rushes her. "Get on if you're going to!" She pushes the button for the doors to close. "No more room!" the ticket taker bawls. "Take the next bus!"

The harried woman keeps trying, unsuccessfully, to get on. He Jiabin reaches out to help her up. The "truck" barrels forward, and the two of them make it onto the bus.

One of the woman's traveling bags bumps He Jiabin and knocks the bottle of orange soda out of his hand; fortunately, it doesn't break.

The woman turns to face him—a red, sweaty face, probably a Northeasterner. She just stares at him, her thick lips parted. Doesn't she know how to talk?

The driver presses the gas pedal; the bus moans, then begins to move at a crawl.

Just then a youngster screams in a heavy nasal twang, "God damn it, don't you know how to stand! Who do you think you're pushing?"

"You kicked my thermos!" So, she knows how to talk after all. She has a thick Northeastern accent.

"Don't you know how to say anything? What's the idea of bumping into me with your butt?"

"Why can't you stand over there?"

"Because I want to stand right here. How did a creature as disgusting as you live this long!"

"How 'bout you?"

"None of your goddamn business! You better watch yourself if you know what's good for you. Get me started and I'll say some things that'll keep you awake at night!"

Some of the other passengers are roaring with what sounds like approving laughter.

"Hooligan!"

"Who's a hooligan? I'm not the one who shoved his butt in someone's face. Talk about nerve!"

He Jiabin's anger is rising. He can't stand it any longer. "Hey, young fellow, watch your language! Don't get sassy with out-of-towners, okay?"

The young man sticks his face, which is sandwiched between long sideburns and looks older than his years, right up next to He Jiabin. "Step aside and mind your own business! Who do you think you're talking to?"

"Aren't you ashamed of the way you're acting? Some man, taking advantage of a woman like that!"

The youngster starts rolling up his sleeves. "You looking for trouble?" He indicates the bus door with his thumb. "Come on, let's settle this outside!"

"I wouldn't do you the favor."

The other passengers begin to grumble.

"He can't get away with that."

"He makes the whole city look bad."

"Ask him what work unit he belongs to."

The young man crouches and assumes a fighting stance, baring his teeth. "So, you want to give it a try, huh?"

Actually, he's so scrawny that even someone as bookish as He Jiabin could probably break him in two.

Someone tries to make peace. "Come on, forget it. The less everyone says the better!" He takes the young man by the arm and leads him away. He's smart enough to know he's getting off easy.

That's when the woman starts up: "There, you see, that's what people from Beijing are like. I'd like to know what makes them so great!" She accentuates her comments by smacking her hands together.

She's not winning any friends among the passengers.

He Jiabin begins to wonder if he was butting in where he shouldn't have. Everyone has such a short fuse these days, as though they're just waiting for a chance to have a good argument.

Thoughts are like wisps of smoke, always shifting and changing.

Déjà vu? Her son just threw up, and the smell lingers. Scattered on the floor are a water basin, a chamber pot, a pair of shoes—one

213

here, one over there—even a cooking pot. The table, which hasn't been wiped clean for a long time, is cluttered with empty medicine packets and bottles and a number of drinking glasses of various sizes and patterns. As chaotic as her life. Fang Wenxuan notices that the curtain in the window is a skirt Wan Qun wore as a young girl. As faded and worn as Wan Qun herself. After such a desperate life, she needs someone to take care of her. But she avoids marriage. Could it be because of him? There's still a spark in his heart. If it were true . . . if only it were true. No, it mustn't be true! He must put it completely behind him. Is that being selfish?

There on the bed, her son, staring listlessly out the window at the blue sky. He has Wan Qun's eyes and far too pretty a face for a little boy. Children don't know how to hide illness. He is very, very weak; if he weren't, he wouldn't be lying there in bed, devoid of all desires, just like a monk. He doesn't seem to hear a thing they're saying. Fang had held him as a baby, and even now, whenever he thinks back to that time, he's struck once again with the warm, tender feeling one gets from holding a kitten or puppy in his arms. He has never held Wan Qun in his arms.

Wan Qun is sitting in a creaky chair beside the bed. Even thinner now than at the cadre school, her hands rest limply in her lap, tendons bulging across their backs. Fang can't tell from her tired expression what his coming over has meant to her.

Why did he come? Of course, her son is sick and she needs help, but is that the only reason? What about that spark he felt just a moment ago? Does that mean that what he hopes is true? Or that it mustn't be true?

"Why didn't you call me when he was discharged from the hospital? I've got a car."

No, the emotion and esteem that were present back then in that dark, dank kitchen room are gone. That earlier feeling has been replaced by pity and indifference. The Fang Wenxuan standing in front of Wan Qun no longer seems so strong to her; if anything he is weaker than she. Even if she had called him, would he have had the courage to send his car? Wouldn't he have been afraid that the driver would talk? Why won't the resentment in her heart go away? She can't fool herself—there would be no resentment if there was no love. Emotions are the hardest thing in the world to make sense of. Stumbling into a trap is bad luck; spotting a trap and continuing to walk ahead is stupidity. Wan Qun knows she mustn't let emotion creep into her voice when she talks with Fang, but does she have the strength to control it? Behind her cold, hard exterior lies a deep resentment that Fang can sense. Wan Qun avoids saying what is in her heart: "There was no need. A taxi was just fine."

"He's so heavy, how did you manage?" Compassionate sentiments like this seldom come from him.

"The cabdriver was very kind. He helped me."

You can't always tell about people by the way they look. The young cabdriver is a case in point.

She walked out of the hospital carrying her son piggyback, a hot-water bottle in her hand and a canvas knapsack stuffed with all kinds of odds and ends for his use while in the hospital slung over her shoulder. The driver was sitting in the taxi cleaning his nails with a pocketknife and humming a popular song by Deng Lijun:

> When I read your love letter my face turned red and my heart
>   leapt,
> I didn't know how to respond to your honest passion,
> Your tenderness and sweetness encircled me like misty clouds,
> I think about you day and night . . .

He looked up, spotted Wan Qun, and jumped out of the car to help her. "Lady, I didn't know you were alone. Why didn't you ask me to give you a hand?"

A typical Beijing accent, as though instead of a tongue in his mouth he had a slippery ball. With that sort of accent, even something very sincere has a false ring to it.

It was a hot day, but he kept the windows closed out of consideration for them. Most people believe that the sick should avoid drafts, no matter what the illness.

Wan Qun sat in the back of the taxi, holding her son on her lap.

All she could see of the driver was his greased hair above the high, stiff collar of his shirt.

Compared to him, Wan Qun looked positively shabby. The strap of her canvas knapsack was completely frayed, the corners worn through; the hot-water bottle, which she'd bought in the cadre school, was nearly rusted through in some places; her hair hung unkempt to her shoulders, and she smelled of perspiration. Her son, whose thin frame was wrapped in a striped cotton sailor shirt, looked terribly undernourished. This was only the second time in his young life that he'd been in an automobile. He had been in a coma the first time and had no recollection of it, so this time he kept staring out the car window, touching the door handles, and digging around in the ashtray on the seat in front of him. Almost instinctively, and in a weak voice, he repeated a rhyme he'd learned as a toddler: "Toot, toot, toot goes the automobile, Chairman Mao's inside for real."

The driver honked the horn for him, then said, keeping his eyes straight ahead, "I'll take the long way around, no extra charge, okay?"

At first she didn't understand, but then she said, "Okay, fine. But I'll give you what the meter says."

The driver laughed with a superior snort. "Hick!" he was thinking.

"How come this car's roof is so low?" the boy asked.

"Because you're so heavy you've forced the car down on its wheels."

He thought for a moment. "Uh-uh, you're trying to fool me!"

"That's the ticket. Don't you go believing everything you hear!"

Their lighthearted conversation had a calming effect on Wan Qun.

When they reached home, the driver thrust his thumb toward his chest and said, "Lady, just watch, I won't even be breathing hard!" He picked up her son and carried him on his back to the third floor without stopping.

After getting her son into bed, Wan Qun went downstairs to pay the cabdriver. He was sprawled across the front seat, singing the same tune:

When I read your love letter my face turned red and my heart
    leapt,
I didn't know how to respond to your honest passion,
Your tenderness and sweetness encircled me like misty clouds,
I think about you day and night . . .

"Comrade driver," she said gratefully, "thank you very much!"

He sat up reluctantly. "What for? Look me up the next time you need a taxi. My name's Gao Zhanhe."

Wan Qun stood in the doorway as he backed the taxi out. He'd probably already forgotten her as he zoomed off.

It seems unfair to compare Fang Wenxuan with the cabdriver. He was just an ordinary fellow who held nothing back—his emotions, his goals and desires, his charm and his flaws, were out in the open for everyone to see. Not much difference between him and Wan Qun.

Fang watches Wan Qun's shoulders sag as she sighs and opens her eyes. "What would you like to eat?" she asks her son. "Mama'll cook whatever you want."

He looks over at his mother and stares at her for a long while. She knows that if Fang weren't there, he'd throw his arms around her neck and kiss her on the cheek. When a young boy starts to grow up, he begins to look upon himself as the man of the house. And no man of the house is about to kiss his mother in front of others. "Some pickled vegetables," he says softly.

Wan Qun feels like crying. Pickled vegetables, not something tasty like a nice buttery cake. But she knows that pickled vegetables is about all she can give him. What sort of childhood is this!

"What else?" Almost a plea, hoping he'd ask for something beyond their means. Maybe she wants that more for herself than for him.

Fang walks over, seeing a chance to do something for them. "What would you like? I'll go get it."

"Just some rice porridge and salted vegetables!" He sounds angry. Perhaps just a touch of pride.

Children have the instincts of animals. They sense the difference between safety and danger, truth and falseness, friend and stranger.

He can tell that Mama is more anxious and ill at ease than usual. He suddenly sees her as a little girl who needs his protection.

Once he watched a couple of schoolmates picking on a little girl. They broke all her crayons. Oh, how she cried. He went over and gave her his crayons.

Why doesn't that man leave? He's making Mama unhappy. "Mama, cook it now, okay? I feel like eating now."

"Oh, sure!" Wan Qun walks over, takes out the rice sack, and picks up the aluminum pot from the floor. There are leftover noodles inside. They don't look very appetizing. No color, probably not even any soy sauce in them. And it's too late for Fang to get anything at the store now. If the two of them were living together, Fang muses, he could take care of things like this. He stands there absorbed in thought. What would she be like if they were together? What would their home be like? . . . He needs someone, and not the shameless woman he married, who is always looking for the chance to betray him. But does he have the strength to oppose the mores of society? Everyone would be alarmed: Divorce? You already have a woman, what else do you want? Besides, this woman's no different from the one you have. People would try to talk him out of it, warning him that it was capricious and contrary to Party discipline, not to mention the legal problems it would bring. They'd try to frighten him with the prospects of a ruined reputation: "What's more important to you, politics or love?" Meaning, of course, "What's more important to you, your official post or love?" As though love were incompatible with the goals of the proletarian revolution, or a guiding principle of capitalism or Trotskyism, or at the very least, out of place for a leading cadre. Ultimately, he would be abandoned by colleagues and friends alike. . . .

Fang Wenxuan should have realized that all these high-sounding arguments, camouflaged as communist ethics, were nothing more than feudal morality. Marxism had risen to such glorious heights that it protected itself even with things it had set out to destroy.

But he somehow failed to realize this. As He Jiabin had frequently remarked to Wan Qun: "All those directors who drive everywhere by car, you'd think they were so busy they barely had time to rest. But the fact is, they seldom have any idea what's really going on."

Fang Wenxuan, so frequently caught in a painful dilemma he couldn't escape, envied people who could drink their way to a good night's sleep or forget their worries at the poker table. He wondered if he'd ever manage to live a carefree, casual life like that.

Wan Qun sniffs the noodles in the pot. "They've gone bad," she says with a frown, as she shuffles over to the bathroom and throws them out.

It's as though Fang weren't even there. Has he become superfluous? If he is being punished, he knows he should have the decency to accept it. He is willing to expiate his sins with the blood of his heart.

He follows her into the kitchen, where he watches her wash and rinse the pot under the tap, then fill it with rice and begin washing it. The sounds and her movement have a powerful effect on him.

"Wan Qun, can you ever forgive me?"

"Forgive you for what?" She stops working and rinses her hands under the water. "We never made any vows to one another, and you never held out any promise. So what's there to forgive?"

She keeps her back to him. He can see that her shoulders are arched under her thin shirt.

"Then try to make allowances for me!"

Of course she's made allowances for him. People always make allowances for people with weak characters.

Something deep in Wan Qun's heart takes flight. Soars like a bird. She looks up. Unable to fly themselves, people always look longingly at birds in flight.

"I think you'd better go!" As though to a bird already flying off into the distance.

Fang begins fumbling in his pocket. He stammers for a moment before managing to say with difficulty, "I think I should leave you some money. You can probably use it."

"You know I won't accept it."

Of course she won't.

219

He stops fumbling in his pocket.

"You'd better go."

He turns to leave.

He touches the peeling paint on the doorframe as he walks out, knowing deep down that he won't be back. This doorframe, the messy room behind it, and the people inside now belong to a different world, as does everything that has passed between them.

Wan Qun watches Fang Wenxuan through the window as he walks toward the bus stop. No car this time. Even this last sight of him leaves a colorless impression.

She walks back into the room. "Mama, are you crying?" her son asks.

"No!" She clears the table and wipes it with a rag.

Her son holds out a bony fist. "Wait till I grow up, then if anyone takes advantage of you, they'll get a good taste of this!"

In the midst of her dejection, she is touched: Thank you, son. But when you grow up you'll realize you can't solve all your problems with your fists.

She raises her head, her eyes closed, and lets a silent sigh escape from the depths of her heart.

He Jiabin walks in covered with sweat. "I've been knocking at the door. How come you didn't answer?" he grumbles. "I let myself in." He puts down his packages and looks at Wan Qun. "How's he doing? All better?"

Wan Qun just stands there with her eyes closed.

"What's wrong?" he asks softly.

She raises her arms weakly, like an abused child, and rushes into his arms, sobbing as she rests her head against his chest, "Oh, Jiabin, Jiabin, why has everything turned out so badly?"

He pats her on the back. "Because we're living in a society that's neither capitalist nor communist, neither fish nor fowl, neither this nor that, neither hot nor cold, always at odds, up and down, where nothing is as it should be, and everything can be interpreted one way or the other. No one ever knows which way to go, and nothing's ever made clear. So why should your own agony be more important than the agonies of an entire society?" He puts his hand under her chin and raises her head. As he wipes away her tears, he says, "It's not the fault of any one person, or even several people. These are the pains that come during a time of transition."

"Mama!" Her son is frightened.

Wan Qun finishes drying her eyes with the back of her hand. She smiles an apologetic, almost embarrassed smile. "Just look at all the nice things to eat Uncle brought with him!"

He pushes aside the box of pastries she is holding out to him. That's not what he needs. He needs to grow up, and fast, till he's as big as Uncle Jiabin. He needs to become the best protector she could ask for.

Thirteen

If there were a degree for schedule management, Liu Yuying could get a Ph.D.

After getting out of bed in the morning, she turns on the radio, and in the ten or fifteen seconds it takes for it to warm up, she has the bed made. She turns the dial to the Beijing Radio Station six o'clock news summary. Then, on her way to the kitchen to get the broom, she picks up yesterday's dirty clothes and dumps them into the washtub and lights the stove to warm up some steamed rolls, which will be ready by the time she finishes sweeping the floor and clearing off the table. She stirs the soy milk, and before it has boiled she's washed her face and brushed her teeth.

By 6:30 Xiao Qiang has gotten himself and Xiao Zhuang washed and dressed.

Monday is always the most hectic morning, since Xiao Zhuang

has to be taken to nursery school where he is a weekly boarder. On other days it is just she and Xiao Qiang, so they don't have to get up until 6:25.

Still, things are a lot less rushed than before.

When Wu Guodong was readmitted to the hospital, Chen Yongming realized how hard it was for Liu Yuying to take care of two children by herself and arranged through his connections in the Personnel Department to have her assigned by the Bureau of Services to a beauty shop closer to home. Now she only has to walk twenty minutes to work, which saves her both the time and expense of taking a bus. He also arranged for Xiao Zhuang to get into a neighborhood nursery school.

Liu Yuying, a simple woman, repaid him with a simple "Thank you."

"Why thank me?" Chen asked her. "You're too easy on me. You ought to be angry that it took so long to get it done. Just look, it took Wu Guodong's hospitalization to get us moving. Besides, all I did was put in the request. If anyone's to be thanked, it's the Personnel Department."

Except for her concern over the hepatitis that is causing Wu Guodong's liver to harden, things have been going pretty smoothly for Liu Yuying. With him out of the house, everything gets done more easily. Her renewed energy reminds her of study hall at school, which she had enjoyed the most, since there was no teacher in the room. Being on her own like that had seemed to make her smarter: arithmetic was a breeze and memorizing her lessons was easy. In other classes, she'd felt unhappy and overly anxious, and she stammered whenever she was called on. But in study hall she reeled off her lessons like a stream flows after a spring thaw, merrily, melodically . . .

Yang Xiaodong and Wu Bin brought a bottle of gas with them the day before, along with Wu Guodong's wages. That Yang Xiaodong is certainly strong. He carried the bottle all the way up to the fifth floor on his back as though it were nothing. He wasn't even breathing hard.

He and Wu Bin also went to the grain shop and bought her some rice, cornmeal, and flour.

"Let me know if you need anything," Yang told her. "We're not very refined people, and there are lots of things we might overlook, so don't hesitate. Look here." He punched Wu Bin playfully in the arm. Although it was already October, Wu Bin's muscular arms were covered only by a thin nylon shirt. "You always know where you can find a couple of strong arms."

"Not so hard, okay?" Wu Bin grumbled. "That's my arm, not an anvil."

Liu Yuying remembered Wu Guodong's frequent complaint: "Those misfits in the workshop don't do anything the way it's supposed to be done, always playing around!"

She didn't see anything wrong with the two lively young men standing in front of her.

But even Yang Xiaodong wondered where Wu Bin suddenly found the energy to stand on his head to entertain the kids, nearly breaking a light bulb in the process. He lifted Xiao Zhuang and twirled him around while Liu Yuying watched nervously, afraid he might hurt the boy. But she was too bashful to say anything, so she just kept a wary eye on Wu Bin while trying to be sociable with Yang Xiaodong.

Both kids were laughing uproariously. She'd never seen them laugh like that.

They never let go like that around their father; they sensed that they should speak softly and be restrained, watch what they said and always hold back. Whenever he was home, their play was subdued as they kept their guard up, and when he had that look in his eye, they wisely headed for bed as early as possible. Even Liu Yuying, his wife of many years, felt constrained around him. Once, before they were married, they sat on a bench together at Beihai Park and studied the Party Constitution for two solid hours. If the young people today heard that, they wouldn't believe it. But that's what their romance had been like back then. Each time they met they discussed their progress in ideological and political issues, pointing out their own shortcomings and making suggestions to one another, before going off to look at the goldfish or row a boat. Quite a difference from young people nowadays, who walk arm in arm and even kiss in public.

Wu Guodong neither smoked nor drank, and he handed his whole pay envelope over to Liu Yuying. He was different from other men, lords of the castle who prop themselves up in bed after dinner and enjoy a smoke, letting their wives run around to clean up after them. Nor was he like those men who insist on having wine with their meals, no matter how tight the family budget, or who enjoy a plate of scrambled eggs, eating and drinking noisily while their wives and children look on, forcing down bites of dry cornbread and tough salted vegetables. There weren't many men like Wu Guodong these days, and Liu Yuying knew it. So why was living with him such a chore? If she was carrying a full bowl of piping hot soup, he'd caution her, "Watch where you're going, don't trip over that stool, be careful, don't spill it," which made her so nervous that sooner or later she'd trip and drop the bowl or spill the soup, and that'd be that.

Liu Yuying rolled up her sleeves to make some pot stickers for her guests. They stopped her playfully. "Hm!" Yang Xiaodong said, "Lao Wu says your pot stickers are the best!" He raised his thumb. "But we've got important business that won't wait."

"What's your hurry!" She stopped them. "It'll only take half an hour. "You've got that much time."

Wu Bin became uncharacteristically serious. "I'm afraid it really won't wait."

"What could be that urgent?" she asked doubtfully.

"We have to find him a girlfriend," Yang whispered conspiratorily.

And off they went.

They didn't have anything to take care of, Liu Yuying thought to herself after they'd left. They just didn't want her to go to the expense.

She stood there wrapped in thought for a long time after they were gone. They seemed like such nice young men, and she wondered why her husband couldn't tolerate them. Was it him or was it them? Her spirits began to sink as doubts about her husband grew. As though she'd finally found the end in a tangled ball of thread and patiently begun to unravel it, she began to sort out her husband's shortcomings. Startled by this train of thought, she felt she was being unfair to Wu Guodong. He was, after all, lying sick in the hospital, and this was no time to be critical of him.

Liu Yuying walks along with a small comforter and mattress in her arms. Autumn is just around the corner and the weather has cooled. Xiao Zhuang needs warmer bedding at the nursery school. She looks at her watch. If she doesn't hurry, she'll be late. "Hurry up, Xiao Zhuang!" she says without even turning her head.

No response. She looks back and spots him bending over trying to tie his shoelaces.

"Hurry up, and don't trip!"

He comes running, his shoe flapping noisily. Still untied. He'll trip and fall if he isn't careful.

"Go ahead and tie it!"

Xiao Zhuang, an obedient child, stops, bends over, and fumbles with the lace. He still can't tie it. Liu Yuying sighs, knowing she'll have to help him. She lays down the bedding and ties her son's shoe for him. She feels like scolding him, but what good would that do? He's just a child, and she got him up extra early this morning. He didn't cry or make a fuss. What else could she ask?

Just then Mo Zheng rides up on his bicycle. He pulls up and steadies himself with his long legs. "Auntie Liu, hand me the bedding. I'll take it to the nursery for you. You and Xiao Zhuang can take the bus!"

Liu feels both uneasy and apologetic. When Wu Guodong was home, Mo Zheng made himself scarce, and she knows that as far as her husband is concerned, Mo Zheng isn't welcome at their place. It's as though in their shabby home they have some hidden gold Mo Zheng is just itching to get his hands on. According to Wu, Mo Zheng is like a stone in a privy—hard and smelly. Wu also has a low opinion of Ye Zhiqiu, finding it distasteful that an old maid like her would raise a thief like him as her own son. It was unheard of!

Now that same hard, smelly stone is trying to be helpful.

"Won't that make you late for work?"

"I'll just pedal a little faster."

"Watch out for cars."

"No problem!" He puts the bedding on the bicycle rack behind him and rides off.

Wu Guodong wakes up screaming, ending the naps of all the other patients on the ward.

One of them sits up. "Lao Wu, what is it?"

"I was just having a nightmare," he says apologetically.

"Scared me half to death!" another grumbles before rolling over and going back to sleep.

Only the young man in the next bed shows any curiosity. "What was it about?"

How can he explain a dream like that?

This neighbor of his, an umbrella repairman, spends his time in the hospital thinking not about his job, but about writing a novel. Unfortunately, his wages are barely enough to keep him in paper. Ream after ream, during the month or so Wu has been in the hospital, this man has produced a manuscript as thick as a brick. He lies there all day long, notebook in hand, jotting down every joke he hears and every anecdote associated with the other men's jobs. It all goes into his notebook, particularly the men's gripes.

Once, when the fellow was in the toilet, Wu Guodong looked through the books piled up on the stand beside his bed. They included a Chinese translation of essays by Plekhanov. Plekhanov? Wu had heard of him at the Party school. A revisionist who had opposed Lenin. Why read him and not Chairman Mao? He should be raising high the red banner of Mao Zedong Thought!

There was another book, *The Art of Sculpture*, with photos of nude figures—male and female—on the cover. Wu Guodong blushed bright red. He tossed it back onto the stand and shot a quick glance around the ward, relieved to see that no one was watching.

The young man's crew cut reminds Wu of Yang Xiaodong. Probably another of those misfits!

* * *

227

Wu takes the towel from the rack above his headboard and mops his sweaty face. He rolls over to avoid the smiling gaze of the young man in the bed opposite him, who is always staring at the other men with a sarcastic look. Sneaky eyes, someone to avoid.

A cool breeze sweeps under his blanket. He is sweating profusely; there's a heaviness in his chest, an oppressive weight that throws him into a panic.

What a bizarre nightmare!

Yang Xiaodong and his crew of misfits were squatting on top of a crane relieving themselves. Then the workshop turned into a gigantic skating rink. Yang Xiaodong and the others skated back and forth in front of their lathes. Everything was different—the lathes, the parts—nothing was as it should be, especially the newly finished parts: like newborn lambs, as soon as they popped out of the lathes, they jumped to the floor and lined themselves up alongside the machines. Nothing was still, everything was moving, making Wu Guodong dizzy. The public-address system blared, "And now, Comrade Ge Xinfa will do some imitations."

"Arf, arf . . . arf, arf." First a dog.

"Meow, meow . . . meow, meow." Then a cat.

"Arf, arf . . . meow, meow." A dog and a cat.

There in front of him, a snarling dog, its teeth bared, and a cat with its back arched, fur standing straight up, menacing.

"Stop!" he screamed. "Stop it now!"

No one paid any attention. They teased him, stuck out their tongues, made faces.

Lü Zhimin dug in his skates and skated up to Wu Guodong. "They won't listen to you anymore! Now we're in charge!"

Wu Guodong ran for the door, but it wasn't where it should be.

Wu Bin pointed to himself with his thumb. "We're the door from now on! There's a new set of skills now, and you'll have to learn them, understand?"

Wu Guodong stamped his foot angrily. He slipped and crashed to the ice. He woke up screaming.

How could he talk about a dream like that?

He sighs unhappily and spots a white chair beneath the window. Yang Xiaodong sat in that very chair when he came to visit Wu that morning.

Yang is now the workshop foreman. He's moved up quickly, but he seems out of place. The way he sat in that chair, legs draped over its arm, leaning up against the wall, the front legs raised off the floor.

The whole time Wu was talking with Yang, he kept looking anxiously at the chair, afraid that the rear legs might give out at any second. His patience gave out first. "Don't sit like that, Xiaodong, you'll ruin the chair."

Yang Xiaodong was a man who took criticism well. He lowered the chair to the floor, but quickly straddled the chair arm with his legs again. That's a chair, not a donkey! This, Wu thought indignantly, is our new workshop foreman!

Word had it that since Yang's appointment as foreman, no new Party secretary had been appointed. So who was to be in charge of political study? Chen Yongming had said, "Let's give Yang Xiaodong a chance."

A worker who's not even a Party member! He'll be in charge of everyone else's political study, but who's going to watch over his?

"What's new at the factory?"

Wu hadn't given much thought to Liu Yuying and the kids during his hospital stay. He didn't have to worry about things at home; women were supposed to take care of that. Besides, Liu was a good wife and mother and had the same work ethic as him. As long as the kids ate well, had warm clothes to wear, and were in good health, everything was okay.

He thought mainly about the workshop. All those men, with their unique personalities, and all those duties to be looked after.

"We had a dance on National Day!" It seemed Yang had decided to tell Wu the one thing he knew would incite a reaction.

"A dance? Who organized it?" Wu quickly raised his head from his pillow.

"The Youth League." Yang stroked his chin with his thumb and watched Wu out of the corner of his eye with a look that said, Let's see if that gets a rise out of you!

"Did you get factory Party Committee approval?" Wu found it all very disagreeable.

"It was Factory Manager Chen's idea." Yang said it like someone who had been handed the sword of authority.

That takes the cake! As if things weren't frivolous enough already, with sunglasses and bell-bottoms and cassette players. Now dances! Wu refused to believe that it had met with unanimous approval.

"What was the general reaction?"

"Reaction! Things were really hopping! Even the factory manager was dancing. Some of the technicians really know their way around a dance floor, not like the rest of us, who just bounce around. They were really smooth, like ballroom dancers. You should have seen Lao Chen and his wife waltzing around like pros. He even told us to dress up, including perfume and cologne. He told the guys to go up to the girls, make a little bow, and say, 'May I have this dance?' He reminded us that this was a good chance to get things started with any of the girls we had our eyes on! He's right, you know. It's a lot better than using go-betweens."

Yang was clearly pleased with how the dance had turned out. His thick eyebrows were hopping as he spoke.

The other patients were listening attentively. There were giggles and clicking tongues.

A college instructor said, "Dancing is a civilized social activity. I wonder why people still think it leads to antisocial behavior. That's the narrow-minded way of looking at it. Antisocial behavior is caused by ignorance. It occurs when there's no outlet for normal cultural urges. . . ."

What he said doesn't matter. Count on an intellectual to line up in support of bourgeois tastes! Just look at what he listens to on the radio: sappy lyrics like "The love of days past is now gone forever," or sentimental stories, like one about a girl who wants to attend a dance, borrows her friend's jewelry (Chen Yongming told them to dress up), and loses it. Pay for it? Sure, she spends the rest of her life working like a slave just to pay her friend back. And for what? For a dance! If that's not a tragedy, I'd like to know what it is.

The young umbrella repairman agreed: "That's right, that's just how it is!" Always ready to put in his two-cents' worth.

The butcher across the aisle said, "I don't know about cultural urges, but I'll tell you this—you can't be happy unless you eat meat at least twice a week." He laughed so hard the bed shook on its frame, filling the room with loud squeaks.

There's a guy, Wu Guodong was thinking, who probably buys plenty of the high-quality, low-priced meat that's available only to the privileged every day. I'd be surprised if he wasn't in here with a case of fatty liver.

Then there was the little old man who was a clerk in some office. They say he's not nearsighted, but when he reads the paper or the prescription label on the medicine the nurse gives him, he sticks it right up under his nose, as though he were trying to sniff the meaning out. Even when people were talking, he seemed to be smelling rather than hearing their conversation. "That factory manager of yours," he snorted, "sure has guts! Did you see in the paper how things have changed from last year? From some of the letters to the editor, it seems that dances are under the gun this year. They say that some work units have held dances in secret. Don't you see, there's something in the wind."

He was right, of course, but you got the feeling that he was in favor of trimming the sails.

People like him were always jumping on the bandwagon: what they railed against yesterday they supported passionately today, if that's what the newspaper advocated. People let them go their own way, like members of the *ancien régime* who had been kept on after Liberation.

Wu Guodong was genuinely concerned about Chen Yongming. If he kept doing things without worrying about the consequences, he was just asking to get tripped up over some minor incident, and that would be a real shame. There were things about Chen Yongming that impressed Wu. He always threw himself into his work, and Wu wasn't the type to write him off just because he disagreed with some of his activities. But the situation was getting worse. "So, how are things in the workshop?"

"About the same. We've separated Xiao Wei and Xiao Qin on the milling machine, and let them organize their own teams."

"Why? Their skills are about the same, so why not just put them on different machines?" Wu didn't like the idea of letting the two workers form their own teams.

"You know how much trouble they had working together, with Xiao Wei always complaining about Xiao Qin's work, and Xiao Qin complaining about Wei's attitude. They never got along. But now that they've formed their own teams, their work is better and so's their attitude." Yang could see that Wu was displeased. Did anything ever please the man? Yang began to feel sorry for him. No wonder he has hepatitis; even in good times like this he makes life hard for himself and is grumpy all the time. If he wants to be grumpy, that's his business, but why does he feel that everyone around him has to be the same? It's not worth it!

Yang Xiaodong had obviously gotten the idea from Chen Yongming's "free organization" policy.

The umbrella repairman jumped out of bed and gave Yang Xiaodong the thumbs-up. "It's like this! Take somebody away from a job he's not doing well and put him in the same kind of job someplace else, and he really starts producing. Why's that? The leaders are always grumbling that the workers are hard to lead, but they ought to ask themselves why they're unable to stimulate the workers instead. That's a talent, and a useful one at that. Like a kaleidoscope, always changing. The material demands of the common people aren't unreasonable. Things don't have to be perfect. Like buying clothes at a department store. If they don't have your size, make do with something a little long or a little short, as long as it's close. But they'd better not play around with the people's minds and hearts. A man's heart is the most precious thing in the world. That's where all hope, faith, ideals, morals . . . what I mean is, it's the source of everything good, and you can't treat it casually. People aren't born with cold, evil hearts. What wears them down is unfair treatment. As I see it, a good leader is one who values the hearts of the masses, and what's so hard about that?"

What business is it of his?

The butcher would have none of that. "Hey, there, you try being a workshop foreman and see!"

The umbrella repairman wasn't going to take that lightly: "If you can be one, why can't I?"

Wu Guodong glared at him. But he had second thoughts. He's right, sooner or later they're going to have to take over, whether the older generation wants them to or not. We can't outlive them.

But when this business of free organization moves into his

workshop, things have gotten out of hand. If everyone in China, a billion or more, wanted to do things their own way, Deng Xiaoping would have his hands full!

But worrying isn't going to solve anything. The workshop is Yang Xiaodong's responsibility now. What Wu has to do is get better and get back to the workshop. If they don't make him foreman again, so be it; but if they do, then he'll still do things the only way he knows how. "If you say it's all right," he said stoically, "then it's all right. But have you thought about what would happen if everybody decided to go to America and do their free organizing there?"

"Why do you have to make everything sound so bad? If people are happy with the way things are here, why should they want to go to America?"

The umbrella repairman laughed. "If you had your way, you'd put everyone, mind and body, into a vault and lock it up."

The old clerk sighed from his wealth of experience. "Young fellow, you don't know what it's like to suffer. If you did, you'd know how inviting a locked vault can be."

Wu Guodong suddenly felt extremely tired, worse than after a hard day at the workshop. He could barely keep his eyes open. After Yang left, he ate lunch and fell fast asleep. Then the dreams came. It's all Yang Xiaodong's fault. Why did he have to come anyway? He just made it worse.

After hanging up the telephone, Yu Liwen can't decide if she is doing Liu Yuying a favor or adding to her troubles. While inspecting the wards that morning, she noticed that Wu Guodong wasn't eating. So on an impulse she rang up Liu and recommended that she bring him some of his favorite food on her next visit.

Liu must be worn out, with a full-time job and two kids at home, and Yu Liwen would do it herself if she knew what Wu liked.

"I asked Lao Wu what he'd like," she said over the phone, "but he wouldn't say. I could make something for him, but even if it was his favorite dish, it wouldn't be the same as yours." Yu Liwen has never been one to joke about things like this. She means what she says. When people are sick, they need love and concern from their own family.

Liu thanked her for her kind thoughts, saying she'd be by that evening.

Just then the phone rings.

"Hello."

"Liwen? I'll come by this evening to pick you up." Chen Yongming. He must be calling from a pay phone, since he's shouting over the street noise—a blaring radio, car horns, even a bawling baby.

"Pick me up?" Strange. He hasn't sounded this romantic since they got married. What's gotten into him today? "Where are you?"

"I'm in town."

"What for?" She sounds a little angry. He only returned yesterday and ought to be home resting. What's so urgent it couldn't have waited a couple of days?

"I've got no choice. I can't talk now. I'll tell you when I see you. Wait for me when you get off, okay?"

Okay, he asks! He's always been in charge. Still he never sounds disrespectful or chauvinistically unreasonable when he tells her what to do. For some men, mutual understanding and love are really nothing more than their own individual feelings.

After getting off duty, Yu Liwen shoves a couple of medical magazines into her handbag and glances into the mirror. She smooths her hair and throws her overcoat over her shoulders, thrusting her arms into the sleeves as she walks downstairs. She has to laugh at herself. Look at her, like a girl going out on a date. Never, during all these years, has there been time for romance in their lives.

She's early. His jeep isn't there yet, so she sits down on a bench opposite the hospital entrance, waiting to see that determined face she never tires of looking at.

A janitor is sweeping away the last remnants of the day's work.

Yu Liwen loves this hospital.

The cream-colored building looks old and weatherbeaten, with puddles of filthy rainwater on the ground and dirty melting snow dripping from the roof. From a distance it looks like a basin overflowing with muddy water.

But to her it's like home. This is where she grew up, where she learned to walk. She met Chen Yongming here, her two sons were born here.

The hospital is like a tiny station on a railroad line where not even ordinary express trains stop. The passengers here aren't the kind who ride around in private cars, dress in fine clothes, and whose secretaries follow them around; nor are they the kind who wear patent-leather shoes and pull fancy suitcases with wheels. Most are working-class people who travel with wicker baskets, wear workpants cinched at the waist with homespun cloth sweatbands, and roll their own cigarettes of strong, homegrown tobacco. This out-of-the-way stop has a stationmaster who doubles as ticket seller and ticket taker; a dispatcher who is also the switchman; a signalman . . . But they are honest, hard-working people who see nothing disgraceful about getting their hands dirty.

It's people like this who make society run.

And she is one of them. She has few talents to speak of, and her name will never appear in the annals of medicine, nor will she ever be asked to speak at a medical convention. But she knows how to take a patient's pulse; she doesn't talk when she listens through a stethoscope; she never sleeps on duty; she refuses to speak to critically ill patients using medical terminology that only increases their sense of helplessness. A doctor's reputation is founded on fulfilling responsibilities to the sick and dying, not on the abstract history of medicine. Genius is nothing but the essence of humanity. All dogs, big and small, bark in the only voice they are given.

Yu Liwen has retained a habit she formed during her student days: at the end of each day she examines her performance to see if she has done everything she could.

Now, in the splendor of dusk, as she waits for her husband, she basks in the satisfaction of knowing that she did her job well that day. The exhaustion after a hard day's work brings her contentment. And that contentment will be complete as soon as her husband shows up.

Seven-fifteen, why isn't he here yet? She is growing uneasy.

Chen Yongming is always punctual; the only way to describe his concept of time is "precise." He demands that his subordinates' reports at factory production meetings not exceed ten minutes. "Strictly limiting your time will encourage you to be brief and to the point. There's no need for long, drawn-out, meaningless reports at marathon meetings. Ten minutes is a lot! If ten people speak at a meeting, that's an hour and forty minutes, not counting the time for voting." So the first thing he did at each meeting was lay his watch on the table in front of him. As soon as a speaker's ten minutes were up, he cut him off and asked him to sit down. It took some getting used to, and some people's problems went unresolved because of it. Since Chen's schedule was so tight, as soon as a meeting was over he was off to take care of other business; so some problems had to be held over to the next production meeting, or the next management meeting, or administrative meeting, or Party meeting, and since that had an adverse effect on the work and production, the person was subjected to criticism. But it ultimately had the desired effect of curbing the verbosity of his subordinates and teaching them to get to the point.

Yu Liwen's thoughts begin to turn morbid—has there been an accident? Chen drives too fast for his own good. Even in town he goes forty or fifty miles an hour. Sixty on the open road. If the roads weren't in such bad shape, or if he weren't worried that the car might break down, he'd go faster than that. He invariably scares the wits out of his passengers.

She walks out to the gate to look for him. Every time she spots a jeep, her hopes rise only to be dashed when it drives past.

Too bad she has a husband who knows how to drive.

She sits back down on the bench, feeling miserable and close to tears.

It's getting dark. A Red Flag limousine drives into the hospital compound. She doesn't give it a second glance. The last thing on her mind is why a Red Flag would be coming to this particular hospital.

"Getting worried?" Chen is standing in front of her.

Yu Liwen raises her apprehensive eyes. She is momentarily at a loss for words. Here's the man she's been anxiously waiting for. What was he doing in that car? And why is he so late?

She is angry and elated at the same time, like someone who's just found something she had lost. "I thought something happened to you!" she says with a pout. She glares at him.

Chen has a satisfied glint in his eyes. His wife loves him and is worried about him. She needs him. "I'm just fine."

"What are you doing in that car? I've been watching for your jeep."

Chen's spirits fall. There is a confused look on his face. The look of righteous indignation of a man who has suffered a blow to his self-respect, mixed with a bitter self-contempt and a cold, uncompromising harshness.

He turns and walks toward the car. "Thanks," he says to the driver. "You can go back now. I have some things to take care of here."

He walks back and sits down beside Yu Liwen, takes out a cigarette, and lights it. There is fire in his eyes. "Minister Tian's car . . ."

Yu Liwen moves closer to him as she waits for him to continue. He puts his arm around her, and she rests her head against his shoulder. Smoke from his cigarette gets into her eyes. Chen notices and blows the smoke away from her. He smokes furiously, without saying a word. She can see he's in a bad mood.

He flips his cigarette butt to the ground, a gesture that seems to say that he is discarding the unhappiness that fills him. He gets to his feet. "Come on, let's go see Wu Guodong."

"So, it wasn't me you came to see, after all!"

"You, too!" He seems to be his old self again. He winks at her playfully.

She follows him into the hospital.

On the way upstairs he says, "Something unusual happened today. Minister Tian called this morning and told me to give a report to the senior personnel at the Ministry on my recent inspection tour of Yunnan, Guizhou, and Sichuan. He came to the plant himself to pick me up in the afternoon. At the last meeting of plant managers held at the Ministry, he didn't even look at me. He went to every plant manager's office to say hello, every one but mine, that is. And don't tell me that was an oversight or that it didn't mean anything—it was nothing of the kind. People like that never do a thing without first thinking it over carefully, step by scheming step!"

"So why the change?"

Chen sneers. "There's talk that I'm being promoted to vice-minister, and Tian wants to make it look like it's all his doing, like he's my biggest supporter. But he's secretly spreading the word that I won't be happy till I'm made minister, and that I had that article published to raise my own stock at the expense of others. He says I'm trying to create the right atmosphere for my own advancement."

"I don't want you to be a minister!"

"Why not?" Chen stops and looks back at her, a couple of steps behind him. Her comment has taken him by surprise.

Yu Liwen looks away to avoid his intimidating, inquisitive gaze. "Because you'll have even less time to love me."

He roars with laughter. So she's afraid I'll get into even more trouble there, make even more enemies. The only person who disapproves of me now is a minister, and that's still making it plenty hard, personally and professionally.

Chen bends over, cups his wife's face in his hand, and kisses her thirstily. Not quite close enough. He puts his hands under her arms and lifts her up to the step he is standing on. Although she's smiling, she tries to struggle free. "What are you doing? What if someone sees us?"

"What are you afraid of? It's not against the law to kiss your own wife!"

She reaches up and smooths her hair. "Will you accept if they ask you?"

"Are you crazy? You'll never catch me becoming a minister!" A tone of longing has crept into his voice. "I want to make a success out of this factory, turn our Chinese motor industry into one that can compete with the United States and Japan." He is sounding more like a fervent dreamer or poet than a captain of industry. "I sure didn't make any friends when I gave my report today," he continues. "I bowled them over when I said that building up industry in the interior was a bad idea. All this talk of preparing for war is nonsense! The next war will be three dimensional, without any front lines or rear echelons, no this line or that. Their plan is a carbon copy of the Soviet model. It reflects a narrow, small-peasant mentality, like looking at the sky from the bottom of a well and taking the view to be true. The benefits of the expenditure of all this time, capital, and facilities are so slight it takes your breath away. I can't believe that the ultra-Leftist line in capital construction still holds sway when it's only led to one disaster after another. We should set up a court for economic crimes and put those irresponsible, wasteful bureaucrats on trial."

Chen is talking with such animation that his gray hair is fairly flying. He chops the air with his right hand to underscore each sentence, as though using a scythe on a field of invisible grass. His swarthy face is flushed. She considers herself lucky to have a man like this. She sighs contentedly.

Most of the patients remain puzzled. How could Wu Guodong have a wife like Liu Yuying? If she hadn't visited him several times already, they wouldn't believe it. She just doesn't look the part.

She reaches into an unfashionable vinyl handbag and takes out a jar filled with a mixture of peanuts, dried bean curd, hot peppers, and some lean pork, all in a thick paste. The bag is fifteen years old if it's a day.

"Feeling any better?"

"A little!" Is he trying to keep her from worrying or just responding mechanically? He is sitting cross-legged on the bed with a blank look on his face, like a monk in meditation.

"How are Xiao Qiang and Xiao Zhuang?"

"They're fine."

Their conversation is simple, muted, as though they want to conserve energy; either that or they are too embarrassed to act like a married couple around other people.

They soon run out of things to talk about. Liu Yuying sits silently in a chair beside the bed, not knowing whether to stay or leave, tucking her feet neatly under her chair like a schoolgirl.

The butcher can't believe his eyes. That woman's got a lot to learn. She comes to visit her old man but just sits there instead of whispering intimately in his ear. She doesn't look very happy, and you can tell she doesn't eat enough meat.

Chen Yongming and Yu Liwen arrive, appearing like two swans, flooding the ward with light.

Liu Yuying stands up and slides her chair over. "Here, Manager Chen, sit here!"

Chen waves her off. "No, you sit." He glances around the ward, then brings over two chairs from between the umbrella repairman's and college instructor's beds. He and Yu Liwen sit down. "Sorry it's been so long since my last visit," he says to Wu Guodong, "but I've been out of town. How are you getting along? Any problems?"

A businesslike smile appears on Wu's face. "No, no problems," he answers firmly and quickly. He seems worried that someone might exploit the situation if he hesitates even for a moment.

"That's good. But be sure to let me know if you need anything."

Liu Yuying turns to Yu Liwen. "Manager Chen is so thoughtful. He arranged for my transfer to a work unit closer to home and got Xiao Zhuang transferred to a neighborhood nursery school. It's been a great help."

Out comes the umbrella repairman's notebook and pen.

Wu Guodong shakes his head at the mention of Liu Yuying's job transfer. "I hear that the Department of Services used that transfer to wangle a truck from the factory."

"Yeah, we sold them a truck," Chen says matter-of-factly.

"Isn't that against policy? They don't have an allotment for a truck and they're not part of the capital construction plan." Wu genuinely believes that it was inappropriate.

"There's nothing wrong with that. The cutbacks in this year's capital construction have forced us to make adjustments in our plans. Some projects have been terminated, others slowed down, and there's been a big decline in contracts for goods. Filled orders have been returned, and if I can't sell trucks I can't meet payroll. We can't keep asking the government to bail us out, can we? The state has enough problems already, so we're on our own. Are we supposed to sit back and live off charity? I'll sell to anyone who has the money." His eyes sweep the faces of the other patients in the ward, as though they were potential customers. "We're going to bring out a new line this year," he says, making a salesman's pitch. "We'll be producing motorbikes. They're going to be a hot item."

Liu Yuying is annoyed at Wu Guodong for being so graceless after all Chen has done for him. "Guodong," she says, not caring that she has interrupted Chen, "that's no way to talk to someone who's trying to help."

Chen Yongming laughs. "Comrade Liu, there are still some things you can learn from Lao Wu. I respect the way he refuses to compromise his principles just because his problems have been taken care of. Whether those principles are correct or not isn't the issue. I don't expect him to sing my praises for helping out. That's what a factory manager is supposed to do."

Wu Guodong nods. On this point, at least, he and Chen see eye to eye. He has no trouble accepting Chen's explanation.

Liu Yuying, on the other hand, can't hide her embarrassment.

Yu Liwen leans over and comforts her: "Don't mind them, that's none of our business."

But Wu Guodong is still concerned. "Does the Ministry approve of supplying outside units with resources targeted for state-plan projects?"

"I made a report to Minister Zheng."

"What did he say?"

"He said that *all* engineering enterprises are going to face shortages and an inability to pay their workers because of this year's plan adjustments and capital construction cuts. A lot of construction units will go under, which will cut into the demands for machinery and force cutbacks in production. Increasing imports from abroad just compounds the problem. Sure, our engineering skills aren't up to snuff, but we also have an inferiority complex. Even though we have the capability to produce some of our own electrical equipment, we don't trust our own products. We have to work together to turn this situation around until we're not only self-sufficient, but competitive in international markets as well. We might be able to turn adversity to our advantage since this is an opportunity to implement some of our reforms. No one's expecting us to turn everything around overnight, but we can start taking a few steps in the right direction. The old methods of production won't work anymore, that's for sure. Now's the time to move. Some people will try to stand in our way, but they'll lose in the end. My first responsibility is to feed my workers. A man will scale a wall when his back is up against it; but a dog will jump over it. Hunger forces people to find a way to get food. I think Zheng hit the nail right on the head. It's up to us to get things done."

The wrinkles on Wu Guodong's brow deepen. Doubt is written all over his face.

The old methods won't work anymore? Why not? Production quotas are filled every year, aren't they? Take the Changchun Auto Works, where they still use production techniques from the 1950s on their Liberation trucks; they haven't had any complaints about not fulfilling their quotas. This reform for reform's sake—who's to guarantee that the new methods are any better than the old? And if they're not, we're worse off than before!

Fend for ourselves? What about our planned economy? Wu had learned at the Party school that a planned economy is one of the superior aspects of socialism. If we abandon that, how are we going to demonstrate the superiority of our system?

But what can he say? He can't argue with the minister and his factory manager.

Talk of surpassing foreign countries, on the other hand, is music to his ears. Nothing can keep us from surpassing the competition as long as we pull together and work as one. If we can recapture the spirit of the Great Leap Forward, within fifteen or twenty years we'll leave those other countries behind. Back then we used to chant, "Overcome difficulties, move mountains, part the sea. We'll beat England, just wait and see . . ." Those were wonderful days, among the happiest of his life. Every day they went out like a military parade on May First or National Day in front of Tiananmen Square, chests thrust forward, marching onward, arms swinging proudly, all those people united in their mission. But it all went downhill after that, as everyone began undermining Chairman Mao's revolutionary line. Now our society has been turned upside down, with everybody demanding "democracy." How could there be anything but democracy under socialism? The landlords, rich peasants, counterrevolutionaries, bad elements, and Rightists don't think so! The Rightists, they've all been cleared, and even the Dazhai-style collectives have been discredited. Now we've got free markets. Someone back home even said that fortune-tellers are back on the scene, and the hated "ox-devils and snake spirits" have been released from their cages. Things would be different if Chairman Mao were still alive! He said there should be a cultural revolution every seven or eight years. What they need right now is military control, so they can arrest all those people shouting about democracy and undermining Chairman Mao's revolutionary line, and put them behind bars.

Wu looks at Chen Yongming and fantasizes about being a military commissioner with the power to decide who will be locked up. Chen's innocent, childlike eyes are busily scrutinizing the jar of food Liu Yuying brought with her, trying to figure out what's in it, the same way he studies the functions of a new vehicle. He is interested in almost everything, and never does anything halfway, which is probably why he looks older than his years. It is his face, that intriguing mixture of childlike innocence and wisdom born of rich experience, that draws people to him.

All the other patients—the umbrella repairman, the government clerk, the butcher, and the college instructor—are mesmerized by what Chen has been saying. You'd have to be dead not to be caught up by this kind of talk.

People like this will never have a chance to meet Zheng Ziyun personally, but after listening to Chen they feel as though they know him. By articulating the things that are in their hearts, it is as though Chen has brought him there to walk among them, to talk with them like old friends.

The umbrella repairman puts down his pen and cups his chin in his hand, wishing he knew the man. It's not enough just hearing others talk about him. The smile on the clerk's face has changed from fawning to affectionate. Sincerity is contagious.

"Hm!" the college instructor says. "That minister of yours is a clear-headed man."

The butcher has his own way of showing respect and responds the only way he knows how. "Dr. Yu, look me up whenever you need meat. I can get you whatever you want."

Yu Liwen covers a smile with her hand.

Chen turns to Wu. "Anything I can do for you?"

"No, nothing. Besides, you're too busy to be coming over here all the time." He gets out of bed to see Chen to the door.

The other men also get up, as though Chen had come by to see all of them.

When Chen reaches the door, the umbrella repairman blurts out, "Drop in any time!"

"We'll see," Chen says. "I'll try to stop by from time to time, but who knows what will happen between now and tomorrow morning. I may be tied up with some crazy business. Don't bother to see me out. So long!"

He knows what he's talking about. The unexpected can happen at any time.

Fourteen

March forward boldly, sweep away all obstacles.

Ho Ting is about to make her eighth phone call.

All the necessary contacts have been made, and now all that remains is to get Vice-Minister Kong Xiang's approval for her second daughter to get a job in Beijing.

She looks at the phone on the desk, a confident smile on her face. It's all but assured.

Too bad there has never been a female general in the army. She's confident she could do as well as any man if she was given the chance.

But then, everyone knows that women have to fight harder than men to overcome the difficulties of possessing or achieving anything.

In the estimation of others, Ho Ting has had a pretty easy life.

She joined the revolution in 1945 as a singer for a radio station in northeast China. Though she's fifty-five now, her voice is still sweeter and more enchanting than most eighteen-year-old girls. She was admitted to the Party without a hitch. An intelligent, aggressive woman, she was determined to give up her work in cultural troupes and make a career in politics. She began her climb in political departments, starting out as a clerk and moving up through the ranks until Vice-Minister Kong Xiang promoted her to department head in 1962. Only the Cultural Revolution kept her from being a bureau director by now. She sneers every time she sees women like Mrs. Marcos or Mrs. Thatcher on TV news broadcasts making their mark on the international scene. Only circumstances kept her from becoming one of them. Although seldom discouraged, at times she turns her back to the TV screen and slinks into her room, feeling sorry for herself, as though her best days are behind her and life has cheated her. Then she gets in one of those moods where everything makes her angry: the movie star's smile on the wall calendar is just a little too pat (like women everywhere, she frequently finds fault with other women); her mother undercooks the braised pork; her daughter-in-law is driving her crazy with that constant plucking on the guitar; her husband, whose debilitating stroke more than ten years earlier ended his career and made his speech almost incomprehensible, is forever asking her to buy some of his favorite foods. His stroke hasn't lessened his appetite one bit. He might shuffle when he tries to walk, but anytime she doesn't satisfy his demands, he's off to the Ministry to accuse her of mistreating him.

Why has she been stuck with a husband like this? Just watching the way he eats, slobbering and drooling, disgusts her so much she could throw up. Every meal is torture. Since he can't control his bowels or bladder, a stench overwhelms her whenever he comes near. But she doesn't want him to die, even with the stench and slobber, not because he's her husband and the father of their children, but because of his monthly salary of two hundred yuan.

Mistreat? He's lucky to have a wife willing to live with a half-dead husband for over a decade. Where else would he find someone to keep him clean? Ho Ting was just over forty when he had his stroke, although she didn't even look that old. Hopes of a life of luxury, marital bliss, and shared responsibilities were dashed. Everything fell to her; she was in charge. Other women with her talents and status relied upon their husbands for an enjoyable life. Her schoolmate, Xia Zhuyun, now the wife of a vice-minister, was a perfect example.

Her own husband would undoubtedly be a vice-minister by now, too, if he'd remained healthy. How could things have turned out so badly? When she married him, he was a tall, handsome thirty-year-old cadre on his way up. He had it all then—status, looks, and talent. For women, marriage is a gamble at best.

But as soon as she walks out of the house, she is like a lioness on a hunt, single-minded and powerful.

Now stalking her prey, she crouches, drawing nearer and nearer, ready to pounce . . .

A knock at the door. "Come in!" Ho Ting calls out impatiently.

The door opens hesitantly. It's that technician again, the one from the hydroelectric station equipment section who applied for a generator. He stops in the doorway, not daring to enter the room, a timid man who is always at the mercy of others. Totally unsuited to his job.

On his last visit, Ho Ting asked him in a seemingly offhand way, "Does that place of yours produce tree-ear fungus?" She'd gotten interested in this delicacy after hearing it protected against hardening of the arteries. By reducing the risk of heart attack, she could look forward to a long life.

"Tree-ear fungus?" As though it were the first time he'd ever heard of it, to say nothing of knowing what one looked like.

What an oaf! Most people who graduated from college before the 1960s were like him. Even though they'd been through the Cultural Revolution, they didn't know the first thing about getting things done. Like that time the power station in Director Feng's hometown sent over some local products after receiving parts for their turbine. It's not as though they weren't paid for, after all! If this fellow hadn't been sent over by Director Feng himself, Ho Ting would have sent him packing long ago. Always sounding so self-righteous. What made them so sure that just because some projects had been in the pipeline for what seemed like forever, they wouldn't ever be completed?

"Department Head Ho," the man says, "when we sent our application for a generator last time, you asked to see the figures on part size and quantities and the blueprints. Now that you've had a chance to look them over, what else do you need from us?"

"God," she thinks, "I completely forgot!" It has completely slipped her mind. She can't even remember where she put the forms. She should have turned them over to the right people at the time. But she'd been too wrapped up trying to line up a job in Beijing for her daughter, who was about to graduate.

"Getting old, can't remember anything," she worries. "I used to be able to remember an entire day's activities without keeping a notebook."

Now what? She thinks for a moment, then says, "You'd better send over a couple more copies of the application. We still have to work things out with the Materials Division and the Machine Tools Bureau, you know, so one copy won't do it. As for what else we'll need, let's wait and see what those offices say. As far as we're concerned here, everything's okay."

"Good," he says with a nod. "That's fine. I'll bring them tomorrow." He doesn't suspect a thing.

"Here, have a seat," Ho Ting says as she pushes an armchair over.

"Oh, no, thank you. I'd better go and get things ready."

"Is there anything else I can do?" She's a bit uneasy.

"No, nothing. You've already done a lot by helping us get our generator." A slight bow to show his gratitude.

Uncustomarily, Ho Ting walks him out to the corridor. The perfect department head.

"You don't have to see me out."

Just then He Jiabin comes walking down the corridor, which reminds her of the purchase voucher for a Sanyo TV set for her section. She's planning to give it to Luo Haitao. Unlike a wage increase, it's not the sort of thing that anyone would object to, so she doesn't anticipate any trouble. He Jiabin is the only one who might make an issue of it, so she decides to sound him out. If he doesn't object, certainly no one else will.

"Say, Lao He, we've gotten permission to buy a Sanyo TV. How do you feel about it?" As though they were old friends, two people who always agreed on everything and had since the first day they met, a couple of staunch allies.

"I wouldn't throw money away on a damned TV! Not for the trash that's on these days!"

Just as she thought! She knew he wouldn't go along. But he hasn't even got enough sense to say something nicely once in a while. A few sugar-coated phrases wouldn't hurt his cause.

"Then what if I give it to Lao Luo?" As though He Jiabin were a Party secretary, and she wouldn't do a thing without his blessing.

"Why him? Because he's a Party member and a member of the branch committee? What about Engineer Xin? He's about to retire, so why not give it to him. There's no way he could buy one after he retires."

He doesn't appreciate anything!

"I'm asking your opinion."

What could Engineer Xin do for her, an old bookworm who's on his way out? No, she has to figure out a way to give it to Luo Haitao.

Ho Ting keeps a rein on her temper. They'll be discussing He Jiabin's application for Party membership at the meeting that afternoon. Just you wait!

She's starting to feel better. She dials a number.

"Hello."

"Secretary Cao, it's Ho Ting." A modest laugh. She works hard at staying on good terms with all the ministers' secretaries. They are the key to success, and even though she outranks them all, the way she speaks to them one might think they were her superiors. But that's the only way to consolidate your position in the Ministry, the only way to get ahead, to pass messages to a minister, or find out what's going on. Getting on their good side is worth any amount of trouble.

"Ah, Department Head Ho, what can I do for you?"

Not a trace of a bureaucratic tone.

"I'd like to speak with Vice-Minister Kong Xiang if he's not busy. Could you tell him I'm on the phone?" As though Secretary Cao had the power to decide who could and who couldn't talk to Vice-Minister Kong. As though he'd be doing her a favor by letting her talk to his boss. Kong Xiang always takes her calls.

"Hold on, I'll check." Just leave it to me is the message his tone conveys.

"Thanks very much."

"For what? You're one of the family."

She hears him put down the phone. Then the call is transferred.

"Hello, who's this?" Kong Xiang's Sichuan drawl.

"Don't you recognize my voice, Chief? I guess you've forgotten those of us in the trenches! A real bureaucrat! It's me, Ho Ting!"

He enjoys the playful complaint.

"Ah, ha, ha, it's you, Xiao Ho. You haven't lost your sharp tongue, have you! Where have you been keeping yourself lately?"

"Xiao Ho, is it? A gray-haired old lady like me! When have I ever failed to drop by when I was at the Ministry?" She is telling the truth. She always pays her respects to the old Buddha. "You're too busy with Party meetings or out of town on official business. Well, I'm calling to give you my self-criticism. You know He Jiabin, the author of that article that did so much damage to the Ministry. Well, he's in my department, and it's all my fault. I haven't been doing a good enough job with political work and should have had the situation under control. Of course, I didn't learn about the article until it had already been published. Vice-Minister Kong, you should be reading me the riot act."

Such penitence! Kong Xiang knows he has to hurry up and say something soothing or Ho Ting's remorse might worsen and ruin her appetite or interfere with her sleep.

"Don't you worry, Xiao Ho, it's over and done with now. Besides, there are things you don't know, such as who might have been using this for his own personal advancement. How could you know? This has nothing to do with you. You'll just have to do more to educate people like He Jiabin in the future."

"I never imagined that one little article could involve so much!"

Ho Ting knows perfectly well that Minister Tian gave the

complete history of the article at the Party Headquarters meeting, and how all those in attendance reacted. She's only brought it up to ingratiate herself and make it easier to get things done later on.

"We can't forget what Chairman Mao said about class struggle and the struggle between two lines. Even today there are people who hold up the banner of the Third Congress of the Central Committee to attack our Four Basic Tenets. They're advocating bourgeois liberalization and attacking the leadership of the Central Committee, as well as the Party line! This is a vicious attack on Chairman Mao himself! We have to bring these people under the dictatorship of the proletariat."

Talk of a dictatorship invigorates Kong Xiang more than a dose of ginseng. His voice has grown clear as a bell, the words begin to flow. He is young again, strong, an invincible tank, rumbling forward; the sound of his own cannon fire is music to his ears. He feels like shouting to the heavens. It is talk seldom heard anymore, and that's too bad. Things haven't worked out as they should have. He may be a vice-minister in charge of political work, but that's meaningless since he has no real authority.

With his qualifications, he feels, the right job would be minister of public security. To begin with, he'd been one of the "Little Red Devils" with the Communist troops at fourteen and made the Long March in 1934. Then there is his lineage: poor peasants for six generations or more. His children are all members of the Party or the Communist Youth League, and the rest of his family all true members of the proletariat. He had taken a Leftist stand in every campaign, even though he was branded a "capitalist roader" during the Cultural Revolution. But that was overturned at the Eleventh Plenum.

During the 1952 "tiger hunts" he shot several capitalists and profiteers. Meanwhile, Wang Fangliang and Zheng Ziyun, both of whom outranked him, were locked up for months!

In 1957, when the Rightists were under fire, he always exceeded his quota. But now the winds have changed, and all those people have been cleared. It sticks in his craw. He has been fighting a losing battle, and now all these people, who should be bowing and scraping before him, are his peers again. How can he

251

work under these conditions? What's happened to the prestige of the Party?

During the Great Leap Forward his goal was to organize all the cadres in the Ministry as military units. That is an area he knows something about. These days, with all their meetings, you can't get them to shut up about production and other business, and Kong never has one goddamn thing to say. But military control, that's right up his alley.

To Kong Xiang's chagrin Deng Xiaoping is back in power. What was so bad about attacking the Rightists? Now the current policies are shot through with Rightist ideas. He frequently goes over to see some of his old comrades-in-arms after work to drink and voice his complaints, angrily slamming his glass down on the table so hard it shakes. Deng, your days are numbered! You're the king of the Rightists, and you'd better watch out!

But come morning, he is back in his office, the wind taken out of his sails. When is this Deng fellow going to slip up? His confidence is growing every day, and over the past couple of years the people have been leading calm, peaceful lives—no criticism sessions, no parades, no slogans, no arrests of counterrevolutionaries. So what is Kong supposed to do? He has nothing but time on his hands, and he hates it.

Last year he managed to nab a technician at the research institute who'd said at one of the political study sessions, "I don't think there's enough democracy within the Party. Some people are promoted on the say-so of one person instead of being elected. What's the difference between that and the imperial fiats of feudal times?"

Kong wasted no time in getting the Political Department to print this comment up as a bulletin and fire it off to the newspaper. The bulletin pointed out that talk like that showed the new direction of class struggle. People like this, who no longer believe that class struggle is the power behind social development, are the embodiment of an ultra-Rightist stance.

He called the Public Security Bureau more than once to urge them to arrest the technician as a counterrevolutionary. He was a busy man those few days, running the Political Department at the Ministry and the Public Security Bureau ragged. It got so bad that no one in the Public Security Bureau would accept phone calls from the Ministry of Heavy Industry. All Kong talked about was labels, intimidation, demands to act on principle and policy line; and his tone of voice implied that if they didn't arrest the technician, he'd accuse the Public Security Bureau of shielding a counter-revolutionary.

One fellow in the bureau quipped, "This minister is out-public-securiting the Public Security Bureau, and if we're not careful he'll have us all put under his dictatorship."

Kong likes to spend his free time reminiscing about his life as a mainstay of the glorious Leftist line. Letting his imagination take over, he dreams about how, as minister of public security, he'd exercise military control over disruptive elements. Daydreams . . .

Ho Ting, who knows exactly what Kong Xiang is getting at, has a broad grin on her face. Why not? He can't see her.

But she doesn't have time to listen to him scratch this personal itch of his, because if he's called away on urgent business, the phone call will have been wasted.

"I also have a personal favor to ask of you, Minister Kong."

Normally, she wouldn't bring up something like this over the phone, nor would she go to his office, since his secretary could be expected to overhear her and might use it against her later. Just one comment can spell the difference between success and failure. These old-timers may be so muddle-headed they can barely speak without the help of their secretaries, but they know how to hold onto their official posts. The minute they're confronted with some-thing they don't quite understand or that looks like trouble, they're off and running—the other way. If nothing else was learned from the Cultural Revolution, everyone agrees that the less you do, the better off you are.

In a matter like this, Ho Ting understands, the more people kept in the dark the better. It's all right to go through the back door, as long as you do it on the sly.

She knows, too, that she can't go to Kong's home. Back in 1962, when he was her boss in the cadre division, she visited his home often, which was normal enough. But her visits became even more frequent when she was bringing him reports on her immediate superior, until she was virtually thrown out by Kong's wife. It still rankles. That wife of his, a nurse who never went to work but still drew a salary, said nastily, "I suppose you think a pretty face is all it takes!" Well, she'd show her. She wasn't someone you could walk all over!

Nothing ever happened between her and Kong Xiang. But women have ways of getting things done when they're dealing with men. And as long as principle isn't involved, what's wrong in exploiting that advantage? She isn't at all like that commonplace wife of his, whose only hold on her coarse vice-minister of a husband is her looks—a pretty decoration in his life. No, she'd use her abilities to climb to the rank of bureau director, or even higher. Who knows, maybe even a minister! If she isn't the equal of that worthless Feng Xiaoxian, something is wrong. The one female vice-minister in the Ministry graduated from college in 1948, after running a flour mill with her cousin. She only has four years' seniority over Ho Ting, and if she is one of the nation's "liberators," Ho Ting is one of its "builders"!

"You remember my youngest daughter, Niuniu?" she continues. "The one who called you her foster daddy when she was little? Well, she's about to graduate from college, and as it turns out, there's an opening in one of our institutes. They've agreed to take her on and have already made a report to the Ministry. They say all they need now is your approval."

"Institute? There was something about that . . ." Kong Xiang is trying to recall.

"Has it already crossed your desk?" Faster than she expected, certainly faster than usual.

"No, it's just that someone came to me with news that one of our department heads and his wife both died recently, leaving three children, two of whom still need looking after. The elder boy is about to graduate, and they hope he'll be assigned to a job here in Beijing."

So that's it!

They want to make a fool out of me, forcing me to scrape and claw for everything!

Kong Xiang shouldn't have been so open, since this involves me. What can I say now? My hands are tied.

Hard to tell if Kong Xiang is making things tough for me or if he's just making sure I know that his word is what counts. He's so casual it's obvious he's not concerned about how the news affects me.

Her pale face grows red and splotchy, as though she has a rash. She feels like slamming down the receiver. But common sense warns her that that would be the wrong thing to do. She releases her anger by yanking the cord and twisting it tight. *Crash!* A teacup is knocked over, spilling tea on her desk, soaking her papers, her confidential handbook, and the edges of the felt pad under the glass top. She sweeps the papers and handbook onto the floor.

She is fuming: Damned hypocrite!

It was she who found a job in her department for his son-in-law, who'd never learned a thing except class struggle in that proletariat college of his! Once they get what they want out of you, people like him just toss you aside. They have no memory. Back in 1974, when the Ministry was trying to restore the level of efficiency to pre—Cultural Revolution days, people were tripping all over themselves trying to get their relatives hired, while every cadre school in the country was packed with competent comrades just waiting to be reassigned. Back home, aging parents and young children were waiting for someone to come and take care of them. But when it was all over, they'd been forced out by people with better contacts and no brains. In times like this only the decent folk suffer.

Anger, indignation, defiance, revenge, schemes crowd her heart. On her Party application she wrote that she had faith in communism, but in day-to-day living she's a realist. Back down? Not on your life!

The three children of that now-deceased couple will be around for a long time, and they'll get their jobs one after the other, handing them down, from one to the other. But her time is limited. In the years left to her there's always the danger that she'll be dragged down by some illness or other. If that happened, would anyone come forward and take care of things for her? She couldn't be sure. The fact of the matter is, human relationships are gradually giving way to materialism. It's getting worse, and there's no end in sight.

But how much damage could one comment by Kong Xiang do? She isn't about to throw in the towel yet. It's all up to her now.

Instead of worrying about his intentions, she'll just play along and wait for her chance to get what she has coming; she won't let him conveniently forget their past.

"You're right, those three kids need someone to look after them. Things aren't as bad now as they were a couple of years ago, when jobs were so tight. With all the new institutes opening up, there's a need for talented people. Honestly, if things were better at home, I wouldn't even have brought the matter up. In all these years on the job, I've never put my own needs first. They're always the hardest to take care of, anyway, unlike the needs of others, which are all in a day's work. You know how things are with me, with an invalid at home. It's hard enough just taking him to the hospital and helping him up and down the stairs. And that's only one of my troubles. Now I'm a department head and I have to set a good example for the others, especially since we're all involved in the Four Modernizations. All this has an effect on my work. I really need someone to help around the house. I didn't know where to turn, since I've never learned how to go through back doors. That's why I came to you. But I've already said too much. You know all about my problems. If you can't do anything this time, would you mind keeping an eye open for your 'foster daughter' just in case something else comes up?"

"Ah, Niuniu!" The changed tone of voice is proof that he knows he's let her down. "She's probably forgotten her old 'foster daddy' by now. Tell her to come see me."

Okay!

Ho Ting has managed to keep the door open, and she can breathe a little easier.

After hanging up the phone, she leans back and sighs. She reaches down and scoops up the papers and confidential handbook she swept onto the floor in anger, then wipes off the damp desk. Several smiling children standing on the Great Wall look up at her from beneath the glass top. They're all grown now, healthy and good-looking, just like their father in his youth. When would their wings finally be strong enough for them to make it in the world without having to rely on their mother?

Shi Quanqing is right in front of Ho Ting in line at the canteen. "Drop by my office after lunch," Ho Ting says to him conspiratorily.

What could she want?

She has him so perplexed he can't enjoy his lunch. He just wolfs down his rice.

Has He Jiabin brought some new charge against him? Did someone object to the subsidy he still draws for his son, who already has a job? Are they going to cancel it? Did Lao Qian report to Ho Ting that Shi had gotten drunk and complained that Ho was so intent on getting a raise for Luo Haitao that she's overlooked his?

Will it be good news or bad? Ho Ting is so unpredictable, you can never be sure. He Jiabin was right on the mark when he said, "She's probably going through menopause."

After giving her enough time to finish her lunch, he goes to her office and knocks on the door.

She is completely absorbed in weighing some tree-ear fungus. He experiences a feeling that's not quite resentment and something other than sadness. He had had a purchasing agent for one of the relay stations buy it, and it just arrived that morning.

Ho Ting doesn't even look up. She fiddles with the scale, raising the steelyard as high as it will go. "See there! When you take the paper wrapping off, each catty is one ounce underweight, altogether two ounces!"

Shi Quanqing keeps himself from saying, "Maybe it wouldn't be if you didn't raise the steelyard so high."

Two ounces short! It would be a bargain even if it were four ounces short. The stuff costs eight-fifty a catty when you can even find it! The man at the relay station said that was the restricted price, but he may have known that it was for Ho Ting and paid for it himself.

257

Is that what she called him in for? This woman can see the dark side of anything! Maybe she thinks he skimmed two ounces off the top for himself. He must be crazy to do her favors like this.

As Ho Ting takes a plastic bag from her purse, Shi rushes over to help her hold the mouth of the bag open, then waits patiently as she dumps in the two catties of tree-ear fungus.

After clapping her hands together, she dusts off her clothes, then walks over and closes the door. "Do you know where Lao Luo went yesterday?" she asks him confidentially.

"No."

"Qingdao. To take care of that business of yours."

The news stuns him.

Prior to Liberation, Shi's father had opened a fabric shop in Beijing with some of his friends. His family had majority control. On the eve of Liberation, his father had sold his stock and opened a mill in Qingdao under Shi's name. There was no way he could deny it, since he'd gotten fixed interest on his investment when the private ventures were bought out by the government.

After joining the work force, he had kept this background secret, and it wasn't found out until he applied for Party membership. His application has been held up ever since because of this incident.

Ho Ting went to bat for him several times at branch meetings: "We shouldn't judge people on the basis of class origin alone."

But Guo Hongcai, a narrow-minded cadre with a worker-peasant background, stuck adamantly to his opposition: "This isn't just a question of class origin. He tried to cover up his past, and that makes it a question of attitude. I don't think he's qualified to join the Party yet."

His view was shared by the majority of the committee, and they made their recommendation accordingly: "Not yet qualified to join the Party."

So Ho Ting waited until Guo was out of town on an assignment to submit the report, changing the recommendation to "Basically qualified to join the Party." Guo was filled in when he returned from his assignment and confronted Ho Ting. "When was the decision made to change the recommendation to 'Basically qualified to join the Party'? Did you hold another meeting while I was out of town?"

No way to hide the truth about this one. "No."

"Then why was it changed?" Guo went immediately to the Party Committee and issued a protest, which gave Ho Ting a black eye.

Now Ho Ting had sent Lao Luo off to Qingdao to look into things there. Her intent was obvious, and the only question remaining was how to smooth things over.

"You've got to come up with a plan to handle this Qingdao matter. Why don't you go to your uncle and try to get some answers out of him?"

Her meaning is clear. She wants him to make an issue out of it again.

"My uncle's not well. His mind's not clear at all."

"Then ask your mother!" She'd lead him by the hand if she had to.

"My mother doesn't remember."

"So help her remember!"

Of course! Why hadn't he thought of that? Another case of onlookers being smarter than players. No, that's not it. He doesn't have the guts to think along those lines. He is frequently shocked by Ho Ting's outrageous schemes. How could she even consider something like that? Further evidence for Shi that he is more qualified to be a Party member than Ho Ting.

But in the long run this might just make the humiliation he has suffered over the tree-ear fungus worth it. He smiles ingratiatingly as he thinks to himself, "Lady, I know what's on your mind. You're not doing me a favor, you're just trying to get another follower. Well, I'll swallow my pride for now, but once I get my Party membership and everything's turned around, I'll get even for all these years of being kicked around. Just you wait and see!"

The marathon meeting has already gone on for three solid hours. Fang Wenxuan can see that the old-timers are tired and bored. They are slumped in their easy chairs, half-asleep. More and more of them have been getting up to go to the bathroom or answer phone calls.

Ho Ting is giving her biased report on the branch committee discussion regarding He Jiabin's Party application. An obvious attempt to influence the Party Committee to overturn the branch committee recommendation.

Ho Ting is a master politician. Fang has heard stories about her unorthodox political maneuvering, but this is the first time he's seen her in action. He is appalled by her behavior. And the fact that she hasn't even glanced at Feng Xiaoxian is all the proof he needs that they are in this together.

Feng, who is sitting opposite, has already poured himself two glasses of strong tea to keep his energy up and his mind clear, like adding fuel to a tank just before it levels the road ahead.

Everyone at the meeting knows that Feng is biding his time.

But they keep their feelings to themselves and sit there while He Jiabin's qualifications are discussed from every angle.

Feng's strength lies in his ability to "brew." The two glasses of strong tea are a sure sign that he's preparing for a long fight.

He hadn't shelled out one-twenty for that magazine for nothing!

If his own son hadn't mocked him, he'd never have bought it. "Hey, Papa, you're famous! There's a magazine article that says you're a coward. You'd better read it."

His own son!

Since he'd paid for the magazine, he read it cover to cover. There was a sordid novella and a bunch of silly writing about "love" among a bunch of degenerate women, and the traitorous thoughts of anti-Party intellectuals. If that wasn't the raving of people who oppose the Four Basic Tenets, what was it? As though He Jiabin didn't cause enough trouble in the Ministry, now he's intent on stirring up public opinion and joining forces with people like this.

Having been informed of Song Ke's speech at the Party Headquarters meeting, Feng concludes that joining the fray at this point won't help his cause. He'll take care of things, but not out in the open. There's plenty of time; he'll just wait for an opening. He knows he won't have to wait long.

Ho Ting's objections fit in perfectly with Feng Xiaoxian's plans. She's putting into words the anger and suspicion that article has stirred in him. There didn't seem to be anything on the surface that lent itself to attack, but it rankled.

All the other objections against the author could be thrown out, since he only needed one: years of public disapproval of He Jiabin's improper relationship with Wan Qun.

These old-timers are always ready with opinions on the usual topics, but on the subject he has in mind, they'll clam up and just sit there with their eyes lowered.

We'll see what tune Fang Wenxuan will sing now.

Wan Qun . . . Fang's thoughts are on his encounter with her that morning at the Ministry gate. Instead of saying hello, she just glared at him. By then he'd been informed that she was being transferred.

How could she blame him? Feng Xiaoxian had arranged to have her transferred to a factory in the suburbs while Fang was out of town. His pretext was to return her to a specialized unit. Fang learned about it only after he returned. It must have been in the works for some time, it happened so quickly. His position as a bureau director was meaningless, since Feng Xiaoxian, who was in charge of personnel, had made up his mind. Fang couldn't bear to think about it. If only she'd raised an objection . . . but she wasn't in the habit of asking favors. This time he really let her down!

Ho Ting's speech today is clearly another veiled attack on him by Feng Xiaoxian.

This time they're going too far. They've been trying to pin this on him for years. What law was broken? What has he done that is immoral? Has he ever slept with Wan Qun? Has he even kissed her?

Oh, how he'd like to get to his feet, bang the table, and pour out all the conflict and pain he's carried with him for years, admit that he has vacillated, has been selfish, has regrets, . . . lay it all out there for everyone to see, and make it clear that what he should be censured for is not what they're talking about, but his inability to be a true materialist and his lack of courage to make a clean break with the past. But that applies to them, too, and they should be censured right along with him.

Fang's face is drained of color, and he is trembling; but he forces himself to keep cool. He's Fang Wenxuan, not He Jiabin. Any show of emotion is a sign of political weakness.

"You say the masses have been critical? Who in particular? Discussing an application for Party membership is serious business, and every allegation must be backed up by solid evidence. Comrade Ho Ting, I'd like you to be more specific."

Fang watches Feng Xiaoxian smoke a cigarette furiously. His decision to stand his ground this time has a calming effect on him. He'd do one last thing for Wan Qun: he'd clear her name. Why the last thing? Wouldn't they ever see each other again? All in all, that would probably be best. Since he has nothing to give her, he can ask nothing of her.

It apparently hasn't occurred to Ho Ting that Fang Wenxuan isn't planning to dodge the issue. That in itself is out of character. She grows uneasy. "That's what Guo Hongcai said."

"Anyone else?"

"Comrade Shi Quanqing."

Fang walks over to the telephone and dials. "Electrical Department? Send comrades Guo Hongcai and Shi Quanqing to the Party Committee meeting right away."

The old-timers, who have gotten their second wind, sit up straight again.

The atmosphere in the room has grown tense. The second hand on the wall clock speeds along, pushing the time reluctantly forward. Even the sound of replacing a tea-glass lid is deafening.

Guo Hongcai enters the room wearing the sort of cunning smile generally seen only on the faces of peasants used to keeping their feelings hidden.

Shi Quanqing, on the other hand, lowers his head as soon as he sees the scene in front of him, a look of panic in his eyes, like a man on trial.

Fang Wenxuan defers to Ho Ting. She's a woman, after all! Let her prove her allegations.

But she freezes and can't open her mouth.

It's up to Fang, after all. "Comrade Guo, Comrade Shi, you told Comrade Ho that you observed improper behavior by Comrade He Jiabin, specifically in his relationship with Comrade Wan Qun. I'd like you to tell us exactly what you know."

"Not true," Guo Hongcai replies. "I never said anything like that. I complimented him for helping Comrade Wan Qun. There aren't many people who would deliver charcoal to someone in the snow."

Fang Wenxuan refrains from turning and looking at Feng Xiaoxian and Ho Ting.

Every chair in the room is squeaking.

Glug . . . glug . . . glug. For some reason, Fang is reminded of the struggles of a drowning man.

He shifts his attention to Shi Quanqing.

Shi tries to look him in the eye, but he can't do it. He lets his gaze wander to the stained wall behind Fang, the tea table in the corner, the red telephone. "I saw them, once I saw Comrade He Jiabin come out of Wan Qun's home late at night."

"What time was it?"

"Um, after ten."

"You're sure you saw him coming out of Comrade Wan Qun's home?"

"It was her building."

"How did you know he was there to see her and not someone else in that building? Lots of families from our bureau live there. I know, I've been there." He turns and looks straight at Feng Xiaoxian. "Comrade Feng, are there any other points you'd like cleared up? Now's your chance."

"Let's hear what Comrade Ho Ting has to say."

He's not going to let the ball stay in his court for long. No sense taking the heat for someone else. But this startling turn of events has taken him by surprise. Too bad!

From the moment Guo Hongcai and Shi Quanqing entered the room, Ho Ting has known what to do. She'll neither admit that she's wrong nor affirm that they're right. "This isn't the place to be discussing matters like this. I'll talk it over with Comrades Guo and Shi later."

Some people's faces don't turn red even when they're caught in a lie. It's a terrifying trait in a woman.

Fang Wenxuan's eyes sweep the room. "Is this matter cleared up then?" He gains a sense of smug satisfaction, if not delight, from the nodding heads.

"Fine then. Thanks for your help."

Guo Hongcai is reluctant to leave. He was hoping that Fang would question him further, so he could expose Ho Ting enough that it would be impossible for her to get back at him.

Shi Quanqing, on the other hand, slinks out of the room like a dog with its tail between its legs.

"Shall we vote now?" The color has returned to Fang's face. He leisurely takes a cigarette from the box in front of him, lights it, and takes a long, slow puff. He's earned this one. "Let's go over things again," Feng Xiaoxian drawls, clearly dissatisfied and displeased with the way things have gone.

"Haven't we already gone over everything?" One of the old-timers has run out of patience.

"But we don't have a unanimous opinion!" Time for him to "brew" again.

"The majority rules here."

Feng Xiaoxian is going to have to brew alone.

Fang Wenxuan finally lets some emotion creep into the discussion. "We're all revolutionary comrades here. Think back to what you were feeling when you joined the Party. We're dealing with a person's political life. Is it right for us to oppose him on the basis of someone else's hidden agenda? Why must we be unanimous? Is it fair to keep good people out of the Party just because we can't reach a unanimous decision? Unanimity is impossible in some cases, and that's just how it is. If two people can't agree on a color for a washbasin, one person gives in after a while and that settles it. But on important matters like this, people just don't give in so easily. I propose that we put it to a vote now." He raises his right hand solemnly.

Passed!

Just then the phone rings. Fang picks it up. His face grows deathly pale. "It's the hospital. Comrade Wan Qun has been hit by

264

a car, and they say it was already too late to save her when she was brought over."

Feng Xiaoxian will never forget the accusing look Fang gave him as he made that announcement, as though he were a murderer. Why glare at him like that? Accidents happen.

But he can't keep slumping in his chair like that. He sits up, then gets to his feet, hardly daring to breathe. He has forgotten his plans to make things hard for Fang Wenxuan. Maybe it *is* his fault. But if so, how? He feels like a prisoner who has been mistaken for a condemned man and is facing a firing squad. What can he say?

Feng is not a believer in all that nonsense about retribution, but he can't shake the images of Wan Qun that seem to have burned themselves onto his eyelids. He can still see her sitting across from him as he informs her of the transfer, her rail-thin arms folded, the skin on her face taut as a drum, her eyes sunken. She sits there with narrowed eyelids as she stares at him with a bitter smile. Her smile puts him on the defensive. Go ahead and smile. You'll be crying soon enough.

She doesn't cry, but the smile disappears. She glares at him obstinately, squinting with one eye as though peering into a microscope.

She can't treat a senior Party official like that! How can he justify not subjecting her to reeducation in order to bring her back into the fold? At this rate she'll make a serious mistake sooner or later, and just being transferred won't be enough.

Feng Xiaoxian has forgotten the bizarre circumstances that put Wan Qun in such a precarious position. She hadn't done anything to deserve what has happened to her.

Now he can't shake the thought that if it weren't for the job transfer, she'd have been sitting in her office instead of riding her bike to get some rope to tie up her suitcase or to take care of the children's school transfer, . . . whatever she was doing at the time. Feng's heart aches as though someone is pounding him on the chest.

* * *

Fang Wenxuan seems unsure of where he's going. Or why. The car is speeding along as though on urgent business, as though someone were waiting for him at his destination. But no one is waiting, no one needs him, he has nothing to look forward to.

Someone waited for him once, there in that tiny, dank room with the low ceiling. "This would be a great place to grow mushrooms!" Who had said that? Probably He Jiabin. And how about their feelings, were they like mushrooms, too, growing in a dark, dank place where the sun never shone?

The buildings, the pedestrians, and the cars whizzing by seem to be collapsing before him, rolling under the wheels of his car. He reaches up and taps the driver on the shoulder. "Xiao Yan, slow down a little!"

The driver slows down, thinking the old fellow must be afraid of an accident.

She's gone, the one person who meant so much to him. No more than a few hours earlier he had been thinking that they shouldn't see each other anymore. Well, he won't be seeing her now; he is going to say goodbye, to look at her one last time. What was she thinking as she passed into that other world? Did she hate him? Or forgive him? People view life as a long, long road. He has already walked that road for several decades, but the distance between life and death takes no longer to travel than the blink of an eye. In less than a second she was gone, and no one could bring her back. Oh why, when she was still alive, hadn't he . . .

". . . We've got the driver in custody," a policeman tells him in the hospital waiting room. What else was he telling him? Where it happened, and how. But what good does that knowledge do anyone? She's gone. Where is he to find her? How long will it take for the world to create another woman like her? When that day comes, will he recognize her? All she'd have to do is sing "Havana Dove," wear that green dress, cock her head, look straight at him with those trusting eyes, and ask him, "Have I got it right?"

The doctors tell him how they tried to save her even though she was dead on arrival. Now who is going to save him? Can't the doctor hear the sorrowful sounds of his broken heart? There is no one to comfort him, since no one knows that he has lost the most

266

precious thing in his life. It's almost comical the way he has to keep from looking mournful or letting tears come. He isn't the first person to be part of a farce like this, nor will he be the last. How he wishes his heart would just stop then and there. He wouldn't have to keep standing there nodding his head, he wouldn't have to say a thing. . . . God, so many people milling around! What are they doing here?

Footsteps echo in the stairwell leading to the basement. Clear, detached, ruthless. The doctor is taking him to the "slumber chamber." It sounds so odd, yet that's what it is: a place for eternal slumber. But what about those they leave behind? Have the others been here already? Is he the last one? How did they manage to get through it?

He Jiabin stops tactfully before the entrance.

Thank you!

If only the doctor would stay outside, too.

But the doctor couldn't know what Wan Qun meant to him. So cold!

All those white sheets, each covering a concluded story. The final calm that follows the storm.

"25832." She has become this number. Her final reward. A good high figure. Will it be cremated with her? Probably not. She'll be given a new one at the crematorium. That final digit, so ironic, he wishes it were true.

They didn't clean her up very well. She is still a bloody mess. Clumps of hair on her crushed head are matted with dried blood, like bundles of rice shoots lying in the fields at the cadre school, waiting to be planted. Is that the same hair that blew in the spring winds? He could still see it flying in the wind like the wings of a bird.

That crushed head had held far more painful memories than happy ones. Where, in all this gore, had he existed? There, in that mess by her ear? Why isn't there some sort of sign? Hard to believe that this sticky, decomposing mess was once the source of her thoughts and feelings, that it had governed her life, body and soul. They say that at this stage people are all the same, but this one's different, this is Wan Qun.

Her face looks like a rubber mask that's been twisted out of shape by a child, then abandoned. Her eyebrows are horribly contorted; her once-expressive lips, rather than giving testimony to her final anguish, are parted in a willful, childish expression.

Why aren't there any chairs here? Fang needs to sit down.

Probably no one had sat by her sickbed and spoken quietly to her. How lonely her days must have been! The narrow white sheet, the shrunken body lying beneath it, the mangled, bloody head, the grotesquely twisted features—they all testify to the unjust fate of a singularly uncomplaining woman. Now she's gone, leaving to him an unspoken condemnation.

You, Doctor, why don't you condemn me, despise me, instead of standing there so patiently and respectfully? People seldom see beyond the surface. There's nothing to be afraid of. Doctor, I want you to remember this fantastic story.

Fang bends over and kisses her swollen, bloodstained lips. The first time and the last. It seems to him that her lips twitched, as though in anger. No, his vision was just clouded by the tears welling up in his eyes.

Fifteen

I t sounds like an American presidential campaign speech!
Why was this meeting called in the first place? What's the point of that pack of lies? You might be able to fool the others, but not Wang Fangliang!

The results of the last round have been announced: 887 to 406. Zheng Ziyun has been elected to represent the Ministry of Heavy Industry at the Twelfth Party Congress.

Tian's speech is disgusting. Wang would be better off going back to his office and signing some papers or reading the unexpurgated version of *The Golden Lotus* he recently acquired.

But Tian has just started, and Wang will have to wait awhile before slipping out.

To keep from yawning up there where everyone can see him, Wang begins studying the faces of the people sitting in the front row of the auditorium. But a fat woman sitting in the corner is already yawning. They say it's contagious, which is apparently true, since her neighbor starts to yawn, too. Feeling somehow seduced, Wang clamps his mouth shut and quickly turns to look at some other faces.

The ass-kissing head of the Housing Department, sitting front-row center, is taking notes and nodding, a reverent look on his face, as though he were listening to an imperial edict. He's doing everything but prostrating himself before the stage. No one knows this act better than Wang. Back in 1958, during all those meetings, every time he heard one of those ridiculous boasts, he nodded and took notes, just like this fellow. Those so-called notes were actually drafts of his own poems, and it was his good luck that things weren't as bad then as they got during the Cultural Revolution, when people fought to come up and look at what you were writing. If someone had done it then, he wouldn't have had to wait until the Cultural Revolution to get locked up.

So this is nothing new to him, and just watching someone else do it brings back intoxicating memories.

During the Yan'an period, whenever one of the Central Committee members gave a speech, there Jiang Qing would be, at the front, right in the center, nodding and taking notes. Wang had had the dubious honor of sharing a bench and desk with her at the Party school. Once he'd managed to get her to sing a song for him, for which he later was locked up for ten years. A case of "ruthlessness is a sign of greatness." One of Tian Shoucheng's favorite sayings.

Before the Cultural Revolution, one of the directors of the Instruments Bureau asked Tian, "Did a Party member say that? It sounds like something you'd hear from a gangster!" For that she was exiled to the Northeast for more than ten years. She learned what gangsters were capable of.

Now here it is again: ruthlessness as a sign of greatness.

Tian Shoucheng would attend the congress as the representative of a certain province. This would be an unusual—comical is more like it—way to handle things. How many members of the Party from that province even know who Tian is? Although he was born there, has worked there, and has even come into contact with many comrades there, what percentage of the Party members in that province belong to his circle? Probably some couldn't say whether he was a Party member or not. But he was chosen to represent and speak for them at the congress. What did he know of their opinions and their desires? Were they aware that he had been a faithful follower of the Gang of Four, a man who always tested the winds? Could they be sure that he wanted to devote himself to the betterment of the people, the advancement of the Party, the enrichment of the nation, and the scientific application of Marxism and Mao Zedong Thought, instead of concerning himself only with his own well-being?

For the time being, his only concern is keeping Zheng Ziyun out of the congress.

There's more to it than just personal animosity. It's a reflection of the current test of strength between the rigid conservatives and the reform-minded progressives. Zheng's election gave the reformers one more zealot.

Tian's speech is not only filled with bureaucratic jargon, but he seems to be stammering his way through it. He sounds as agonizingly remorseful as a model child who's neglected to help his blind grandfather because he was in too big a hurry to go to a movie.

He's outdoing himself this time; his name should be added to the list of great actors.

"Many people joined the Party after the Cultural Revolution. Some were not completely qualified. And the qualifications of some old Party members have come into question. I'm one of the latter."

The audience stirs. Wang Fangliang glances at the Housing Department head, who appears so touched by the admission he is nearly in tears. He turns to his neighbors to proclaim his admiration for the speaker. He's acting like a shill.

"I've fallen down on the job, my thoughts have lagged, and I've sought special privileges. The people are justifiably indignant. I've already written a report to the Central Committee and have sent my self-criticism to the appropriate authorities. Now I want to do the same in front of everyone here. I promise to work hard to mend my ways!"

His voice nearly cracking with emotion, Tian seems on the verge of tears.

The Housing Department head begins to applaud, and in no time the entire hall resounds with applause, most of it spurred by genuine emotion.

The people, so good and so forgiving! And so easy to manipulate.

Just prior to the meeting, Tian railed at Lin Shaotong. "You want me to move? Not so fast! I'm not moving until decent housing is found for me! Am I supposed to sleep on the street? They can criticize me if they want; I'll just criticize the person above me, and we'll see where it goes. Everyone else has more living space than I do, but they've decided to make me the scapegoat!"

The more he thought about it, the more he fumed. Years of experience told him that more than housing was at stake here. This was the way things were always done in China. He had a premonition that the pyramid of power he had spent an entire lifetime building was threatened. They were closing in on him. He was reminded of summer clouds that slowly envelop the sun, casting dark shadows to spoil the light mood of people enjoying a sunny day. Tian had always been afraid of those clouds, ever since childhood. He'd often fled, thinking he could outrun them. But they always caught up with him and wrapped him in their gloom.

This was no case of women's intuition, which has no basis in fact. Ever since the Third Plenary Session of the Central Committee, he had been feeling more and more penned in, and had been losing faith in himself. He was acutely aware of how times had changed, and of how difficult it was to skate by as in the old days. Back then, all you needed was powerful backing to weather any storm. Now political chicanery and a glib tongue weren't enough. You needed to gain the confidence of the Party and the people by knuckling down and doing a good job.

As for what he had done in the past, as the Buddhists say, "The reckoning will come when the time's right and not before."

He was surrounded by enemies.

Old friendships no longer counted; a person was judged now by his record during the Cultural Revolution.

The fall of the Gang of Four had thrown Tian into a panic. One of his old comrades had become a powerful figure in the Planning Commission, and was very close to one of the vice-premiers. Every time Tian ran into him, he'd say, "Chief, drop me a line any time you have ideas about how the Ministry of Heavy Industry is being run."

Once it became clear that he was out of danger, he called a mass meeting to announce, "No one in the Ministry of Heavy Industry was involved with the Gang of Four!" Not long after that, two of his vice-ministers, both protégés who had enjoyed meteoric rises to the top, were singled out for criticism by the Central Committee.

There had been two factors behind Tian's association with the Gang of Four. Back in the 1930s, when Jiang Qing was a Shanghai movie star and Tian's wife a famous athlete, the two stars had become close friends. The other factor was the close relationship between these two vice-ministers and the Gang of Four.

He was positive that he was the real target of the attack on these two men. Even though no one could prove he had joined the rebel faction, the accusation that he'd sold his honor for patronage would certainly stick. Although he felt obliged to offer these men his protection, since the Central Committee had criticized them by name, and more than once, he had to do something to save his own skin.

Claiming that the men couldn't be isolated because of a shortage of space in the Ministry, he made it easy for them to compare notes and get their stories straight.

The struggle sessions were little more than formalities, restricted to small groups and closed to all members of the opposition, in order to keep from opening old wounds and turning the proceedings into a full-blown criticism.

On paper more than fifty struggle sessions were held, but in fact they only consisted of one or two people reading out the charges. Tian himself made it clear at these meetings that, "Since both men are ministerial-level cadres and have had little contact with the rank and file, only department heads and above need participate in the exposure process. Given the duties of their offices, state secrets are involved, which can only be protected by keeping the meetings small."

The accused were told, "As long as you come clean, your ministerial rank isn't in jeopardy. There are others in the same boat, including provincial secretaries and Central Committee members, and they've managed to keep their positions."

But the men weren't impressed by this display of brotherly sympathy, and in each struggle session, they pointed at their accusers and shouted: "That's a bunch of horseshit!"

The team assigned to investigate the men was a joke, since it included the same hacks who had staffed the "Repudiate Deng Xiaoping Office" in early 1976 and, after the crimes of the Gang of Four were exposed, the "Repudiate the Gang of Four Office." They eventually settled on the name Investigative Team, but they were referred to by local wags as "new wine in old bottles," or "fresh prescription, same old medicine."

Someone actually sent over—anonymously—a door sign that had Repudiate Deng Xiaoping Office on one side and Investigative Team on the other. They could flip it over as their mood dictated.

"Anyone who doesn't have faith in us is free to write a report and send it up the chain of command," Tian said.

The investigation went on for a mere five months or so. Tian wrapped it up with a report to all the workers: "In the campaign to expose the Gang of Four, the Ministry of Heavy Industry, like the rest of the nation, is taking giant steps in the right direction. Our investigation is now complete, and the twenty or so people in the Ministry who had ties with the Gang of Four have been thoroughly investigated and given a clean bill of health."

When Tian subsequently learned that the Central Committee had removed both vice-ministers from office, and was informed of the decision by the leaders of the Ministry Party Headquarters, he knew it was the beginning of the end for him.

If only he could do it all over again.

He began to take a backseat to his subordinates, whether it was Wang Fangliang or Zheng Ziyun, who kept the pressure on him. They went over his head or issued their own restrictions, no matter how small the matter. What were they after? His job?

He endured it all. He'd get his revenge, even if it took ten years. Self-control was something Tian knew all about.

But under no circumstances would he let Zheng Ziyun be a delegate to the Twelfth Party Congress. The first round was not decisive, and now it was up to him. This might be his last hurrah. Given the circumstances, his age, and the times, there would be no more chances after this. This was it. If he was going to take a fall, he wouldn't mind so much if he could take Zheng with him. What made him, Tian Shoucheng, worse than anyone else? And what made Zheng better than Tian? It looks as though they're all set to kill the donkey now that the milling's done. Didn't his contributions count for anything?

If they expected him to lay his head down on the chopping block, they were in for a surprise. They didn't know him very well.

Even a chicken gets in his last hops before he dies. And he was a man, a man of no small ability, not one to be kicked around. Just try it and see!

The smug look on Tian Shoucheng's face reminds Wang Fang-liang of a stage actor receiving bouquets from his audience after a successful performance. How he'd love to go over, push him aside, and declare, "It's a pack of lies!"

Trying to pull the wool over their eyes in broad daylight!

For more than two months, Tian Shoucheng and Kong Xiang suppressed the Central Committee document of censure, keeping it from the membership of the Ministry Party Headquarters. After receiving several inquiries about the results of the investigation, Kong finally was forced to show it to Zheng Ziyun. But when he reported to his superiors, Kong stretched the truth: "Since this affair involves our Party secretary, people have been reluctant to speak up. And the assistant Party secretary, Vice-Minister Zheng Ziyun, is on sick leave, so we haven't been able to submit it for discussion."

Kong could never have dreamed up something like this. No, it had to be Tian's idea.

Now their hands were tied. It was time to show it to Zheng.

He was furious. "On whose authority did you suppress a Central Committee document? And what right do you have to mislead our

Party Headquarters? I'm warning you, this is a flagrant dereliction of duty. If I were you I'd make a full admission in front of the entire Party Headquarters. I want you to send this immediately to every member of the Headquarters and convene a meeting to decide how to handle the matter, as you were told to do in the document, then send in the proper report."

Kong Xiang had no choice but to show the document to each Party Headquarters member, but he sent Lin Shaotong along to make sure it didn't disappear. He treated it as though it were the minutes of a Politburo meeting, which all the local Party members were just itching to get their hands on and pass to their secretaries, friends, or relatives for sale to foreign agents. He was actually afraid that his enemies would copy portions as ammunition for the future.

In order to ensure the early convening of the Party Headquarters meeting, Zheng wrote an open letter to all members, commenting on the intent to derive the truth from the known facts, and urging them to study the document well to reach appropriate conclusions. The eyes of everyone in the unit were on them, so it was important that their attitude be proper and that they remain true to principle, take firm action to strengthen the existing principles and correct erroneous tendencies, stimulate revolutionary fervor, and contribute to stability and unity. If the Party Headquarters didn't face the workers' complaints squarely, or if their attitude was less than clear and they hedged on their actions, the workers would be further alienated and morale throughout the Ministry would suffer.

So what happened? Tian stalled until Wang Fangliang and another vice-minister were out of the country on a fact-finding mission and most of the Party Headquarters members were away from Beijing. Then he called a meeting at which no decision was reached. No report was made to the Central Committee detailing their machinations, which included violations of law, resistance to the investigation, deception of the Central Committee, and submission of false reports. No action was taken, and the fact that the Central Committee document was withheld from some of the cadres was hushed up.

Wang Fangliang wouldn't have handled it that way. He would have waited for the next inquiry from the Central Committee, and if he felt they were really committed to getting to the bottom of things, he would have done everything in his power to resolve the issue once and for all. But if he thought the inquiry was all for show, nothing but an attempt to defuse an explosive situation and make themselves look good in the process, then Zheng's complaints would serve no purpose. If the opposition fired first, Zheng would be the first victim. So why force the issue? After all, people still had to work together, and there would always be differences of opinion.

Tian Shoucheng had it all over Zheng Ziyun in matters like this. How else could he have become number one? Being number one depends primarily on having a knack for analyzing a situation. Few people are blessed with this knack; Wang Fangliang, for one, knew that this was not his strong suit. Still, he did better than Zheng Ziyun.

"Owing to the ideological chaos stirred up by the Gang of Four, some comrades are confusing right and wrong, good and bad, fair and foul, . . . staying away from work to stir up trouble or going to the office only to be attacked . . ."

Here we go! This is what Tian has been leading up to.

He has his sights on Zheng Ziyun.

Getting to his feet, Wang Fangliang scrapes his chair noisily and walks across the rostrum with his hands behind his back. He heads back to his office to read *The Golden Lotus.*

Wang Fangliang has always hated this office building. The windows are too small, giving the place the appearance of a big face with tiny eyes. Sturdy as a heavy bomber. The Tangshan earthquake didn't even make a crack in it. God knows how many tons of cement went into the foundation.

Because of the small windows, the lights are kept on in the corridors no matter how bright the day—it's like the passageways in the Ming Tombs.

Apparently, many people are missing the meeting. Typewriters, people talking in the corner, muted but still loud enough to be overheard. "Tough luck for Song Ke. They say he's not on the list of candidates for vice-minister."

"Serves him right! He thought he could squeeze out Chen Yongming and take his place. Was Chen on the list?" Wang stops to hear the rest of the conversation.

"I think so."

"Looks like the Party Headquarters is standing tough. Tian Shoucheng and his cronies might not have their way this time."

"Hard to say. They're pretty evenly matched and keep jockeying for position."

Wang Fangliang smiles. Where did they come up with those two camps? But all in all, the people are pretty well informed about Party meetings and the topics under discussion.

He is unlocking his office when Xiao Yi, Tian Shoucheng's junior secretary, comes down the corridor with a sheaf of papers in his hands. He nods to Wang as he unlocks the office across the corridor.

Xiao Yi's trousers, as always, are too short, exposing his colorful socks and leather shoes. The hangdog look on his face, which reminds Wang of Christ on the cross, always makes Wang feel sorry for him.

Wang knows that something has been bothering Xiao lately.

Tian is pitting factions against each other again, and Xiao has become one of his victims, another pawn to be sacrificed in this political chess game.

It's 1980, what's he doing playing that same old game!

Ever since the two Gang of Four accomplices were removed from their positions in 1977, the remainder of the people in their faction have been grumbling about Tian Shoucheng, complaining that he pulled all sorts of shenanigans in order to consolidate his own position as minister. "You can burn your bridges behind you," they were thinking, "but you'd better not forget how you got where you are!"

More and more accusations against Tian, along with damning evidence, were coming in these days. There was no question that he had risen this high solely on the basis of this faction's power toward the end of the Cultural Revolution.

But their grumbling didn't worry him. What harm could it do? Did they think they could drag him down just by grumbling? Take away his status? His salary? His housing? They'd be better off putting the past behind them. You can't move forward if you're weighted down with old issues.

What bothered him was the fact that his accusers were his onetime confidants.

So he devised a scheme to boost the morale of the rival clique and get them to attack Xiao Yi's faction's record during the Cultural Revolution and undermine their prestige.

Xiao Yi, who had never enjoyed any of that prestige, had been a devoted follower; his greatest regret was that he'd been born too late to participate in the revolutionary struggle. Then came the Cultural Revolution, and a chance to offer up his life in defense of Chairman Mao's revolutionary line. Now that was over and done with; yet there were still people out to settle old scores and write his political epitaph. His only mistake had been to let himself be used in the attack on innocent victims. He'd done stupid things that he'd regret for the rest of his life.

Every time he ran into a comrade from the opposing faction, he felt a sense of shame. What had turned them into such bitter enemies? Like lunatics, completely devoid of reason, using the right hand to cut off the left—they'd all been lunatics back then. The world was filled with lunatics.

"Comrade Xiao Yi," Wang calls out to him. "It's been a long time. Has the verdict come in on your case?"

"They decided I made a serious political mistake during the campaign," he stammers. "They said I came out in opposition to a certain vice-premier."

The news enrages Wang. Sooner or later, opposing even a vice-minister would become a serious political mistake. Will there never be an end to these ultra-Leftist tactics? "Did you sign?"

A smile. "No. I'm not going to accept the verdict. It's all trumped up. Right now, it's a standoff."

Wang knows he'll have to help him out, since standing tough

isn't the answer. He knows how to deal with Tian Shoucheng. His position is the most important thing to him, so he can be led by the nose with an appeal to his selfish interests.

An assistant director of the Design Institute who had once offended Tian was frozen out of all work for three years. He came to Wang Fangliang for help, who went to Tian: "Is it true that the assistant director of the Design Institute attacked you during the Cultural Revolution?"

What's this all about? Tian thought. "No," he answered cautiously.

"Well then," Wang exclaimed with a show of surprise, "someone's out to get you! People are saying that's why he hasn't had any work for three years. They say you're getting your revenge." Tian took care of this business the next day.

Another friend of Wang's, a bureau director, was also blacklisted. Wang went to Tian again and told him solemnly, "You have to give Lao Zhang something to do."

"Why?"

"If you don't clear the case up, the Organization Department will do it for you sooner or later. Are you going to let them take the credit? Besides, he has quite a network with his knowledge of traditional 'medicine' and his ability to make difficult diagnoses, if you know what I mean. Some of his 'patients' are very well placed." He lowered his voice and moved closer to Tian. "And I've heard he sometimes talks before he thinks."

Bureau Director Zhang was assigned work within the week.

"You take that piece of paper to Minister Tian," Wang says to Xiao Yi. "Tell him that since opposing a vice-premier is a serious political mistake, you'd like to know what opposition to Deng Xiaoping is considered."

Just then one of the custodians walks up. "Minister Wang," he says, "last night you forgot to close your window when you left, and the office was covered with dust. It took a lot of work to clean it up."

"You're right, I did forget. Sorry you had to go to all that trouble."

* * *

280

Xiao Yi dumps the pile of mimeographed documents he's just gotten from the duplicating room onto his desk. Some of the ones on top fly off, but instead of reaching down and picking them up, he just kicks them into a corner.

No heading and no signature, but every word is an evil eye staring up at him defiantly.

1. The Ministry of Heavy Industry has already elected one minister as delegate to the Twelfth Party Congress. Neither of the remaining two delegates should be of ministerial rank.
2. Delegates must not be over the age of sixty-five.
3. The remaining two delegates should be chosen from among the ranks of professionals.

The word "Confidential" is printed in the upper right-hand corner above the code numbers of the sections slated for distribution.

Since they obviously have no shame at all, why mince words? All they need say is, "Zheng Ziyun cannot be elected!"

How dare they! Here in Beijing, in the shadow of the Central Committee, a Ministry directly responsible to the State Council!

Xiao Yi feels like sending the whole stack up in smoke. He paces the office, his arms crossed. Of course, it's all part of their plot, all planned out, including the mobilization report that Tian is making that very minute in the lecture hall. Mobilization? Mobilize them to not elect Zheng Ziyun!

His heart is racing, his temples throbbing. "Calm down," he cautions himself. "Calm down. This has nothing to do with you. What difference does it make who's elected?" But an angry voice inside him keeps shouting, "What kind of Party member are you if you just stand by and watch what's going on?"

But he refuses to weaken as he recalls how his innocence was beaten out of him during the Cultural Revolution. Why suffer for someone else?

Someone else? Who? Since when is being chosen a delegate one person's personal glory? Making the correct choice is both the right and the duty of every Party member. If they don't elect

Zheng, does that mean that the self-serving Tian Shoucheng will represent all Party members in the Ministry of Heavy Industry and maybe even worm his way into the Central Committee itself, where he can abuse even greater power? Xiao Yi picks up the telephone.

Oh, the hell with it! He's only one man, after all! He puts down the phone.

But what if the decision on a critical issue comes down to a single vote?

He pounds his head with his fists. Too melodramatic. He lowers his fists.

The telephone rings.

It's Tian Shoucheng's wife. "Where's Lao Tian? He's not there? Well, tell him to come home a little early today. We've been invited to dinner by Minister H——."

Not even a how are you? or a thank you. As though Xiao Yi were an answering machine.

Xiao knows this Minister H——. At the Fifth National People's Congress, he was the one who proposed making it constitutionally mandatory to add the words *wise* and *great* before certain leaders' names.

What's this crowd up to now? Probably cooking up something for the Twelfth Party Congress.

Xiao Yi takes one of the documents from the pile, folds it in two and puts it in his pocket. Then he takes the remainder into Tian's office and sets them on his desk. He locks the door behind him, walks downstairs, gets on his bicycle, and rides to Zheng Ziyun's home as fast as he can pedal. Don Quixote?

Zheng can't believe his eyes. He picks up the crumpled sheet and reads it again. Three points, all clearly aimed at him. He tosses it on the table and settles back into his chair. The sound of a clarinet in the dusk reminds him of a bugle call sounded at the frontier in ancient times.

He hears his wife return with their grandson. The flat is quickly filled with the sound of machine-gun fire and his grandson's shouts. She must have bought him a new toy. He gets up and closes the door.

"Don't climb on the sofa with your shoes on!" he hears his wife yell.

"Don't pull the cat's tail!

"Oh, you bad boy! Why did you put soap in the thermos bottle?

"Don't mess with that pot of flowers!

"Don't . . .

"Don't . . ."

Always something going on. If she knew he'd sent in his resignation again, there'd be another fight for sure. A man's finished when he's got a woman around. Never a moment's peace.

Bang bang! His grandson banging on the door with his gun, no doubt.

Zheng opens the door. Sure enough, he's standing there, legs akimbo, eyes covered by a helmet several sizes too big, and his toy machine gun jammed up against Zheng's ribs. "Hands up! Surrender or I'll shoot!"

God! Go play somewhere else! Zheng thinks, but he raises his hands. "Okay, I surrender. Now go play somewhere else!"

A final burst of fire, a triumphant stamp of the foot, and off to the next conquest singing a made-up battle song.

Surrender! Zheng smiles. The word isn't in his dictionary.

He'll have it out with Tian over these three points.

Tian is surprised to find Zheng sitting in his office. He should have known that something was up by the look on Xiao Yi's face as he passed through the outer office.

Looks like trouble!

"Feeling a little better?" Tian asks with a bland smile. "Why don't you take a few more days off?"

Zheng smooths out the cigarette in his hand, but doesn't light it, like a soldier solemnly rubbing his rifle before a big battle.

"Have a seat!" Zheng says as he reaches over and picks up the crumpled sheet from the tea table beside him. "Can you tell me what this means, Comrade Tian?"

Tian stands there looking like he doesn't understand Chinese. "This thing, where did you get it?" he demands, like a foreigner trying out the few Chinese words he knows.

"Where I got it is unimportant. As vice-secretary of our Party Headquarters and a vice-minister, I have every right to ask you that question." Zheng lights his cigarette and takes a long, slow puff without looking up at Tian.

Take your time, no hurry, Tian cautions himself.

An oppressive silence. Tian can hear his own heartbeat: a slow, heavy thumping. A thousand eyes are boring into him; retreat is out of the question. He'll have to tough it out. "That, uh, we want to have the broadest possible representation by our delegates to the congress for the masses. It's a congress, after all, a congress!"

"Was this passed by the Party Headquarters?"

Tian takes out a cigarette. His lighter won't work, even after several attempts. Zheng tosses him a matchbox. Tian stubbornly keeps trying his lighter until it finally lights. He lights his cigarette and tosses the matchbox back to Zheng.

He takes a puff. "Some of us discussed it."

"All right, then let me see the minutes." Zheng sticks out his hand. There is a frown on Tian's greasy face. "Um . . . well, we discussed it privately . . ."

"How many of you? Who besides you?" Zheng stands up and walks over to him.

Unable to speak, Tian is like a spent cannon.

"Since when can a few people meeting in private put out a directive that's supposed to represent the entire committee? Who gave you the authority to tamper with the Central Committee's regulations on electing Party delegates? No wonder everybody says the Ministry is ruled not by the Party Headquarters, but by four individuals." Zheng is so angry he grinds out the cigarette he just lit. No need for an answer. Tian knows which four he's talking about.

"We didn't publish this in the name of the Party Headquarters!" No heading, no signature. He knew what he was doing. No incriminating evidence. He, more than anyone else, knows what awaits people who violate a trust.

"Why didn't you have the guts to sign your names? There's nothing wrong with issuing a document in your own name. It's obvious that you wanted to make people think that a decision made by a few men was that of the entire Party Headquarters. You planned to use the organization to force your decision on the workers. I demand a Party Headquarters meeting and an explanation of what you've done to the committee and all Party members. As far as I'm concerned, anti-organization activities constitute a serious mistake. This isn't the first time something like this has happened in our Ministry. It's not normal Party politics, and it shows an utter disregard for Party principles. To say one thing at a meeting, then think and act altogether differently is no way for a member of the Communist Party to act!"

High-sounding words from someone whose only concern is to get himself elected as a delegate! Maybe he's set his sights on becoming an alternate member of the Central Committee at the congress. Sick as he is, he's running himself ragged making speeches, talking up reform, and recommending adjustments, instead of recuperating at home. Always looking out for himself with his constant harping on "making political work more scientific" and saying that it requires changes in personal relationships, all the while waiting to make his own move. Some of the higher-ups like that kind of talk. If that's not stacking the cards to get himself elected a Central Committee alternate, what is it?

Tian stifles the urge to sneer. Look who's talking about saying one thing, then thinking and doing something else! But he keeps his anger in check. "If you have a complaint, we can deal with it. Why let personal feelings get in the way? Someone in your condition shouldn't get too excited."

He has to calm Zheng down because he knows Zheng's capable of doing almost anything without a thought for the consequences. After all these years in public office, Zheng still hasn't learned the ropes. It's better to keep a distance from people like this if you want to avoid being knocked for a loop; what do they care about infractions? Besides, this isn't something Tian wants made public. He might be able to fool the world, but he can't fool himself.

Zheng sees at once what Tian is getting at. He smiles faintly. He knows how the man's mind works; trying to get him to think differently would be foolhardy.

"Don't change the subject. Let's not just dream up ways of dealing with things. We're supposed to seek truth through facts. I mean to settle this business once and for all. Either you revoke this at once or I'll report it."

A real stone in a privy, hard and smelly. Who was it who'd said that about Zheng? Oh, yes, an old-timer, now dead and buried, said it at the beginning of the Cultural Revolution. The speaker may be gone, but the comment lives on. Everyone gets something right once in a while, and this is a case in point.

"If you feel that strongly about it, we'll look into it."

Look into it! Spoken like a real pro. That gives him plenty of room to maneuver.

"Okay, I'll be waiting to hear from you." Essential to give Tian a way out.

Tian's face has that greasy look again. He is incapable of feeling awkward. Zheng, too, for that matter. That's for children.

The atmosphere has changed completely in the time they began talking up to the time Zheng leaves Tian's office.

As soon as he's alone, Tian walks over to the tea table and picks up the crumpled sheet of paper, which he rips up and flings into the wastebasket.

Damn! That was quite a fight; score one for Zheng.

But Tian is a patient man. He'll bide his time until Zheng slips up. Sooner or later it'll happen, and when it does, Tian will be there to turn the tables on him.

Calmer now, Tian still can't drive out the feeling that in recent months he has had one setback after another, for which he has only himself to blame. He must be more patient and regain control of his temper. It doesn't look good, not good at all. He's losing his grip, his intelligence, and abilities like so many fallen flowers flowing away in the stream of life. It saddens him to realize that his golden years are now all behind him. Has he really gotten so old? He and Zheng are about the same age, but Zheng still has a lot of life in him, no matter how sick he may be.

Tian takes a sip of tea. Bitter, and much too strong, but

surprisingly refreshing. He drinks some more, slowly, as though a glass of strong tea were all he needed to rid himself of his bad luck. He's been drinking stronger and stronger tea over the past couple of years, and smoking and drinking more. As though strong tea, tobacco, and alcohol could make up for an increasingly insipid life. A glance at the tea table. Sure enough, Zheng didn't touch his. He doesn't care for strong tea. The man lives a temperate life— simple, neatly ordered, dull, drab. Disgusting! What sort of marital life can he have? How did he manage two kids? He should have been a monk!

Tian looks up to see Xiao Yi standing in the doorway. He must have been there a long time. What's he up to? Trying to worm his way into Tian's mind? Fortunately, even with all the recent techno-logical advances, you still can't read people's thoughts. Things would really be a mess if you could. Even though people's feelings and desires are essentially the same, if you could get into someone else's mind, there'd no longer be any distinction between sacred and profane, between master and subject. Where would Tian Shoucheng be then?

There's something strange about the way Xiao Yi looks, like someone with a dagger hidden in his belt, trying to decide whether to whip it out and stab the man or wait awhile.

"What is it, Xiao Yi?"

I hate it when he stands there like that! Tian thinks.

"I'd like a word with you." Xiao Yi's chin is quivering. "I didn't want to interrupt while you were talking to Vice-Minister Zheng. I heard you ask him where he'd gotten that thing." He has himself so worked up he can barely get the words out. He's making Tian nervous. "He got it from me, I gave it to him."

Tian can see how hard it was for Xiao Yi to say this. He looks like a man who is prepared to be thrown out on his ear. That would be too easy. Tian has known all along that Xiao Yi never wanted to be his secretary, that he's always felt ill at ease around him. But if he left, where would Tian find anyone to replace him?

Even with this admission, Tian isn't about to let him go. If word got around, it would make him look bad. He can keep him around and make it work to his advantage.

Still, he has to admit that this development has taken him by surprise. After watching him for the past couple of years, he'd come to the conclusion that Xiao Yi had become an unworldly man. Now it looks like he was wrong. He'd have to be more careful from now on.

He weighs his words carefully: "Comrade Xiao, what you've done has disrupted stability and unity. But there's no sense crying over spilled milk. Just be more careful from now on."

Xiao isn't taking any handouts. "What has disrupted stability and unity is this entire business, not what I did. It's been mishandled, and no decent communist should stand for it. I'd like to be transferred to a different job. I haven't got what it takes for this one."

Right again! But Tian isn't about to discuss it with him. What would be the point? What difference does it make what Xiao Yi thinks? He isn't one of the Central Committee discipline inspectors.

"It was all for the sake of the work," he says self-righteously. "We'll talk about this later."

After excusing Xiao Yi, Tian feels that the whole morning has been wasted. Everyone's ganging up on him. They're dumping all their slop on him as though he were a garbage pail.

And all he can do is stand there and take it!

He's had to put up with so much. They say it's easy being an official. Like hell!

The exercise bell rings. Ten o'clock. A man's voice booms authoritatively from the loudspeaker. Like a field general. Certainly more impressive than this minister.

"Exercise time. Ready! One, two, three, four . . ." Just listening to him you know the fellow is strong and dynamic, not someone you'd want to make angry. Not if you wanted to keep your face unbruised.

Still, if you want something, you have to pay the price. All in all, his gains have outnumbered his losses. Otherwise, he'd have been out of the business long ago.

Sixteen

Zheng Ziyun and Xia Zhuyun have been sitting tensely in
the living room for two hours, ever since finishing dinner.
They seem ready to pounce on Yuanyuan the minute she walks in
the door.

Xia Zhuyun looks at her watch every minute or so. Then she
sighs and rubs her chest as she looks angrily at the photographs on
the tea table. She's been digging through Yuanyuan's drawers
again, he tells himself. She's impossible!

In one photo Mo Zheng is whispering something in Yuanyuan's
ear as she leans against his shoulder, her head thrown back, her eyes
squinting. Bright sun?

In another, taken from behind, they are walking hand-in-hand
toward the setting sun on the horizon. The grass and shrubs are
bent by the wind in what appears to be a vast, deserted plain.

There is another in which Yuanyuan is trying to force a popsicle into Mo Zheng's mouth. She's laughing happily. . . .

Yuanyuan's masterpieces. The photojournalist. They aren't half-bad. They have the artist's touch, are well conceived, capture a mood . . . but none of the photos she takes are ever published in the papers or in magazines. "I just can't seem to get the right effects," she always says.

Right effects? For a news photo? Aren't they all right as long as you don't cut off the top of the subject's head or one of his limbs? But she's like her father: Do something right, or don't do it at all. Neither of them will settle for mediocrity.

When Zheng returned home from work that afternoon, Xia Zhuyun rushed up to him the minute he stepped in the door, waving some photographs under his nose. "Look at these! Just see what your daughter's been up to!"

His daughter? Anytime Yuanyuan did something her mother disapproved of, she was *his* daughter.

What she was saying, was it true? Women seem to have a sixth sense where things like this are concerned. She must have done some checking to be so sure. What else did she have to do around the house all day?

"Mo Zheng has served time for stealing. He's the adopted son of that Ye Zhiqiu of yours." Victorious, Xia pronounced judgment on her husband.

Now even Ye Zhiqiu has become *his*.

He frowned. He avoided arguing with his wife whenever possible. In matters like this it was essential.

The photos showed that Yuanyuan and Mo Zheng had become very close. This came as less of a shock to Zheng than to his wife.

Yuanyuan had already hinted as much to him.

One night Zheng was having more trouble than usual falling asleep. He lay in bed wide awake, listening to the rhythmic beat of his own heart and feeling his temples pulse. He had been tossing and turning for a long time, like someone with so much on his mind that he's overcome by mental fatigue and wants desperately

290

to clear his head. Holding his head in his hands, he wished he could hide himself in a corner, but he knew that wouldn't do any good.

He wished for some other sound—any other sound—to come and drown out the inescapable thumping of his heart.

He listened carefully.

He began to count: "One, two, three, four, five . . ."

He tried breathing exercises.

Nothing worked.

Finally he heard the sound of a key in the door. Yuanyuan was home. He jumped out of bed and opened the door. He could imagine the sight he presented: his gray hair a mess, pajamas all wrinkled, a jacket thrown over his shoulders, like a man begging for help.

A guarded look immediately appeared on Yuanyuan's normally uninhibited face, like a soldier braced for an enemy charge. She was prepared to receive the wrath of her father.

"Had dinner yet? There's some stewed duck's feet." A coaxing smile to get her to stay up awhile. He didn't want her to go to bed just yet. He knew this was one of her favorite dishes. For reasons no one could pinpoint, they hadn't been eating very well recently.

"Really?" She arched her dark eyebrows, which were a carbon copy of her father's. Every time he looked at his daughter he could almost see himself as a young man, and that made him nostalgic. Life is such a mystery.

He waited patiently as she hung her huge canvas backpack on the coatrack. He wondered what she stuffed that big thing full of every day.

She kicked off her high heels and changed into a pair of slippers.

He followed her to the bathroom and watched her wash her hands, then followed her into the kitchen. She opened the cupboard, looked inside, and took out the bowl of duck's feet. "Actually, I already had dinner," she said as she nibbled one of the duck's feet, "but . . ."

She slid a stool out from under the table with her foot and pushed it toward him. Then she slid out another one for herself. They sat down.

"Has Mama been screaming about me again?" she mumbled as she spat out a bone.

"No."

Her skeptical smile said that he didn't have to say anything, she could guess. She stopped eating and licked the grease off her fingers.

"Papa, if I fell in love, would you trust that he was someone worth loving?"

This caught him off guard. He didn't say anything about how important it is to have the right ideological preparation for something like this. He was a lonely old man starved of happiness in life.

Her sly, capricious questions often stumped him.

The youngsters of her generation are smart, but they have their shortcomings. No matter what they do, form is more important than substance.

Deep down, he knew he could trust Yuanyuan. She wasn't one of those youngsters who never took anything seriously. She had a good head on her shoulders, even though people usually thought her nonchalant. But Zheng didn't want to say too much, particularly since this was something that concerned her happiness. Were there times when she was carried away by her emotions, too? Love follows its own rules.

"That sounds like a riddle, Yuanyuan. You know I never make up my mind on a whim. You probably think I'm an old stick-in-the-mud, but you and I grew up in different times. At first I was involved in underground work, then I went into economics. The realities of life haven't given me much time to dream. The only way I could give you an answer is if I knew what kind of person you're talking about. Do you have someone in mind?"

She smiled at him. "Not yet, but someday I will."

"Will you tell me when that time comes?" Almost a plea. He wasn't a man of steel, especially where his darling daughter was concerned.

"Of course!" She got up and kissed him on the forehead, her lips still greasy from the duck's feet. "Papa, I love you. No one understands me like you do."

292

He wiped his forehead with his hand. It was damp and a little greasy.

Of course! she says. Like hell! The little schemer.

Apart from these photographs—and who knows where Xia Zhuyun found them—Zheng is completely in the dark.

Once again he's been caught off guard.

He picks up the photos and studies them closely.

The boy certainly would have been worth loving if he hadn't been arrested. Why else would Ye Zhiqiu have taken him in? Why else would Yuanyuan have fallen in love with him? What was it about him that made them feel that way? Were they just a couple of foolish women? Worse than Xia Zhuyun? Hard to figure.

He's never seen his daughter laugh like the girl in the photos. He sighs softly. He'd never laughed like that, he suddenly realizes, even in his youth. Maybe that's because back then everyone was too busy trying to survive to spend time laughing.

That laughing face could only belong to someone out there somewhere, standing at one of life's crossroads.

It certainly doesn't belong to her mother, nor to her father. Yes, she was born and reared in their home, but this young man has easily taken her away from them.

"I want you to get to the bottom of this," Xia Zhuyun says sternly. Almost as though it's he who wants to get married.

Get to the bottom of it? Easier said than done. He sighs. Nothing's ever that simple. Recent events at the Ministry have caused talk in senior circles, and both he and Tian Shoucheng have to assume the responsibility.

Things are still up in the air at the Ministry and, it seems, with Yuanyuan as well. Zheng isn't feeling very confident about the outcome.

"Don't get so worked up. We'll talk to her. Things like this can lead to confrontation, and no one benefits from that."

"You always let her have her way. This is what you get by spoiling her." Xia Zhuyun turns and notices that the curtain isn't drawn. She's fit to be tied. She storms over to the window, but the cord is snagged and she can't draw the curtain. She can barely contain herself from yanking it down and ripping it to shreds.

Zheng comes over to help, but she pushes him away and tugs with all her might on the cord. *Rip!* There goes one piece. But she's not giving up. Finally, she yanks the curtain down and stomps on it.

Hysteria!

Zheng sits down on the sofa without a word. He's fed up with this kind of life. Some people find it easy to destroy themselves and everyone around them. He looks down at the curtain lying on the floor, torn down for no reason at all, looking like a burst balloon. It seemed all right when it was hanging, but now he can see that it's just a faded, dusty piece of cloth.

As Mo Zheng races along on his motorbike, Yuanyuan rests her head against his back.

She's tired, tired and happy. She closes her eyes and forgets where they're going. With him she'd go anywhere. She smiles and holds her hand up to his lips.

Mo Zheng kisses her hand lightly. It's small but as rough as a boy's. A mischievous girl who nearly drives him to distraction. With her behind him, all the streetlights ahead become precious stones, the motorbike a vehicle to transport him to Nirvana.

Mo Zheng believes he can make it. He has to, now that he's responsible for the delicate flower whose head is pressed against his back, and who has unconditionally given herself to him. Yuanyuan has given him more than the love of a young woman— she has cleansed him.

People are capable of leaping back through time. Mo Zheng is starting life all over again; he is that boy in the light blue flannel shirt, his hands washed clean.

A fresh start, but this time she's with him.

Yuanyuan can sense what he's feeling. She pats him on the chest and whispers something in his ear, but the wind swallows her words. He envies that wind. It must have been something he yearned to hear.

He turns his head back. "What did you say?"

Yuanyuan grabs his ear and pulls his head down close to her. "I said I want to lean my head against your back for the rest of my life."

He can feel her warm breath against his ear. The warmth goes straight to his heart.

He smiles.

Thank you, you decent, passionate little girl!

Human desires are virtually indestructible. All they need to come to life is something one can believe in.

Mo Zheng's heart, an old tree shattered by bolts of lightning, has suddenly put forth new branches, tender and green, full of life. They will grow, their leaves rustling in the wind, and provide a haven for hungry, thirsty, tired travelers. He wants to love this world, and all the people in it, more than ever. Now, even if lightning strikes again, he's rooted in the soil, drawing nourishment from Mother Earth. In years to come there will be more new branches, and the endless cycle of life and death will continue.

Mo Zheng shakes his head.

"You don't want me to?" She pounds his back. "You think you can stop me!"

More, hit me more, my little tyrant.

Red light! They've already crossed the line.

Damn! He wasn't paying attention. Well, this is no time to hesitate. He zooms through the intersection, then quickly turns down a side street, just in case there's a traffic cop waiting for them at the next light.

Yuanyuan tiptoes inside. Hm, why is the light on in the living room? Isn't Mama watching TV tonight?

She picks up her mirror. She barely recognizes the lovely face looking back at her: darker eyebrows, brighter eyes, rosier cheeks. She looks at the lips—they're different, but only she knows why.

She puckers up until her mouth looks like a tiny red trumpet. Then she smiles, revealing two rows of even, white teeth behind red lips that seem to shine. All this now belongs to him!

She is in love! She gnashes her teeth and rolls her head. People always gnash their teeth in anger, but you can do it for love just as easily.

Is she getting carried away?

She laughs and throws herself on her bed, burying her head in her pillow. She said yes—she's going to marry him!

Marriage! Even though she looks forward to it, it scares her. The big doll on her bookcase stares down at her disapprovingly. Her cocked head seems to be asking, "Are you going to give up your childhood so simply?"

Yuanyuan jumps off the bed and looks beyond the long lashes and straight into the doll's beautiful, sightless eyes. "No," she says softly. "You'll never understand!"

How could a doll understand that when two people become one it's not a loss but a gain, the creation of something new? They'll build a life for themselves with their hands and their minds.

Mo Zheng told her he wouldn't become a part of her family, nor would he give up Ye Zhiqiu, who had been both a mother and a sister to him, not to mention his best friend. After he married Yuanyuan he could do even more to ease Ye Zhiqiu's loneliness. And they would have a child, who would call Ye Zhiqiu "Grandma." Yuanyuan covered the embarrassed smile on her face. He was going to make translation his profession, which would allow him to become the head of a real family. Yuanyuan shook her head. But he'd already translated two or three short stories, which Ye Zhiqiu was going to have an old schoolmate, the editor of a foreign-literature magazine, look at.

Yuanyuan and Mo Zheng had already agreed that if the translations were sold, they'd use the money to buy their new quilt for the bed, a green satin one. When Yuanyuan was neither laughing nor angry, her eyes were deep green. They'd buy lots of beds and lots of quilts in their lives together. . . .

"Yuanyuan!" Xia Zhuyun shrieks, bringing Yuanyuan back to reality.

"What do you want?" The impatient tone of a dreamer.

"Come in here. Your father and I want to talk to you."

Something's wrong.

Yuanyuan straightens her hair and takes one last look in the mirror, seeing nothing her mother can pick on. Reluctantly, she walks into the living room.

She glances quickly at her parents. Something's up, all right.

Zheng Ziyun watches his daughter close her mouth tightly. A bad sign. She's ready for a fight before they even begin.

"Sit down!" Xia says in the superior tone she uses at the Ministry when she's speaking to a subordinate who has done something wrong or is in trouble. "Lao Zheng, you go ahead."

Such a delicate matter. How can he convince her to give up this young man without hurting her?

Why do people have to fall in love, anyway? It just complicates life. All those tears, the love letters, the dates, the explorations, the vows of undying love . . . all at the cost of enormous time and energy. Love belongs in novels. He and Xia Zhuyun have never been in love, yet they've lived together all these years. When the time comes, a man gets a woman, a woman gets a man, and that's that.

"Yuanyuan," he says to ease the tension. "You seem awfully busy these days. You hardly ever eat at home."

Yuanyuan shrugs her shoulders.

Oh-oh, that was the wrong thing to say. He sounded sarcastic. Better not beat around the bush.

"Your mother and I are very concerned about you. We know that people want to get married when they reach a certain age. When you're considering a future husband, the most important things to look at are political stand, character, professional initiative . . ." Damn! Even to him it sounds like a speech. No, his speeches come off better than this. He senses that Yuanyuan is forcing back a pitying, ridiculing smile. She must be thinking that there isn't much difference between this and a discussion over someone's qualifications to join the Party.

By this time Xia Zhuyun is glaring at him impatiently.

Zheng decides to try to describe his ideal son-in-law to her with a bit more of the human touch. "You should choose a faithful man who has more than his self-interest at heart and has a love for things that are proper and correct. He should be talented but not flashy, an understanding and forgiving man with whom you can work out your differences. You can live and work happily with a man like that."

Yuanyuan laughs. How can she laugh over something as serious as this?

"Papa, you're talking like someone who's picking out a pair of sneakers at the store. These white ones? No, they get dirty too easily, and have to be cleaned all the time. But they *are* good-looking. That blue pair? No, the soles are too thin. They'd be uncomfortable for a long walk . . ."

"Yuanyuan, be serious for a change! Lao Zheng, you'd better leave it to me." Xia Zhuyun reaches behind her and takes out the photographs. "You listen to me. I forbid you to bring pictures of this person into the house ever again, and I want you to have nothing more to do with him!"

Yuanyuan rushes over to take back her pictures, but Xia puts them on the chair and sits on them.

"Mama, you should be in the KGB!" Yuanyuan says through clenched teeth, the color drained from her face. "What right do you have to search through my things? That's unconstitutional, it's a violation of my rights. Give those pictures to me! I want them back!"

Her voice has risen, like all women when they're excited.

"We can talk about this without acting like that. Give the pictures back to Yuanyuan."

"Give them back?" Xia Zhuyun takes the photos from under her, rips them up, then tosses them in the spitoon. "KGB, huh? Violate your rights? How dare you! Cuddling up like that for a photograph before you're even married, have you no shame at all?"

"Lao Xia!" Zheng has heard enough. She's talking like a street brawler.

Yuanyuan, on the other hand, has her anger in check. She stands there with her arms crossed over her chest, her legs trembling slightly. "Go ahead and tear them up. I'll just take some more. Cuddling up? I'll take a picture of us kissing! I'm going to marry him, and there's nothing you can do about it."

Xia Zhuyun reaches out and slaps her, leaving five red marks, which soon merge into one large red blotch. "You little tramp!"

God, has Xia forgotten her own affair when she was young? Zheng never used such language with her; in fact, using it has never crossed his mind. What right does she have to be so self-righteous with Yuanyuan?

"You'll regret this!" Yuanyuan has never felt such intense hatred for anyone before.

Zheng knows that Xia has truly lost her daughter at that moment. His own beloved daughter. Never, not even as a child, did he raise a finger against her. Now her mother has slapped her. Afraid she might do it again, he pushes his wife aside. "What's gotten into you? That's enough now. We'll talk about it later." He starts nudging Yuanyuan out of the room.

"Push me, will you? You almost knocked me down. Do you think you two can gang up on me? No way! We're going to settle this here and now. Yuanyuan, I've fed and clothed you in this house since you were a baby. What makes you think you can blow up at me now and not do as you're told!"

"I didn't ask to be born. People who want children have a duty to raise them. I don't owe you a thing!"

Xia Zhuyun picks up a stool and rushes toward her daughter. Zheng can't hold her back. She's like a crazed animal.

Yuanyuan snatches the stool out of her mother's hand and throws it into the corner. Someone downstairs bangs on the radiator.

"Try to hit me, will you? How dare you!" She flings herself onto Yuanyuan, who weighs about half as much as her mother.

"Keep it down! Okay! Stop fighting! What'll the neighbors think?"

Yuanyuan gives her mother a shove that sends her staggering. "That's enough of that. I didn't hit you, and you know it!"

"Get out of my sight! You're no daughter of mine!" Saliva drips from the corner of her mouth. She is dizzy with rage.

Zheng closes his eyes, unable to bear the ugly sight in front of him. How had he never noticed it before?

"Yuanyuan, don't take her seriously, she doesn't know what she's saying." He tries again to nudge her out of the room.

"I'm going, don't worry. You don't know how long I've wanted to leave this hateful, hypocritical home. Do you think I care about your status, or your home, or your life-style? I just felt sorry for Papa, that's all. But, Papa, it's your own fault. You're a hypocrite, too. You know Mama's faults better than anyone else, and you look down on her because of them. There isn't a bit of pleasure for you to come home to. Ever since I can remember, you've stayed away as much as possible, just coming home to sleep, shutting yourself up in the office all day long. Sure, you're busy—I know that—it's your job. But I've known all along that home to you is a place to sleep and that's all. On the rare occasions when you do come home, you head straight to your own room. But in front of others, you act the loving husband, pouring tea for Mama, or pulling out her chair, helping her with her coat, or opening the door for her. You might be able to fool other people, but not me. Does Mama love you? She only loves herself, not you, not me, and not Fangfang. Has she ever lost any sleep over your problems at the Ministry? Mama, all Papa's ever meant to you is a meal ticket. Because of his position, you have a car at your disposal, nice living quarters, and the prestige of being the wife of a vice-minister, which means other people have to give in to you whether you're right or not. If you married someone else, do you think you could keep drawing your salary month after month without doing a lick of work? Are you on approved leave? Hah! Look at the way you dress, Mama, all the satins and silks you could ask for. Now look at Papa. What other minister dresses like that?" Yuanyuan walks over and picks up the hem of Zheng's jacket, exposing the worn lining. "If you won't buy him a new one, at least you could mend this one; but no, you're not even thoughtful enough to ask Auntie Wu to do it." Yuanyuan raises the cuffs on her father's pants, which are as frayed as a fishnet. "He bought these in 1971, and they haven't ever been mended. Just feel these pants. You tell me how anything this thin could be warm. That sweater of Papa's, I bought it.

Nobody'd believe it if you told them. If I didn't see it with my own eyes every day, I wouldn't believe it myself. You know that decorum is important enough to Papa that he wouldn't say a word to anyone, so you figure you can get away with murder." Yuanyuan turns to her father. "I know what kind of person Mama is. I have no illusions about her. But you, with all your talk about making political work more scientific, behavioral science, respect for others, trust in others, this theory and that . . . yet you refuse to believe that Mo Zheng is a decent person. What is stealing? It's taking something that doesn't belong to you or something you don't deserve without anyone knowing about it. In that case, Mama is stealing her salary, since she never goes to the office. You won't catch me living this kind of hypocritical life. Mo Zheng and I are going to live like real people. We love and respect each other. We're going to make our own way, without depending on anyone else. We may be poor, but we'll live honest lives. Don't you worry, Mama. Even if the sky falls or the earth opens up, no matter how tough things get, I won't come back looking for your charity. That's all I have to say. I'm leaving now—for good."

Zheng Ziyun sits in the nylon-covered chair beside Yuanyuan's desk, watching her pack. Strange, but he can't think of a single argument that might change her mind. He must know deep down that she is doing the right thing. If it weren't for the fact that he'll miss her, he'd be glad that she's found a way out of this stifling environment.

Yuanyuan has calmed down. She owes nothing more to this family. She might have had some qualms if not for that ugly scene. That has made what she's doing so much easier. She tosses her light-blue down parka to the side and fishes a brown and red jacket out of her closet. She puts it on over her sweater, and since it's a little small, she takes out a bulky corduroy coat and slips it on over the jacket.

Zheng knows without being told that Yuanyuan wants nothing to do with anything her mother has bought for her. How sad that it's come to this. He knows her well—she means what she says, and no regrets. Once she makes up her mind, she never looks back. He goes to his room, gets his padded military overcoat, and hands it to Yuanyuan. "Take this overcoat. That jacket isn't warm enough for this cold weather, not to mention all that riding around on the back of a motorbike."

"No, I won't be cold." Yuanyuan bites down on her lip.

"It's *my* overcoat." His voice seems to tremble.

Yuanyuan takes the overcoat, buries her face in it, and bursts into tears. But she quickly bites down on the overcoat to stifle her sobs and turns her face away, just as she did as a child whenever she cried. "Papa," she sobs, "can you ever forgive me? I just can't live here anymore . . ."

Zheng's heart is filled with shame. It's his fault that Yuanyuan, a sensitive girl eager to understand what life is all about, was born into a family like this. Everything that followed has been inevitable. But he is powerless to change the environment that's been all wrong for her. Worst of all, he was a part of that ugly scene a short while ago, indirectly at least. It was as though his wife had picked a beautiful flower and thrown it to the ground for him to trample.

He hugs his daughter and strokes her short, wavy hair. How long has it been since he's done that? She's grown up so quickly, and in his muddling way he's gotten old. "I should be asking you to forgive me."

He doesn't know how to cry like Yuanyuan. He can't remember the last time he cried. All pain, no tears. Like now: his cheeks ache, but the tears won't come.

The motorbike's taillight disappears in the night, but Zheng Ziyun stands there in the cold, dazed.

Is that him talking? Is that his voice? Pleading. "Yuanyuan, don't go, don't leave me here all alone."

He knows he has his weaknesses, just like everyone else. Why didn't he find the nerve to say it to her a moment ago? He was afraid that she'd have asked him, "What is there worth staying for?"

What could he have said?

Yuanyuan's right, he is a hypocrite. She's probably the only other person who knows that. Just a little while ago she completely exposed his hypocrisy after he'd spent a lifetime hiding it from himself.

The things he's put up with, the compromises he's made, all for the sake of appearances. That includes Xia Zhuyun's youthful infidelity; he has always known that Fangfang—his cruel, vulgar, politically backward daughter—isn't his child. And for what? Because he loved his wife and was willing to forgive her? No, she isn't a woman who deserves love or respect. It was for himself, to create a flawless image, to make himself appear larger than life. All his theorizing about scientific Marxism and society only masked the fact that he lived his personal life in accordance with the old ways.

Why did he feel he had to appear larger than life? Was it possible that behind his professional dedication there lurked a hunger for personal fame? Of course it was possible. Why not have the guts to face up to the fact that he's forsaken his own natural instincts to make himself appear saintly, halo and all.

He lacks Yuanyuan's courage. She chose to leave, without hesitation, to seek her own happiness, wherever that took her. He has no one to blame but himself.

"The right to my own freedom!" Just that, going where I want, that's all, like Yuanyuan. Could he do it?

He yearns for it, but he knows it is too late.

Maybe it isn't all that hard to break free of external fetters. It is the self-imposed fetters, trying to overcome your own intellectual barriers, that usually leads to failure.

Zheng would be happy to turn the clock back, to become, say, Yuanyuan's age. Everything is easier for her than for him.

The wind has picked up, and Zheng feels the cold in his hands and feet, even in his chest. He is lonesome. He's never felt this lonesome before. And not just because he's lost a loved one.

He walks ahead aimlessly.

It begins to snow. Huge snowflakes swirl in the wind. Zheng is reminded of small, white butterflies.

Butterflies!

Yuanyuan was six years old. She was in the hospital having her tonsils removed. As she slept soundly, he sat there for hours listening to her even breathing and looking at her chubby little face, feeling responsible for her and her whole generation. Wasn't there more to those responsibilities than mapping out a path for them?

Yuanyuan woke up. "Where's Mama?"

"She's busy. Now, you're not supposed to talk." That was when he began lying to Yuanyuan. But what could he do, tell her that her mother was dancing at the Beijing Hotel?

"Tell me a story, Papa!" she begged him in a raspy voice.

He was no good at telling stories, and he had never imagined that besides mapping out a path for Yuanyuan, he'd also have to tell her stories.

"What kind of story?" He searched his memory, but he came up blank.

The look of disappointment on his daughter's face perplexed him. What good was a father who didn't know how to tell stories or a mother who went dancing while her daughter was having her tonsils taken out? After a moment, Yuanyuan asked him, "Papa, where do butterflies come from?"

"Butterflies? They come from caterpillars."

"Don't try to fool me." She didn't believe him. How could a thing of such beauty come from something as ugly as that?

She probably forgot this little incident long ago.

An ugly caterpillar turns into a beautiful butterfly after a great deal of toil. But all the toiling in the world won't turn every caterpillar into a butterfly: some perish in the cocoon. He wonders how many actually make it.

That's what he is: a caterpillar trying to become a butterfly.

"Yuanyuan, don't think that you have a wonderful father. You have to accept that I am a caterpillar going through the agony of metamorphosis, and that I may die before I become a butterfly." He kept these thoughts inside him.

Why did he keep them inside? He should have said them openly to his daughter and to Mo Zheng, to whom he has brought pain before they have even met.

What time is it? Nearly eleven. He can still get the last bus.

* * *

Liu Yuying yawns as she drags herself upstairs on legs that feel like blocks of wood.

New Year's Eve. Things have really been hopping the last few days, with all those perms and the overtime. Working from eight in the morning till ten at night, standing until her legs are numb. Her own hair is filthy, but where can she find the time to wash it?

What did Xiao Qiang eat for dinner? That morning she cooked some food and left it in the steamer with some buns. She even put some water in the pot on the stove. All he had to do was light the stove and warm the food until it was ready to eat. But Ye Zhiqiu probably took him to her flat for dinner again. She hated to put her to so much trouble. Time and again she urged Ye to let her give her a perm and make her look really nice.

But Ye would just hold her head in her hands and say, "Please, just let me have a peaceful day or two!"

Clothes make the woman, and Liu believes that with a little work she could make Ye quite presentable. She really ought to find herself a husband instead of spending all her time alone, wearing herself out with work.

Liu pauses at the third floor to catch her breath. What's that? A moan? It was very close. She looks under the stairs. No one there. She hurries up the stairs. Oh! An elderly man lying on the stairs.

"Comrade, what's wrong?" She tries to help him up.

Zheng Ziyun looks up at her and motions her off. He doesn't want her to move him. He points to some white pills scattered on the stairs, then to his mouth.

Liu Yuying understands. She scoops up several pills and stuffs them into his mouth, then rushes over and bangs on Ye Zhiqiu's door. "Lao Ye, Lao Ye!"

The door opens to reveal three smiling faces: Ye Zhiqiu, Mo Zheng, and the pretty young woman named Yuanyuan, who drops by regularly.

"Hurry, someone's collapsed on the stairs. It looks serious!" Liu Yuying is frantic.

The three of them hurry downstairs after her.

Ah!

"Papa!" Yuanyuan rushes to her father's side.

"Lao Zheng! Quick, Mo Zheng, call a taxi!"

Zheng closes his eyes, as though his journey were over.

What a way to meet Mo Zheng for the first time. It's like a soap opera. He prays that Mo Zheng and Yuanyuan won't think he's come to make a scene.

Yuanyuan is crying. It's all her fault. All because she'd made him angry. "Papa, Papa!"

"Stop that crying!" Ye Zhiqiu orders her. "And don't shake him like that. Let him lie there. He mustn't move!" She kneels down and cradles Zheng's head in her arm. "Go inside and get a pillow."

Yuanyuan, too stunned to move, doesn't hear her. Still a little girl! Liu Yuying rushes off to get a pillow.

What's taking the taxi so long? Ye wishes she could make time stop, feeling that every passing second brings Zheng closer to the brink. Beads of sweat dot her brow.

Please don't let him die, not a wonderful man like this! There are already too few people like him.

Yuanyuan presses her cheek against her father's cold, clammy hand. "Papa, please don't die, you have to let me make this up to you. Papa, I'll love you better than ever. Please, I beg you, forget everything I said. You're a wonderful father. I understand, Papa, I understand you . . ."

"That's enough, Yuanyuan. He needs rest." Ye Zhiqiu is losing her temper.

The taxi finally arrives. Mo Zheng carries Zheng Ziyun downstairs.

Such a strong young man! Full of life. Mo Zheng's powerful arms infuse Zheng with fresh strength. It's wonderful. He is an infant cradled in the arms of a giant. Don't worry, he's not going to die. Zheng opens his eyes to find Mo Zheng gazing down at him. The magnetic, unyielding power of those sapphire eyes seems to be calling him back from the brink of death.

Zheng struggles to smile at him. How wonderful to have a son like that!

The telephone rings.

Who the hell could be calling in the middle of the night? Don't they know people are sleeping!

Tian Shoucheng opens his eyes. The phone has been ringing for what seems like ten minutes. It must be urgent. He sits up, swings his legs out of bed, and tries to find his slippers. Shit, they're on the wrong feet!

"Hello!" he answers impatiently.

"Minister Tian? Sorry to wake you up like this." Ji Hengquan is a smooth talker. He doesn't value his words so much as he always knows just whom he's talking to.

"What is it?" Tian drawls.

"Minister Zheng had a heart attack and was rushed to the hospital." Ji makes his voice sound tense so as not to sound too happy. He doesn't want to sound like his usual self.

"Oh!" This wakes Tian up. "How'd it happen?"

"They say it happened at that woman reporter's place, sometime after eleven o'clock." He rattles this off, as though he's afraid of running out of breath before he gets the news out. God forbid he should die before broadcasting this to the whole world! He is like one of those agents in the movies who has returned from the enemy camp with an armload of intelligence to report triumphantly on sweeping military successes.

"Ah—" The bottom falls out of Tian's exclamation. "Make sure you tell the hospital authorities that I want him given the best possible care, personnel, medication. After all, Minister Zheng is one of our most respected, dedicated, and influential comrades in economic circles, and they must do everything they can to save him. The political consequences of his loss would be enormous. Where are you now? At the hospital? Good. I'll be there as soon as I can!" He sounds genuinely concerned and burns with anxiety.

As he hangs up the phone, the results of the final tally for delegate to the Twelfth Party Congress flash through his mind: 1,006 to 287.

After Tian had risked his reputation and worked so hard to concoct those three regulations of eligibility for delegates to the Twelfth Party Congress contrary to Central Committee policy, Zheng Ziyun seized the opportunity to undo him, and when the carnage was over, his ballot count had gone from 887 to 1,006. Tian had played his best hand and lost.

Thinking it was all over for him, he gave up. Who would have thought that the tables could turn so suddenly?

Zheng Ziyun would not be a delegate to the Twelfth Party Congress after all.

Tian seats himself in his car more solemnly than usual. Even though it's the middle of the night, not a hair on his head is out of place. He is dressed as neatly as if he were off to a state dinner.

He glances at the luminous dial of his calendar watch: 3:41, New Year's Day, 1981.